PERSPECTIVES ON RACE AND CULTURE IN JAPANESE SOCIETY

The Mass Media and Ethnicity

PERSPECTIVES ON RACE AND CULTURE IN JAPANESE SOCIETY

The Mass Media and Ethnicity

Peter B. Oblas

The Edwin Mellen Press
Lewiston/Queenston Lampeter

Library of Congress Cataloging-in-Publication Data

Oblas, Peter B.
    Perspectives on race and culture in Japanese society : the mass
media and ethnicity / Peter B. Oblas.
        p.   cm.
    Includes bibliographical references and index.
    ISBN 0-7734-8986-X (hard)
    1. Ethnology--Japan. 2. Japan--History--To 645. 3. Mass media-
-Japan. I. Title.
DS830.025   1995
305.8'00952--dc20   94-38356
                                                                            CIP

A CIP catalog record for this book is available from the British Library.

The Edwin Mellen Press   The Edwin Mellen Press
        Box 450   Box 67
Lewiston, New York   Queenston, Ontario
    USA 14092-0450   CANADA L0S 1L0

The Edwin Mellen Press, Ltd.
Lampeter, Dyfed, Wales
UNITED KINGDOM SA48 7DY

Printed in the United States of America

Dedicated to the memory of my Father

TABLE OF CONTENTS

INTRODUCTION:

Race and Nation

"Nihonjinron" or the theory of Japanese culture is a subject which has been considered from many different angles by intellectuals in a variety of disciplines in Japan and abroad. It's well worn and fits comfortably into discussions on Japanese society. Nihonjinron scholars seek to reveal the core of what it means to be Japanese by closeting together unique cultural values into a holistic enterprise. For the nihonjinron specialist, the point of departure for a survey is the ambience of the group within an environment of consensus rather than contention. Yoshio Sugimoto and Ross Mouer, who have unleashed a pioneering exploration of nihonjinron literature, contend that academic writing on the theme will continue to prosper.[1] They refer to three reassertive perspectives in the 1980s fueling renewed discussion. For instance, there is a focus on the "ie" (home) or "mura" (village) mentality as a cultural norm in Japan and the promotion of Japanese society as being fairly homogeneous. The ie organizational factor, not the American occupation, consequently, is the evolutionary thread in Japanese democracy and this thread extends back into the post-war period. Then, there is the assertion that Japanese and Westerners are psychologically distinct, the former being contextual within an orientation of social relationships, the latter being self-centered and individualistic. Finally, among the approaches of the 80s is "nihon bunmeiron" or theory of Japanese civilization. According to Sugimoto and Mouer, this emphasis on civilization expands the unit of analysis from social values and national character to include social organization, structures and institutions, but the standard of analysis remains unchanged. In their estimation, nihon bunmeiron is merely a new label for comparing native culturalism and foreign individuality.[2]

The pioneering efforts of Sugimoto and Ross are limited to a particular genre of academic literature. They tend to eschew mass media publications and popular culture. Also, although the racial implications of the holistic perspective are touched upon, they are not heavily weighed in their appraisals. The object of this book is not to reexamine the analyses of these authors or pursue nihonjinron within the realm of the media but to follow in the wake of a short digression of this authoritative team which for a single paragraph found themselves enmeshed in popular racial imagery. At that instance, they related that there is reason to believe in the existence of a "very strongly ingrained racism" in some quarters of Japanese society. They also described their documentation as bringing "attention to the depth of the folk belief that Japanese 'uniqueness' is biologically based."[3] The issues to be pursued henceforth relate to the following: How popular racial perspectives of uniqueness are within Japanese society and how strongly such folk beliefs are held?

The paragraph in question dealt with the racially-charged remarks of a Japanese politician, Yasuhiro Nakasone. Even as prime minister, Nakasone would slip into comments pertaining to the superior qualities of the Japanese society because of the homogeneity of its people. His utterances offended Japan's Ainu population when he denied the existence of minority races and therefore discrimination in Japan and Americans when he associated America's minority populations with inferior education performance. Later, when he was taken to task for these assertions, there were always the convenient fallbacks of being misinterpreted or quoted out of context.[4]

Other politicians have gained notoriety with similar off-the-cuff asides. Nakasone is definitely not alone. More recently, the mayor of

Kawasaki (a city within commuting distance of Tokyo) gained media attention when he joked that dark-skinned Asian immigrants posed a danger since they were difficult to see at night. He later expressed astonishment that his words had been misunderstood. Then, there was the indiscreet observations of the justice minister concerning the problem of foreign prostitutes in Tokyo. He equated prostitutes with black Americans, alleging that they both destroyed good neighborhoods. Later, he contended that he had not meant to talk about racial issues.[5] One can definitely amass political anecdotes to reveal racial values within Japanese society. Yet, a series of disconnected stories do not provide significant descriptions for revealing a systematic pattern within Japanese society. Furthermore, political remarks might reflect racial attitudes within some quarters of Japanese society, but the problem remains as to the number of these quarters or just how pervasive such attitudes are. Moreover, there is the matter of how intensely racial views are held or how central they are to the world view of the average person. With anecdotes, one can never really rid oneself of the impression that perhaps they really are just slips of the tongue. Or maybe it's merely a lack of sensitivity to the feelings of minorities since racial discrimination isn't an important aspect of Japanese society – a consideration often mentioned.

Consequently, instead of stringing together statements of individuals on a variety of racial subjects, the supposition is that it would be more analytically appropriate to consider racial perspectives by focusing on the source of Japanese racial identity and how the media communicates racial origins. The assumptions set forth therefore are media related. Since generally the mass media seeks to reach the broadest of audiences to deliver its message, the assumptions are also average-person oriented. Regarding media reach, certain statistics are revealing. *Asahi Shimbun's* circulation of the morning edition in 1989 was over 8 million. The combined circulation of two of this newspaper organization's weekly magazines was over one million.[6] The percentage of TV's daily viewing audience in Japan is 94%. Average viewing time is between three and four hours daily, with the audience concentrated in the 7:30 PM to 11:00 PM time period. Advertising expenditure in Japan especially underlines the reach of TV broadcasting, with outlays accounting for one-third of the national advertising total.[7] In a more general sense, it is noteworthy that in a land where leisure is consumed in sips rather than gulps, a government public opinion poll shows the largest proportion of respondents in weekday, weekend and 3 or more days off categories spend their leisure time watching television, listening to radio, and reading newspapers and magazines.[8]

Within this hypothetical orientation, the consistency with which the media draws upon a specific formula to attract the average person reflects the general acceptance of such a perception among the viewers or readers. The continual patterning of origins' information within a specific historical time zone and according to definitive images indicates a lack of segmentation within the media's perspective of what the audience anticipates when Japanese racial origins is considered. Furthermore, the media's inclination to distort information in its treatment of origins and to send out a dissonant-free message of racial uniqueness documents not only the pervasiveness but also the depth of belief of such a popular perspective.

Nevertheless, there is still the question of where racialism should be positioned vis-à-vis cultural uniqueness. For Mouer and Sugimoto, biological nihonjinron is deposited in a peripheral realm of naïveté within their intellectual categorization. They relegate it to odd ideas on the uniqueness of the Japanese brain or the relationship between herbivorous habits and ways of thinking. They even go so far as to place it at the very fringe of holistic thought.[9] They write: "it is in this intellectual climate that the anti-Semitic literature has served to deflect attention from the conflict of economic and social interests by suggesting that the trade friction between Japan and the United States and the ensuing economic trouble in Japan has resulted from a Jewish conspiracy."[10]

To handle racial uniqueness in such a way is to overlook the symbiosis of the two variants. Both culturalism and racialism draw upon similar holistic values in nurturing their presence within society. Racial uniqueness is not just brain size or innate thought habits. Although it might be easy to separate culture and race in academic paraphernalia, it is impossible to do so within the mass media. They tend to flow in and out of one another and bolster each other. It does not follow that cultural uniqueness is the mild cold, so to speak, of Japanese society and racial uniqueness is pneumonia. This is true even though one agrees to a certain extent with Sugimoto and Mouer when they observe that "the symbols of racial difference are so powerfully part of the colonial and post-colonial experience, and of the occupation and post-occupation experience, that they are easy to conjure up again as internationalization brings the national interest of the Japanese state into conflict with the interests of other states."[11]   The extent of disagreement pertains to the lack of interpolation of a powerful part of present-day experience within this quotation and the failure to identify racial uniqueness as inherent within the social fabric of modern Japan, thereby continually influencing Japan's international perspectives regardless of current intensity of impact. There is no need for conflict to awaken the evil demon.

The symbiotic relationship between cultural and racial uniqueness within Japanese society is evident in the distinct cultural definition that colors popular understanding of the word "race." Actually, in whatever language or from whatever social level, race is a word which is exceedingly situational in definition. Scientists faced with how to apply race to divide the human species for description are confronted with any number of alternatives. One expert on the diversity of scientific conceptualizations using race, Stephen Molnar, refers to the confusion surrounding the race idea in biology and anthropology in this way:

> Many people take for granted that they know what race means and assume that scientific investigation has long ago proved the existence of significant human racial differences. But, each time the term is applied, a definition must be provided so that the reader will know what concept it represents. There is even considerable confusion over the number of divisions of humanity; as few as three and as many as thirty-seven races have been described. Two carefully written studies published in 1950 listed six and thirty races respectively.

Just what constitutes a race is a hard question to answer, because one's classification usually depends on the purpose of classification, and various approaches to taxonomy often have a built-in bias, especially when applied to humans. It is usually assumed that there is an actual structure or collection of organisms in the natural world awaiting classification.[12]

Molnar proceeds to provide a listing of top specialists on race and their varied definitions. It is also quite easy to reproduce such definitions from the works of scholars, Westerners and Japanese alike, cited within this study.[13] On a worldwide basis, two distinct polarities can easily be observed. At one end, there is Stanley Garn's classification of race which emphasizes the importance of geography or spatial distribution of human variation as delineating racial groups.[14] At the other, there is disagreement with definitions which posit geographic isolation as playing a role in origins.[15] At this polarity, "the origin of race involves estimating population size and dispersal rates, two favorite parameters of the population geneticist."[16] Actually, Garn conceived of his nine geographical races, which closely conformed to the older root-stock divisions of Mongoloid, Caucasoid and Negroid, as collections of local races which were in turn defined as breeding populations, the number of which were very large. Race, therefore, in scientific circles, is like a Caucasoid-Mongoloid-Negroid accordion being stretched back and forth along lines of human variation. There is also a recognition among scholars that the term race is highly susceptible to erroneous and prejudicial linkages regarding human worth and ability.[17]

Race can also be defined primarily according to sociopolitical criteria. According to Molnar, this frequent use of the term entails a delineation of a cultural or political group followed by an explanation of its existence in biological terms.[18] Consequently, racial boundaries delimiting populations are distorted by social demands. It is this definition which creates a quandary for Japanese scholars who are quite aware of the strength of attachment toward such a perspective within their own society. The world of Japanese origins' research is confronted by a sight defect within mass culture. The tendency is for Japanese to view race as nation and nation as race. The prominent paleoanthropologist, Kazuro Hanihara, in his introduction to a paper on the origins of the Japanese put the problem in this way:

> In Japanese, the concepts of 'nation' and 'race' are often referred to by the same term. The term is used to denote two clearly different meanings, and the resulting ambiguity does cause some confusion. For instance, the word for 'racism' is also used to denote 'nationalism' in Japanese, and the term for 'Aryan race' is used to refer to the Aryan nation (people) and the Aryan linguistic family. In this paper, we intend to discuss the origin of the Japanese from the point of view of physical anthropology. Therefore, the subject is not the Japanese nation, but the Japanese 'race.'[19]

A quick glance at a Japanese-English high school dictionary would turn up the meaning of the word "minzoku" as people, race or nation. Recognition of the confused state of race and nation within the Japanese perspective is also evident in the observations of another senior professor of anthropology, Takao Sofue. In a round-table discussion with other scholars on the subject of race and nation (and/or ethnicity), Sofue referred to a symposium which was held in 1973 concerning education and the diffusion of anthropology and ethnology within the universities, high schools and society in general. He explained that during the meeting the matter of a large number of inaccuracies on race and ethnicity within high school textbooks was raised. As a result, two years later, he noted that the Ministry of Education considered the situation serious enough to provide funding for the establishment of an investigative committee of anthropologists and ethnologists. At that time, according to Sofue, a survey of seventeen high school textbooks on world geography revealed that all possessed a similar misunderstanding of race and ethnicity. In his estimation, therefore. there exists at the high school level a number of textbooks which can promote bias, such as the ones which identify Jews as a race.[20] During this discussion as well, the genetics expert Ryutaro Otsuka evaluated the sociological significance of the race-nation confusion by dividing academia from mass culture on the question. He maintained that such matters are often misunderstood within the general society. but there appears to be a common understanding among scholars on the differences between the two concepts.[21]

Popular culture in Japan is therefore beset with not only a highly fluid, scientific definition of race, but also with a crisscrossed race-nation perspective. Consequently, the idea of a race-culture symbiosis rather than just culturalism itself as activating a Japanese image of their uniqueness would appear at face or "word" value to be appropriate.

CHAPTER I

MYTHICAL HOUSE OF THE RISING SUN

It has been said that the Japanese have been eminently successful in engineering better products than in the West. But can it be contended that they construct better myths as well? If the Japanese myth of racial origins was an automobile, one might hear the consumer refrain that it outperforms the western model in terms of long-term reliability, flexible handling ability and attractive features. One would learn that the western myth depends on an abstract concept for its basic plan and utilizes scientifically gathered and verified information as the main materials while the competition relies on the force of imagery in design and makes optimum use of ancient historical texts and modern mass media creativity. Consideration of the West-Japan performance differential in myth manufacture concerns mankind's obsession with its "specialness" in nature, with the continuing saga of why man or a group of humans stands out from the rest of the creatures on this planet.

According to those experts, especially anthropologists and molecular biologists/geneticists, who have to do battle with myth in their professional pursuits, the conceptual framework of the contemporary operative myth on man's self-image in the West is based not on the heroic tales of the ancient Greeks, Norsemen or Hebrews nor the Christian vision that man, a special part of God's grand design of the universe, was predestined to occupy the tower apartments of a hierarchical chain of being. Instead, from where they stand, the popular myth which weighs heavily upon Western society is a gift of the industrial revolution, a residue of Victorian times, i.e., the myth of progress. The 19th century had witnessed man's harnessing of natural energy to prosper as never before and society's economic future appeared boundless. The betterment of the human condition was conceived as inevitable but not revolutionary, not destabilizing – an unacceptable course for the growing middle class. The world would instead become more and more efficient, little by little. This myth of progress was bolstered and knighted by the theory of Charles Darwin.[1]

Darwinian evolution or the proposition that organisms are related and new species develop out of older through the natural selection of variations in traits in the struggle for survival is one of science's most highly verified theses. Evolution is not a myth. According to Niles Eldredge and Ian Tattersall, both curators at the American Museum of Natural History, evolution which has been subjected to close scrutiny for over a century now "emerges as the only naturalistic explanation we have of the twin patterns of similarity and diversity that pervade all life." But, in their estimation, "*how* life has evolved is another matter entirely."[2] Scholars and commentators continually encounter the standard expectation of a slow, steady, ladder-like climb through time. They discover obstacles in the path of observations and theories of nonchange and stability in evolutionary development or of development in fits and starts. Even though data continues to be forthcoming on the predominance of nonchange in organisms' genetic histories, the expectation in evolutionary-scientific circles remains of a constant progression to a new breakthrough.[3] In posing the question "how not to think about evolution?," the biologist Christopher Wills notes that two of the main fallacies are movement toward a goal and the smooth and direct evolution from one species to another. Regarding the former, he explains that natural selection could be nondirectional, for the status quo. As for the latter, he explains that smooth changes in the fossil record do not seem to involve the appearance of novel structures and functions and the possibility is, as a number of researchers suggest, that dramatic changes can occur only during violent upheavals in the gene pool of primarily small populations. One of these researchers is the Harvard biologist and *Natural History* magazine commentator, Stephen Jay Gould, who co-authored with Eldredge the theorem of punctuated equilibrium, i.e., of long periods of evolutionary stability punctuated by much shorter periods of rapid change in the gene pool.[4] In his study of biases inherent in past scientific inquiries in the development of man's mental powers, reference is made to the propensity for ordering a complex variation as human intelligence on a scale of gradual ascent. He notes in this regard that "metaphors of progress and gradualism have been among the most pervasive in Western thought"[5] and generalizes on conceptualized scientomyths or what he calls imaginative visions. He relates:

> Science, since people must do it, is a socially embedded activity. It progresses by hunch, vision, and intuition. Much of its change through time does not record a closer approach to absolute truth but the alteration of cultural contexts that influence it so strongly. Facts are not pure and unsullied bits of information; culture also influences what we see and how we see it. Theories, moreover, are not inexorable inductions from facts. The most creative theories are often imaginative visions imposed on facts; the source of imagination is also strongly cultural. This argument, although still anathema to many practicing scientists, would, I think, be accepted by every historian of science.[6]

Although Gould didn't mention it as an example in this regard, one of the world's most prominent anthropologists of the past, the American, Carleton Coon, fell right through this pitfall of imaginative vision into an arena of blatant racial prejudice, although a highly popular form of this commodity, in the West when he began to hypothesize on how Africans fell behind the other races in the progress through time.[7] The tendency to reach out for such discoveries extends back to the Darwinian eruption of the 19th century[8] and continues to plague interpretations of human evolution. The molecular biologist and anthropologist, Vincent Sarich, whose research achievements will be described below, was recently sharply criticized by students and faculty members of the University of California, Berkeley, for making statements demeaning to women, nonwhites and homosexuals. According to the *New York Times*, "these statements, made in an introductory course, include suggestions that women have smaller brains than men, that race makes a difference in academic ability and that homosexuals prefer jobs where a woman is boss."[9]

In the 1980s, when a team of molecular biologists associated with the University of California, Berkeley, set forth their findings that modern man had not evolved over millions of years through progressive stages but had made a quantum leap in Africa in rather recent times and thereafter had occupied the niches worldwide previously held by other homo species, *Newsweek* ran a story highlighting the controversy which engulfed their findings. The reporters related that the most controversial implication of the results was not biblical, although the article was entitled "The Search for Adam and Eve," and the explanation was given that the 200,000-year-old common, maternal ancestor of modern man was being called Eve by the scientists themselves. What was a bitter pill for many anthropologists to swallow, according to the article, was the idea that man didn't emerge after a slow and inexorable process in different parts of the world.[10] From the opposite corner of the ring, *Newsweek* quoted Gould, as saying: "If it's correct, and I'd put money on it, this idea is tremendously important."[11] In the opinion of Michael Brown, an investigative journalist, "Gould seemed nothing short of in love with the Eve proposition" – a jubilant witness to a stone thrown through the window of the myth of progress.[12]

This merger of myth and science, which gave rise to a battle of will within the Western academic theatre, represented a parting of the mythical models – Western and Japanese – on human ancestry. The former entered a conceptual, scientific universe while the latter remained sequestered behind in the world of the "image," the planet of the superheroes. A kind of splitting of the atom had occurred. Western myths are highly structured performers reflected in the efforts of the analytical mind to tame the physical environment. These performers combine with civilization's technological contours to provide man with a sense of security within an environment in constant flux. Scientomythic man takes solace in the tale that science is bigger than life and order after order will be revealed as science fills in the pages of the book on the relativity of the world of experience, making life a commodity of smooth progression.

The philosopher Leszek Kolakowski notes such a duality in his book *The Presence of Myth*, although he is intent on distinguishing metaphysical from scientific questions and beliefs. He holds that the presence of the nonempirical unconditioned reality (metaphysics) "cannot in principle be the object of proof, because the proof-making ability is itself a power of the analytical mind, technological oriented, which does not extend beyond its tasks."[13] For Kolakowski, the two different energizing activators in man's conscious relation to the world are the scientific and the mythical. But Kolakowski's schematic design depends on two extreme reference points, the eternal and the ephemeral: myth is eternal while science is continually excavating new ground and disregarding old traditional values. However, even the strongest myth cannot resist time and the impact of civilization. The tall tales of the ancient Greeks are now just old stories, museum pieces. And the perimeters surrounding the paradigms of science share the following features identifiable as mythical within the Kolakowski framework:[14] (1) There is a need to rescue meaning from fleeting contingency by reference to an unconditioned reality. A paradigm, according to Thomas Kuhn, the author of *The Structure of Scientific Revolutions*, possesses the power to resist alternatives and "to force nature into the preformed and relatively inflexible box that the paradigm supplies."[15] The difference between paradigmatic mythical forms and the metaphysical is that the latter has the capacity to envelop the universe as a totality and resist modification on a holistic basis, e.g., the biblical, omnipresent God. (2) There exists a disposition to search for values which transcend time, ones that will remain even after the individual has departed from this planet. Once again, a paradigm-related myth might not be around forever, but it could, like the myth of progress, be around for generation after generation. (3) Another requisite relates to the organization of the world in which we live, to the desire to make nature continuous and thereby eliminate surprises. In this regard, the myth of progress also would come very close to meeting the Kolakowski understanding of myth. Herein it functions as a safety valve against the tyranny of time and the terror of mere happenings.

Nevertheless, Kolakowski is entirely correct on the point that when myth combines with science it degenerates in terms of resistance to the conditional reality.[16] A scientomyth is conceptually based and possesses a definitive structure. Although a concept can be broadened to include dissonant inputs, the nature of a conceptual form is like that of a highly earthquake-proof building subjected to an unforeseen, catastrophic upheaval – quite insecure. Once a myth is attached to detailed boundaries, it becomes difficult to rearrange points of reference without disregarding the unconditional reality. For instance, the myth of progress lacks the flexibility which would permit incorporation of the geneticist's "out of Africa" thesis. As such, this evolutionary finding possesses the potential for being a 12 on a mythical quake scale of 10.

There is also the matter that a scientomyth can never be one-hundred-percent unconditional. The shadow of a doubt is ever present in the continual reassessment of what is true, an action dictated by the scientific search for better models to explain the realm of expanding knowledge. The dictum of falsification is the hangman of scientomyth. And therefore such a mythical form can never completely conquer the soul of man as the primordial heroes did. The anthropologist Donald Johanson who in 1986 discovered a skeleton in Africa which added an innovative ascent to the early stages of human evolution found himself simultaneously accepting and resisting the popularity of being the new idol of the scientomyth of progress. He wrote that in his lecture tour of the United States he was possessed by the feeling that his words were being inhaled as if they held some special authority. He notes that it was as if he had just returned from the Mount and was offering a new version of the path which man was destined to follow. Afterwards, when he found himself bombarded with questions concerning the nature of man's humanity, the development of human morality and the future of mankind, he recoiled from all the notoriety, explaining:

> Rather than inspire me with self-importance, the questions only filled me with a nagging sense that something was going wrong. I am an anthropologist, not a priest. Donald Johanson's opinions on the future of mankind have no more intrinsic worth than those of any other reasonably informed individual. More to the point, even my views on human origins – including my firmly held interpretation that Lucy's [the name given to his discovery] species was the direct ancestor to the human line – are necessarily tentative. I would be the first to reject that hypothesis if new evidence proved it false.[17]

While the Western world grapples with scientomyth, Japan has remained in the distant past. Japan today still envisions origins rather than conceptualizes them. Japan's passage through the industrial revolution, the drastic changes in political and socio-economic structure, the welcoming of Darwinism, anthropology, biology, etc. and the achievement of international recognition as a national developmental model of growth and progress have failed to dim the image of an unconditional reality inherent in the origins of man.

This is not to say that the science of human evolution and its accompanying scientomythology have not impacted on Japanese society, popular and academic. However, the influence of the conceptual universe has been kept at the periphery of the dominant reality through the division of origins into Western-related and Japanese, the former primarily the domain of science, the latter of a vision. Furthermore, although various scientific technologies have been allowed to invade the core of Japanese origins, they have not altered the myth. Their penetration of the core has been along acceptable paths, ones which would add color to old tales rather than challenge their legitimacy. In the case of Japan's mythical core, knowledge, whether historical or scientific, is to be utilized according to the myth's dictates rather than in accordance with an objective method or procedure.

Myth in Japan still fits snugly into the definitive framework set forth by the mythologist Mircea Eliade. The dictates of the "origins" in Japan are conjured up by the properties and functions illuminated in Eliade's works. Firstly, myth is the historical account of sacred time, a narrative of the "beginnings" in which Godlike heroes created reality.[18] Myth relates not only the origin of the World and all living organisms but also those primordial events which confer upon man his social character and future destiny. Secondly, myth functions to reveal models for man which give meaning to the World and human life. Myth unfolds the activities of superhumans behaving in an exemplary fashion by performing grandiose and glorious deeds.[19] These performances since they pertain to man's rite of passage can be partly recovered through imitation of paradigmatic values and archtypes which is the end-result of the repeated telling of the tale. Through repeated recitation, man transcends his own limitations and realities and is able to take his place with the Gods and the mythical heroes in a perfectly articulated and intelligible Cosmos.[20] In Eliade's own words, "the copying of these archetypes betrays a certain discontent with one's own personal history, an obscure striving to transcend one's own local, provincial history and to recover some Great Time or other – though it may be only the mythic Time of the first surrealist or existentialist manifesto."[21] It also stimulates the true believer to strive toward a higher self-esteem by transforming himself as best a possible into a child of the Great Time in his perception of his everyday life.[22] Thirdly, the Eliade myth is insulated against time and history. Time cannot unveil the mystery or dispute the revelation of values embodied in the myth. The myth is a cradle in which man can seek shelter when the course of events outruns his capacity to cope. The outside world cannot challenge the Sacred Time of creation. "As a summary formula," Eliade says, that by "living the myths one emerges from profane, chronological time and enters a time that is of a different quality, a 'sacred' Time at once primordial and indefinitely recoverable."[23]

The typical Eliade-defined myth and the origins' myth of the Japanese interface within the realm of the image. Japan's myth complements Eliade's above designated properties and functions with the following: a flexed Great Time and composite archetypes. The Japanese myth or elements of it can penetrate or appear within a highly diffuse time period of 8 centuries or more. However, the thematic treatment of the origins rests within a single cradle. Although some alteration in the style of the myth may be required, the structure is never jeopardized. The participant in the Japanese myth is just about given the choice of what style – Chinese, Northeast Asian, etc. – of information is most provocative in evoking the image within the psyche. The way of the image is an affective response along any point within a continuum of suggestive touches of color, tonal shadings and emphasis. Japan's image myth is a vision of ancient history outside of Time. Time loses its sanctity; the sacred lies in legendary history. The tale unfolds within a set context, but time is not a set fixture. Consequently, the fluidity and movement of the image is the myth's ultimate protection against conditional reality. The Japanese myth is a dramatic happening with no single date or dates. It travels lightly, making use of the winds of selective bits of information to guide its time-zone landings and extensions. The myth doesn't seek out information or rationality but instead attaches itself to the dramatic, since the Creation is an event of overwhelming significance. Of extreme importance in the mythical penetration of time is the correct mood or atmosphere, a magical or theatrical incident, for instance. Mood information rather than substantive information sets the stage for the rise of the image myth and mood information is more in keeping with a flexed Great Time. Mood modifies the psychological climate of the individual participating in the myth, sweeps away the disposition to know more about the details of reality and substitutes an affective response for one of understanding. Mood is the lever by which the participant is drawn away from the mundane and fully caught up in the image scenario.

Mood is also associated with the second significant property of Japan's image myth, the composite archetypes. These mythical superheroes radiate lessons on how man should behave in spite of the conditional realities of everyday life. In the world of the image, all is possible and all who take part in the performance carry with them into real time the heritage of the Becoming. They breathe in the value-rich episodes of the myth and breathe out tales on perspectives of their own real-time actions. In this way, the image myth is carried forward into individual roles in business, politics, international relations, etc. By composite archetypes, it is meant that the archetype image is an image within an image (and perhaps within a third or forth). To uncover the other reality, assistance is often required and that's where mood enters the picture. Mood makes everything transparent. Mood stereotypes. A suggestiveness within the atmosphere can reel the participant from one focal point to another and place him in the midst of a totally different portrayal. For instance, a narrative description of a 3rd century Japanese madonna, the legendary Queen Himiko, whose queendom is described in the Chinese dynastic records of the time, can zap one into the presence of forceful horseriding invaders from the continent by means of stereotyped visual-leads, e.g., the beating of horses' hoofs followed by an incoming tide, within a TV story which doesn't require such additions. In this way, the myth-rider moves on to the flip side of a Queen Himiko episode and mentally replays the heroic exploits of Japan's nomadic conquerors.

Nevertheless, mood is not always required since composite archetypes are such a standardized feature of the mythical format. The composite offers a means of legitimizing images as well as providing a context for variations in the rendering of the myth. An example is the composite of Queen Himiko, a symbol of unification extracted from the old Chinese records, and Amaterasu, the Sun Goddess, who according to the ancient Japanese chronicles, sends her grandson down to earth to reign over the inhabitants. In this regard, Himiko's name can be interpreted as a rendition of Himeko which in Japanese means Sun Princess to suit the format. Biten Yasumoto, a professor at Sanno University in the Yokohama area who has found a niche in mass culture publications on ancient Japan and has written prolifically on the subject, "images" Amaterasu as Himiko. His tale centers on the story of Amaterasu's withdrawal into the cave of heaven, thereby throwing the world into darkness. To Yasumoto, this signifies the demise of Queen Himiko since the cave is a symbol of death. Afterwards, in the tale, Amaterasu is enticed out of the cave by the festivities of the deities. In Yasumoto's rendition, the "coming out" sequence is a reference to the succession of a new female ruler, Himiko's niece.[24]

Another popular writer on ancient Japan is Masao Okuno, a nonacademic who tends to believe that there is a place for myth in history and that mythical inquiries need not be unscientific.[25] Both Yasumoto and Okuno can usually be found packaged in mini-sized paperbacks, usually half the size of the usual kind, or booklet-style volumes, targeted for commuters' and travelers' easy reading on city and long-distance trains.[26] In fact, although Okuno's approach to mythical veracity tends to differ somewhat from Yasumoto's, their paths do cross. For instance, Okuno highly evaluates Yasumoto's imaging of the mythical descendant of Amaterasu, the Emperor Jimmu, as the embodiment of a reference in the Chinese records to a king who followed Himiko.[27]

Sometimes, composite archetypes seem more complex than they actually are for the Japanese enthusiast of interpretations of the ancient records who has come into contact with the form many times before. For instance, a common form has Himiko's niece and successor, Toyo, as the counterpart of Yamatototohimomosohime, of the Japanese sources. This aspect of the composite is derived from the close political relationship between Himiko and her brother – a type of sister-brother, queen-king relationship. The Emperor Sujin, the 10th emperor, and his aunt/priestess, Yamatototohimomosohime, are pictured as having a similar kinship-imperial relationship and consequently, the Toyo of the Chinese records becomes the mask beyond which the Emperor Sujin lurks, giving greater reality to the existence of this legendary ruler.[28]

This "Eliade-ized" storybook of the origins of the Japanese with its flexed Great Time and composite archetypes can be conceived of as being divided into three interdependent sections. One can think of it as a triple layer cake. The foundation layer is the ancestral mythology collected in 8th century Japanese texts. The center layer mainly contains 3rd century Chinese observations on Japan. And the final layer, with a topping which spills down over the lower layers, is the secularized, updated version of earlier storybooks. In other words, all three divisions are interdependent, but the modernizing division is more style than form, functioning to enhance the attractiveness of the mythical context.

The texts of the foundation layer are the *Kojiki* (712) and the *Nihon Shoki* (720). A popular controversy, which exists even today, concerns whether the *Kojiki* was an imperial compilation or not, or whether it was originally a nonimperial family work, with the preface being fabricated to make it seem to be otherwise.[29] In any event, the *Kojiki* lent support to the more politically-oriented *Nihon Shoki*. Through the mythical embroidery of the *Nihon Shoki*, we are taken back to a sacred time when the islands of Japan were created by the coupling of the primal pair, Izanagi and Izanami. The Age of the Deities of Heaven and Earth in the mythical history was a miraculous period in which a highly productive natural universe was created for the benefit of the earthly god-children, the Japanese people.[30] In this context, the heavenly gods deemed the land below to be too valuable to be ruled by just any deity. It was therefore decided that the grandson of the Sun Goddess was to exercise political control. However, before he could descend, it was considered necessary to restore order since the islands had been thrown into turmoil by the actions of "numerous Deities which shone with a lustre like that of fireflies, and evil deities which buzzed like flies."[31] By means of magical and heroic exploits, the deities carved out an orderly kingdom in Kyushu to receive the descent of the august grandchild. The son of Japan's first god-ruler covorted with the dragon-daughter of the Sea-God and to them was born a boy who would be the father of the *Nihon Shoki*'s conquering Emperor, Jimmu.[32] When Jimmu reached the age of 45, he addressed his elder brothers and his children, explaining the need to bring to complete fruition the design of the heavenly deities. He related that when his heavenly ancestor descended, the area around them was desolate and in upheaval, but now order has returned to the western border (Kyushu).[33] He continued: "But the remote regions do not yet enjoy the blessings of Imperial rule. Every town has always been allowed to have its lord and every village its chief, who, each one for himself, makes division of territory and practices mutual aggression and conflict. Now I have heard ... that in the East there is a fair land encircled on all sides by blue mountains. ...I think that this land will undoubtedly be suitable for the extension of the Heavenly task, so that its glory should fill the universe. It is, doubtless, the centre of the world."[34] Emperor Jimmu and his imperial forces then proceeded from one glorious adventure to another, proceeding with the Sun (or Sun Goddess) at their backs, following her rays and trampling under foot all who weren't neutralized by magical ploys or imperial alliance. At one point, when the imperial forces were stymied in their advance by confusion as to what direction to take, the Sun Goddess sent down a sun-crow to guide them through the mountainous terrain. Victorious, the Emperor Jimmu established the imperial reign of Japan in 660 B.C. in Yamato, the area centering around Nara, a short distance inland from Osaka.[35] The *Nihon Shoki*, then, turns to the reigns of the emperors that follow Jimmu and the chronicle ends at the turn of the 7th century.

The *Nihon Shoki* was not intended as an historical treatise in the modern sense, but was to serve as an instrument of political propaganda designed to glorify and legitimize the rule of the hegemonic Yamato clan chieftain who was the direct descendant of the supreme deity, the Sun Goddess. In this framework, facts were to be used whenever necessary to enhance the intensity of the origins' myth and to assimilate the lesser clans and their deities into a hierarchical ordering under the children of the august grandchild.[36] The facts which appear in the *Nihon Shoki* are so enmeshed within the mythical framework that they are difficult to see and it is almost impossible to understand how, when and why they were placed in their existing locations. However, there are writers, such as Yasumoto and Okuno, who believe they possess the vision and have sought to extract from the foundation layer factual relationships for blueprinting the chronological flow of events by logical reasoning. But such an endeavor overlooks a structural standard; i.e., the primary objective of an origins' myth is its telling, all other elements being accessories to be placed wherever appropriate. And although an analyst may read all that he wants into it and attach archaeological finds to the interpretation, there is no way for confirming whether that individual is not merely verifying his own biases given the paucity of evidence external to the myth.

Another complication which modern-day commentators confront or seek to bypass relates to a further sprinkling of intricacies and ambiguities brought about by the association of the Japanese texts with the highly respected Chinese dynastic histories. Magical Chinese dating techniques were adopted to arrive at the founding of the imperial reign in Yamato in 660 B.C. The reigns of the Emperors were lengthened considerably to accommodate this approach and at least one major, glorifying event was liberally assigned to each reign. In addition, events were transcribed with year, month and day, although the calendar was obtained from China in the 6th or 7th century A.D. And for good measure, Chinese classical quotations and terms were liberally dispersed throughout the text, which was written in Chinese. This use of a stylistic model outside of the ancient Japanese traditional way of thinking must have violated any number of historical continuities and relationships and led to an even greater alienation of facts from their original moorings.[37]

Nevertheless, regardless of the validity of efforts to analyze the myths by selecting out for special attention the contents of the ancient records themselves, such appraisals, as those of Yasumoto and Okuno, foster modernization, if only within a narrow textual spectrum, through the application of logic and modern-day-compatible creative styles. Yasumoto has popularized his search for mythical enlightenment by transforming the quest into a game or a puzzle. Yasumoto is like a knight trying to find a way through the labyrinth of tales and the reader is continually presented with new and possible passages as the storybook proceeds. Yasumoto tends to evaluate the *Kojiki* somewhat more highly than the *Nihon Shoki* at times because he believes that the nonpolitical, native-style *Kojiki* represents a purer commodity for analysis. However, this point is a moot one in view of Yasumoto's assertion that regardless of whether an analysis is based on either of the ancient texts, the results would be the same. In any case,

Yasumoto initially packages his quest along rational lines by describing the nature of the game in a rather psychological fashion. He explains that the *Kojiki* and *Nihon Shoki* are like old memories of one's childhood in that one is aware of the occurrence of a past event but is unable to fix a date to it. He states further that the accounts in the *Kojiki* and *Nihon Shoki* are similar in clarity to memories of where events occurred in one's childhood, e.g., having taken place either at home or in kindergarten. This analogy between the reality of childhood and the mythical tale of creation, intentionally or not, updates the myth and personalizes it for the individual, making it part of his life history and his condition of being. The reader is not merely proceeding to undertake a search into legendary time but is descending to his roots, to the cradle of cradles. This assumptive and connotative prologue leads to another assumption in the form of the conclusion that the location of a great Yamato power initially in Kyushu represents a relatively clear memory.[38]

The Yasumoto game or puzzle of origins centers on a list of place names in the *Kojiki* and references to places in the 907 A.D. *Engi-shiki*, a record of court and provincial conditions at that time. One should keep in mind that Yasumoto is assuming that the place names in the *Engi-shiki* were in place several hundred years prior to this compilation. One name which is not included in the game is that of Yamato itself since Yasumoto concedes that Yamato can be placed in either Kinai or Kyushu depending on one's reading of the *Kojiki*. In certain respects, the Yasumoto game resembles a word association quiz. A popular long-run TV program in Japan presented members of a panel with associated word hints until a participant identified the correct word. Yasumoto provides similar quandaries. For example, he gives the reader the word "unabara" from the *Kojiki* and refers to its relationship with the ruling god-king of San-in (western Honshu centering on Izumo), Sanno no Mikoto, prior to the descent of the august grandchild. Unabara means seaside, but in conjunction with Sanno no Mikoto, another definition can be gained. Yasumoto, in framing the question for the reader, explains that Izanagi no Mikoto, in the *Kojiki*, ordered Sanno no Mikoto to govern unabara. The hint having been given, Yasumoto confides in the reader that unabara is a place name like Yamato and although he doesn't say so, considering the relationship with Sanno no Mikoto, it would be in San-in. In commenting on the complications of his listing of localities in his book, Yasumoto asserts that if one checks carefully the place names in Kyushu and San-in, a lot of places mentioned in the *Kojiki* become apparent.[39]

An excellent example of how creative Yasumoto can be in his presentation is evident in the inferences which he draws from the *Kojiki*'s use of "kudaru" and from the alternative name for one of the two gods sent to San-in to prepare for the august grandchild's descent. Nowadays, trains departing from the capital are "kudaru" while trains arriving from outside Tokyo are "noboru." For Yasumoto, the use of kudaru hints at a hidden meaning concerning the gods' descent from heaven to earth, i.e., from a center of power to an outer area. Also, Yasumoto explains that one of the descending gods went by a name of "fast as a bird, strong ship" (Torinoiwakusubune no Kami), indicating that their movement to an outer area or San-in was made by ship.[40]

Aside from word associations, number crunching also enters into Yasumoto's game plan. For this purpose, Yasumoto sets his magnifying glass to the first volume of the *Kojiki* which recounts the age of the gods and compiles a list of "actual possible place names." The reader then discovers that there are nearly three times as many actual possible place names as there are mythical names and that Kyushu names are mentioned 36 times for a 29.5% ratio and San-in names, 34 times for a 27.9% ratio. As such, Kyushu-San-in area names predominate. In addition, Yasumoto surmises that the actuality of these place names is enhanced because they are associated with the deeds of superheroes and are not just points on a scenic tour map. Actual deeds, in his estimation, necessitate real names. However, when Yasumoto transforms, by his own account, the mythical place names for Earth (Ashiharanonakatsukuni) and Heaven (Takamanohara) into actual possible place names in Japan, his game becomes very mysterious. At this point, he likens his effort to those of a character in an Edgar Alan Poe short story who uses ciphers to break a code hidden within a message. The reader learns that hidden within the 13 sentences in which Earth appears is Izumo country or San-in and that, in view of this conclusion, Heaven refers to Kyushu. Somehow, the fact that Earth and Heaven are the two most preponderant mythical names in the first volume, 27.7% and 38.3% respectively, heightens his resolve in this regard.[41]

Furthermore, although Yasumoto believes that the Japanese texts are capable of decodification, he doesn't neglect the second section of the mythical format, the Chinese record. As noted previously, all layers interface quite easily through a variety of terminals. And there exists an apparent effort on Yasumoto's part to integrate the two sections. It's almost as if it's a ritual requirement, something which the audience expects. He thereby sets before his readers the 3rd century chronicles of the Wei Dynasty (compiled about 297 A.D.) or more specifically the Japanese section of the *Wei Chronicle*, the "Gishiwajinden."[42]

The basic ingredients of the Gishiwajinden which form the junctions between the passages connecting the first and second sections are as follows:[43]

·   1.   Introducing Wa (Japan)...
"The people of Wo [hereinafter cited as Wa] live in the ocean to the southeast of Taifang [Chinese commandery in central Korea]. Because of mountains and islands, it is divided into countries. Formerly, Wa had more than one hundred countries, some of which came to pay respect as subjects of China during the Han Era. Now, thirty countries send their [tribute] missions."

2.   Regarding politics and defenses of the kingdom of Yamatai...
"Originally, the queen's country was ruled by a king who had been in power for seventy or eighty years. A major revolt took place in Wa, and people attacked each other for many years. Later, they acknowledged a woman as queen. Her name is Beimihu [hereinafter cited as Himiko]. She is good at performing *gweidau* [shamanism] and enjoys the confidence of her people. She has come of age but has no husband. Her younger brother helps her govern the country. Since she became queen, she has been seen by few

people and is attended by 1,000 female servants. Only one man approaches her to bring food or to convey messages. They built a palace, watchtower, and a fence. It is always guarded by armed men."

3.   Regarding Himiko's tributary mission to the Wei court in 238... [In the twelfth month of the same year, the Emperor of Wei sent an Imperial edict to the Queen of Wa.] "Although the place where you live is far, you sent a tribute mission. This shows your loyalty. We have great affection for you. Now We appoint you Queen of Wa, Friendly to Wei and give you a gold seal with a purple ribbon. We will wrap the seal and ask the chief of Taifang to deliver it to you. We wish you to soothe your people and be loyal and obedient. ...We will also give you 5 *pi* of brocade with the dragon pattern on a red background, 10 sheets of red wool crepe, 50 *pi* of crimson cloth, and 50 *pi* of deep blue cloth in order to balance your tribute, and We especially give you...8 *lyang* of gold, two 5-*chr* swords, 100 bronze mirrors, 50 *jin* of pearls, and 50 *jin* of powdered red lead."

4.   Regarding delivery of edict and seal to Himiko in 240... "They arrived at Wa and met with the queen of Wa and gave the edict, gold, silk brocade, woolen fabric, swords, mirrors, and colorful things. The queen of Wa gave a letter to the mission and asked them to convey her words of gratitude to the Emperor."

5.   Regarding a war with a neighboring kingdom beginning about 245 and the fall of the queendom... "When Himiko died during the war, a huge mound was built. It is more than one hundred paces in diameter and more than one hundred slaves followed her in death. Thereafter, a king appeared, but the people of the country did not obey him and fought with each other. At the time, more than 1,000 people were killed in the war. So Yiyu [Toyo], a female relative [perhaps, niece] of Himiko, thirteen years old, was acknowledged as queen. Then, the civil war came to an end."

The Chinese record is generally considered by the average Japanese to be more authoritative than the *Nihon Shoki* or the *Kojiki* in its historical accuracies. As such, reference to the *Wei Chronicle* serves to testify to the historical legitimacy of an undertaking to reconstruct Japan's past. Yet, the Chinese record, like the Japanese legendary accounts, presents mass media investigators, such as Yasumoto, with quandaries of its own. There is the matter that the Gishiwajinden is a mere annex within an annex to the main body of the record and therefore quite brief.[44] Since the information provided is highly selective, there is cause to wonder about the value of what the compilation might have left out and how such facts would have altered the tale. Besides, there is no reason to assume that the information presented fell within the dates of 238-247 A.D., the time given for the period of intercourse between the Wei Dynasty and the Japanese kingdom of Yamatai. The source could really be second hand with regard to various specifics. One scholar has even suggested that descriptions of people's lifestyles would seem to be more attuned to an earlier period.[45] The fact that Japan is included in the section on Eastern Barbarians, plus the brevity of the description, raises the spectre of Chinese ethnocentricism controlling and influencing the credibility of the historical account as well. Therefore, the question remains as to whether there's too much Chinese civilization, too much distortion, in the Japan story. For instance, the chroniclers relate that in Japan, "when they meet, people sit together, and there is no distinction between the seats of father or son or between man and woman."[46] Since such a portrayal contrasted with the five sacred distinguishing relationships of Confucian political and social harmony, i.e., ruler and subject, father and son, husband and wife, elder brother and younger brother and friend and friend, this morsel of information would have confronted a Wei student of Confucianism with material for a lesson on the differences between an advanced and backward society. China's idea of international relations, especially with a country such as distant Japan, was quite inward looking and was valued as long as it reflected China's cultural superiority. This lack of internationalism is also probably related to why–although Chinese preoccupation with magical numbers to signify good and bad omens is more than likely the main culprit–the distances and directions between Korea and Yamatai are quite incorrect. Through a differing interpretation of the coordinates, one can locate Yamatai in Kyushu, in Kinki or in the sea or ocean. This shortcoming also makes for some difficulty in matching the Gishiwajinden with the Japanese sources.[47]

Before integrating the Chinese record into his creative rendition of Japanese origins, Yasumoto presents a logical framework – the logic of political rationality – for considering the relevance of what the Wei chroniclers have to say about Japan. He explains that the *Wei Chronicle* can only be partly trusted, but when the Chinese record deals with politics, there is reason to credit the authenticity of such accounts. Herein, Yasumoto is postulating that the Chinese weren't so interested in accurately detailing the customs and values of Japan, but they were very much interested in Asian geopolitics. For this reason, he believes that since the *Wei Chronicle* referred to relations with Yamatai (for Yasumoto, the Wei's Yamatai is the mythical Yamato) country, such a country existed. In addition, he holds that the political date in the Wei record of 238 A.D. for the sending of a delegation from Yamatai to the Wei court is an actual date, one which pinpoints the existence of Yamato in real time.[48]

This pull to follow the *Kojiki-Nihon Shoki-Wei Chronicle* format for telling the story of Japanese origins becomes fully apparent at the end of Yasumoto's book when the author puts the final touches on his product by including a section on how to come to Yamatai using the Gishiwajinden, which means trying to make sense out of coordinates which are highly equivocal.[49] This weaving of an analysis by meandering from Japanese source to Chinese source while coloring in the supporting details with liberal assumptions and associations represents in a certain respect a tale within a tale. Yasumoto is not merely interpreting the "origin" myths, he's imitating the 8th century chronicle's freedom to fly. How many times in the *Nihon Shoki* are stories repeated in a modified fashion with the introduction that "in one writing it is said" or "another version is?" The difference is that Yasumoto is a modern flyer and the repetition which he brings to the subject makes the mythical format not just a product of the ancients but a new, improved product for the modern consumer. Indeed, Yasumoto is creative, dramatic and popular.

Unlike Yasumoto, Okuno doesn't rely so heavily on the foundation texts themselves, but depends more on the historically oriented instrument, the Gishiwajinden, to define the reality of Japanese origins. He explains that when we consider the first ruler of the first established imperial power in Yamato, everybody reflects upon the building of the country by the Emperor Jimmu as described in the *Nihon Shoki* and the *Kojiki*. Therefore, Okuno writes that he will analyze "Jimmu Tōsen Denshō" or the eastern movement of Jimmu, a topic which was kind of taboo after World War II. In Okuno's estimation, there may be some facts hidden in the story of Emperor Jimmu which would throw some light upon the establishment of a country in Yamato. He then goes on, referring to Jimmu's given name of Kamu-Yamato-Iware-Biko (Jimmu is the posthumous name), meaning man in the Iware area of Yamato, and plays a word association game which traces the location of the Iware part of the given name to a place in the Nara area, Japan's ancient historical imperial center, where the first capital might have been built. The Okuno route has Jimmu starting his eastward campaign from Hyuga in northern Kyushu. However, he does indicate that many people consider Hyuga to be in Miyazaki or southern Kyushu. From Hyuga, Jimmu's movement is mapped from Usa in Oita to the Fukuoka area and onward to an admitted unverifiable location and afterwards to.... Okuno's awareness of the dubiousness of reaching firm conclusions based on the Japanese texts alone is apparent in his rather honest appraisal of his own word/place name games. At this point, Okuno concedes the need for confirmation through excavation, but his emphasis is on confirmation, not falsification. He's waving the flags of the *Wei Chronicle* and the Japanese texts, not preparing to stamp them in the dust. Okuno demands that excavated finds should be recognized as the proofs of the facts written in the documents. The document which he identifies as most important for determining the source of the eastward movement is the Gishiwajinden. In this respect, Okuno is highly critical of Yamataikoku Kinkisetsu people (those scholars who argue that Yamatai is in the Kinki area). He refers to them as nonbelievers in documentary evidence who seek to recreate the past only upon archaeological evidence and points to the findings of a very notable archaeologist who, in his opinion, has reaffirmed the credibility of the Wei record. The scholar in question is Makoto Sahara of the Nara Cultural Properties Research Institute who has been active in analyzing the findings of Yoshinogari village, a recent archaeological site in northern Kyushu, which has attracted nationwide attention in terms of mass as well as academic appeal. Okuno exclaims that Sahara has shown that the Chinese document is reliable by stating Yoshinogari possesses attributes mentioned in the Gishiwajinden. As such, Okuno uses archaeological evidence not to embellish but to make a U-turn right back to the narrow modernizing tactic of textual interpretation.[50] In June 1991, Okuno would turn the few pages of the Gishiwajinden into an historical novel of 341 pages replete with heroes, exotic journeys, political conspiracies and turmoil for *President*, the publisher of one of Japan's most prestigious executive business magazines. The title of the book is *Himiko: The Yamataikoku Heroic Story*.[51]

Sahara, however, is much more skeptical, much more attuned to the principles of falsification, than Okuno's portrait admits. In an article in the *Yomiuri Shimbun* in 1989 in which he analyzed the Gishiwajinden in light of the Yoshinogari excavation, Sahara laid out the pros and cons from recent archaeological evidence and he did so in more of an academic-open-minded than a myth-modernizing manner.[52] The media might have had something to do with the concept and the heading. But since the article was under his name, the contents of this famous archaeologist's examination were under his own dictates and his approach tended to be more inquisitive than provocative. In any case, as for the analysis, Sahara recognized a distortive configuration in the Gishiwajinden but related it to idealization, not so much as to Chinese ethnocentricism as postulated above. He explained that the ancient Chinese favored an idea of an ideal country in the eastern area and there was some possibility that this thinking was reflected in the Gishiwajinden. According to Sahara, evidence of such could be read into the reports that the people of Wa lived 100, 90 or 80 years; that a high-ranking person had four to five wives and even one not so high had two to three; that females in Wa were not jealous. Regarding the latter point, he wrote that in the *Kojiki*, jealous wives were found and therefore, "there is a big difference between the *Kojiki* and the Gishiwajinden." For Sahara, the passage indicating that people ate off of a pedestal ("takatsuki") was an expression used to suggest that the people of Wa valued ceremony. A further attempt at idealizing Wa could also be noted in the overestimate of the number of houses, or population, in his view.

In addition, Sahara intimated that a more broader dating of the information from the Gishiwajinden was required. He referred to the statement of the famous scholar Namio Egami that the descriptions in the Gishiwajinden were from the Han period in China and predated Yamataikoku. In this respect, he related that there were a lot of descriptions, such as diving for fish (special fishing tools found), eating with fingers (no chopsticks uncovered and use not known until 8th century), types of arrowheads (iron and bone known), people walking barefoot (rice field footprints discovered and pictures on mirrors of the 4th century), divination through the reading of cracks in organic material by using deer bones instead of turtle shells as in China (deer bones from Yayoi; turtle from next period), which fitted into the Yayoi period archaeological record. Sahara indicated that tattooing the face with circular forms with a real tattoo or coloring makeup was quite fashionable in the 2nd and 3rd centuries in Japan and earthenware evidence as well as a lid of a stone coffin had been excavated revealing such a practice. He noted that the passage concerning the absence of cows and horses in Wa appeared to be correct since the bones of cows and horses found in Jomon and Yayoi sites had been proved by laboratory testing to be of a later date. In his opinion, horses and cows, even if they existed earlier in Japan, didn't become important livestock until the 5th and 6th centuries respectively, an interpretation which he believed would be in line with the account in the Gishiwajinden. Furthermore, the archaeologist pointed to the failure to mention pigs in the Chinese record and, in view of their presence in the Yayoi period, he maintained that this oversight was full of possible meaning. Also, from an analysis of cloth by one specialist, Sahara presumed that the silkworm was being cultivated to produce silk since Japanese silk differed from that of China and Korea.

Unlike Okuno, Sahara picks at the morsels in the Gishiwajinden and spreads them out over a period rather than arranging them in sequential time. Consequently, the mythical format doesn't get caught in his throat. He's more intent on examining culture than in molding layers of information into a structured totality. However, archaeology has a competitor or a usurper within the modernizing sector of the mythical format. Aside from mythical modernization through strict adherence to textual arrangement and interpretation, there is a liberal form which absorbs archaeological, anthropological and scientific finds to support the general story and which functions to integrate diverse bodies of information into the formatted contours. Since the modernizing section primarily stylizes information to match the demands of the foundation and contributive/affirmative sections, stylization can so strongly work upon the information that symbolization occurs. Myth modernizing is as much a world of symbolic images as it is of original material, the objective being to appeal to a modern mass audience.

Since the liberal modernizing section is highly media compatible, allowing for greater versatility and creativity in the treatment of subject matter and inviting a variety of media, including television, into its fold on a regular basis, one might propose that the section should be recategorized as a propagandizing ingredient. Modernized media presentations of the Japanese origins do indeed resemble what Jacques Ellul has referred to as the propaganda of integration, which he describes as aiming to solidify the individual's participation in society.[53] Herein social institutions rather than the state are the propagandists. He explains:

> It is a long-term propaganda, a self-reproducing propaganda that seeks to obtain stable behavior, to adapt the individual to his everyday life, to reshape his thoughts and behavior in terms of the permanent social setting.[54]

However, in this particular case of Japanese origins, the media doesn't produce "pseudo-needs" in the Ellul vein.[55] The needs are there. They are put in place by a ritual tradition which pre-dates mass communication in shaping the identity of a people. They are long-term and self-reproductive because they are an inherent aspect of people's lives. The media is the instrument of myth. It modernizes the myth and makes it more palatable for consumption by a rationally-inclined, fashion-oriented affluent society. The media is a function of the myth rather than vice versa. It reinforces society's telling of the tale and modernizes it through imaginative ways of presentation, ones which would attract the broadest audience participation. The producers, directors, publishers, editors and writers are as much children of the myth as their target audience. In producing or publishing the mythical concept, they themselves are reaffirming their primal identities.

Yet, one must add a political reservation in downplaying the propaganda factor since racial identity is a need which can be made amenable to manipulation for political purposes. The media as a modernizing instrument can be coopted for attaching mythical images to ends which would serve to mobilize support for state interests. As Ellul notes: "propaganda cannot create something out of nothing. It must attach itself to a feeling, an idea; it must build on a foundation already present in the individual. The conditioned reflex can be established only on an innate reflex or a prior conditioned reflex."[56]

During World War II, the media linked the mythical origins of the Japanese and the primal qualities of the Japanese race to notions of a new world order in Asia under Japanese rule. John Dower, in his study of race and power during the war, provides insights into media linkages at the time.[57] He writes:

> Whatever reasons may be offered to explain differences between the racial and racist thinking of the Japanese and that of their Western enemies during World War Two, one overarching generalization seems difficult to challenge: whereas racism in the West was markedly characterized by denigration of others, the Japanese were preoccupied far more exclusively with elevating themselves. While the Japanese

26

were not inadept at belittling other races and saddling them with contemptuous stereotypes, they spent more time wrestling with the question of what it really meant to be "Japanese," how the "Yamato race" was unique among the races and cultures of the world, and why this uniqueness made them superior.[58]

In view of this past record of propaganda linkage, the hypothesis that the present role of the media in modernizing the myth preempts future abuse of mythohistory to manufacture consent for state interests cannot be sustained.[59]

Still, nowadays, Japan enjoys a relatively free and unfettered media. As a matter of fact, the Japanese, like any population in the developed world, is continually bombarded with a variety of information on so many fields of investigation through a wide range of printed and nonprinted sources. One wonders how the mythical format can succeed in its stylizing ventures, which must encounter wide-ranging dissonance in the Age of the Information Revolution. How can a cradle constructed in the Age of the Gods, even though it offers security and identity benefits which are superior to the present-day mythical origins in the West, continue to bend to its will the continuous onslaught through the media of new discoveries, explorations and analyses arising out of our high-tech environment? Is the cradle insulated in some way, in some direction? Is the mythical format protected in some way by the media, resulting in the neutralization of certain viruses which would erase the popular-culture memory of superheroes? There has to exist a close compatibility between the paradigm inherent in the high-profile modernizing section of the mythical format and media marketing requirements which would code information in such a way as to channel nonsupportive new knowledge into other sectors of popular interest.

CHAPTER II

NOW ENTERING JAPAN-TIME

Although human evolution is understood and accepted in Japan (every schoolchild knows), the media is drawn to the Yayoi/Kofun periods, the time frame of the mythical paradigm, for embroidering the story of Japanese origins. In this sense, the media becomes the captive of the myth, adding value to the paradigm by creating and fostering new informational and emotional linkages.   In addition the media is so enchanted by the popular-interest merits of the cradle that it generally behaves positively within a sphere of potential dissonance, studies in human ancestry, to support the boundaries of the mythohistorical cradle. Such positioning of the media's message doesn't mean that other avenues are formally closed, for instance, because of some social taboo, to media creativity. However, these escape routes into lines of descent predating Yayoi (from ca. 300 B.C.) lead story development to bridges of ambiguity which lack the mythical supports to transform them into cultural realities for the media's mass audience.

By and large, the media's response to circulating news on man's evolution and Japanese origins is to divide and rule. The media doesn't ignore the former but processes human ancestry in such a way as to make it a subject of public curiosity rather than national identity. Within the media's environment, there are two anthropological clocks ticking away. one is calibrated to Western time, the other to Japan time. Efforts to merge the two time zones are centered within educational circles and institutions, but, in terms of popular culture, commercial or market-oriented interests find it beneficial to separate the two figuratively through different stories or literally through interpolating a contextual screen which desiccates pre-historical roots.

The momentum toward worldwide time was observed in the proceedings of an anthropological symposium at the University of Tokyo in 1990 and at an origins-of-the-Japanese exhibition at the National Science Museum in Tokyo, which preceded the symposium. If events such as these are successful in influencing the dictates of the mass media, the potency of the Japanese mythical paradigm will be diluted as a result of the association of imagery and symbolism with events which these elements cannot manipulate or exploit and by exposure to public scrutiny through contrast with the mythical patterns which permeate Western anthropological pursuits.

The University of Tokyo Symposium, which was held from November 14-17 in 1990, was titled "The Evolution and Dispersal of Modern Humans in Asia" and brought together a broad spectrum of the leading world specialists in the search for early man. Among the universities, academies and institutes represented were: Western Australia, Australian National, London, Hamburg, Bordeaux, Beijing, Jerusalem, Haifa, Novosibirsk (USSR), Damascus, Hanoi, Nagpur (India), Kyoto, Sapporo Medical, Tokyo, Tsukuba (Japan), Queen's (Canada), Michigan, Stanford, Arizona State, Southern Methodist, Harvard, Hawaii, Illinois, New Mexico and Utah. The convening of this meeting was associated with a four-year project on prehistoric mongoloid dispersals, which was initiated in 1989 under the direction primarily of Takeru Akazawa, professor of paleoanthropology at the University of Tokyo, and funded by the Ministry of Education. The project involved the cooperation of 43 institutions in Japan, including universities, museums and research institutes, and the participation of 85 Japanese specialists representing the fields of archaeology, paleoanthropology, genetics, etc. Akazawa's intent in organizing the symposium was to integrate the Mongoloid dispersals project into a more general approach on human evolution, to internationalize and broaden Japanese studies of racial origin. In this sense, his aim did not suggest the delivery to the media of a tailor-made product on origins, one which was Japan-time or geographical-race oriented, but hinted at one of greater complexity. It is interesting to note that the framework for the symposium was not worded in prehistoric Mongoloid terms. Instead, "Modern Humans" was used and evolution was married to dispersal.[1]

In his introductory remarks on the opening day, Akazawa evinced his objective to utilize the symposium as a centrifugal force for galvanizing Japanese scholars along an axis of worldwide rather than parochial controversies as well as to increase awareness among Western scholars of the potential of Asian research contributions. He related:

> In recent years we have seen increasing debate over both the evolution and prehistoric dispersal of *Homo sapiens*, and a number of international conferences have been held on these subjects. The resolution of various conflicting theories regarding human lineages and migration patterns are all fundamental to such discussions. However, largely because of language, the evidence from the huge geographical area comprised by Asia has yet to be fully incorporated into international anthropological exchange. In holding this symposium at the University of Tokyo, we hope to present a truly Asian perspective on the problems of human evolution, and so encourage the integration of Asian scholarship with that of colleagues from the rest of the world. The presence and participation of outstanding scholars and researchers from many countries throughout the world, who will be presenting current and innovative research, promises that our efforts here will be highly and mutually beneficial.[2]

In the letter of invitation to symposium participants, Akazawa was more specific on the nature of the international debate, referring to conflicting theories of single-source and multiregional origins. Furthermore, the letter evinced Akazawa's intent more explicitly of incorporating the Western evolutionary issue into the main topic of his project. He wrote:

> As you will see from the conference schedule, the three days of the symposium are equally divided into three major themes. On Day One we plan to look at the origins of modern humans

with special reference to the Levant region. ...Day Two the center of interest will move further East with what we hope will be an extensive discussion of the 'Out of Africa' *versus* independent local evolution models. ...Day Three will see a further shift of emphasis to the evolution and dispersal of modern humans *within* the East Asian region and into the New World. As many as you will be aware, this topic is of particular interest to us as we are currently involved in a multidisciplinary project here in Japan on Prehistoric Mongoloid Dispersals. The present symposium is, in fact, organized as part of this project.[3]

Akazawa's reference to the out of Africa controversy pertained to an uproar triggered by geneticists in the United States, one which threatened to upset the jigsaw puzzle of human fossils which paleoanthropologists had been working on for decades to delineate the evolution of man. In the past, there had been disagreements within the field on where particular pieces fitted, point counterpoints influenced by scientifically controlled observations and by preconceived models concerning humankind's step-by-step forward advancement. But none of these were so intense as to upset the paleoanthropological apple cart.

One past line of contention had focused on whether man had emerged body first or brain first, i.e., on the value of the signature of a ladderlike expanding mind on frontiers of human progress. The dispute began with the discovery in South Africa in 1924 of the skull of a child by Raymond Dart of Witwatersrand University. The Taung child, which was named after a cave from which it was taken, was believed by Dart to be bipedal. However, it possessed an inconvenient small braincase and a small humanlike lower jaw. The experts of the time couldn't accept such an image of a missing link and dismissed Dart's child as just another ape. Instead, they held fast to the Piltdown skull discovered in 1911 in England with its big brain and large apelike teeth and to the idea that brain enlargement had preceded erect posture. Some thirty years later, Piltdown man would be dismissed as a fake and further discoveries in South Africa would eventually confirm the Taung child as being an early hominid fossil, hominid being a general classification in evolution in which man is associated with man-apes.[4]

A second but more recent non-profession-threatening dispute, one which will probably raise its head again in the future, hacked at the trunk rather than at the branches of the hominid tree. The heated exchange in this case witnessed the tendency of origins' issues in the West to become very personal – a factor which was probably taken into consideration in the invitation of participants to the Tokyo symposium to avoid acute disharmony in the proceedings. The trunk controversy involved a famous paleoanthropological family, the Leakeys, a relative newcomer, Donald Johanson and Lucy. Lucy like the Taung child is an Australopithecus or a member of the man-ape species in the hominid line. Her name derives from a Beatles' song, "Lucy in the Sky with Diamonds," which was playing in a camp in Hadar in North-Central Ethiopia at the time of her discovery, her skeleton, that is, in 1974. Her discoverer was Johanson. Lucy was rather short, under four feet, and long armed, and her brain was not very much different from that of a chimpanzee. However, she walked erectly and bipedally. And, at about three million years, she was older than the Taung child and its genus by some million years. This in and of itself was not very controversial, but Johanson's claim that Lucy was the common ancestor of Australopithecus and Homo – the evolutionary line of habilis, erectus, sapiens and sapiens sapiens – set the stage for the Johanson-Leakey bout.[5]

The roots of the Leakey tradition extended back to the thirties and to the late Louis Leakey's explorations in East Africa, in Tanzania. Louis' goal was to extend the Homo line back millions of years to a primitive hominid which was definitely human and not a brainless Australopithecus. By the 1960s, he succeeded in tracing the lineage back 1.8 million years. These remains with a much bigger brain capacity than Lucy received the name of Homo habilis or handy man. In 1978, Mary, Louis' paleoanthropologist wife, came across the fossilized footprints of bipedal hominids made over three and a half million years ago in volcanic ash. Also, hominid fossil bones were found in the surrounding ash layers. Were these hominids ancient Homo or just another batch of Lucy's relatives? Johanson claimed them for his side of the ring and Mary and her son Richard, who were working to further the trek begun by Louis, were enraged. Although Mary admitted that Lucy was a man-ape, she held that other Johanson finds in proximity to Lucy resembled her hominids and were clearly Homo. Johanson was not to be outtaunted and labeled his 1986 Homo habilis discovery from the Leakey backyard of Tanzania as Lucy's child.[6] In addition, he left no punches unpulled in a book detailing the quarrel. For instance, he referred to Richard Leakey's belittlement of Lucy in this rather below-the-belt manner:

> It's his privilege, of course, to believe anything he wants and someday he may well find the proof he seeks. For my part, I am quite happy not having a legacy to uphold. My own father – a barber by profession – died when I was two; I scarcely even remember him. I'm sure I bring prejudices of my own to the worktable when I examine a fossil, but I'd like to think that my belief in a more recent birth to humanity has arisen from the nature of the evidence that we have in hand.[7]

But despite the tendency for in-house paleoanthropological quarrels to degenerate into personalities, this fallout from past disputes fell within the framework of ladderlike progress and concerned issues of assembling (What species, characteristics, etc. came first? When did it all happen? How did the tree grow?) rather than disassembling of the model. The concept of categorical-cumulative improvement itself was not an issue. In the 80s, museum walls, print media illustrations and cartoons, and school textbooks in the West still pictured a standardized version of human evolution in the form of a slow-motion, frame-by-frame Clark Kent to Superman style horizontal chart of human evolution which was far more consistent than warranted by actual fossil discoveries given the existing gaps in time, distance, quantity and variability of the finds.[8] For instance, the National Geographic's 1985 issue on "The Search for Early Man" presents a 4-page fold out featuring nine hominids in an olympic race through evolution with Australopithecus types passing the torch of increasing resemblance to Homo habilis, who in turn gives it to erectus and so on until modern man with the greatest stride of all crosses the margin of the final page triumphantly.[9] It was this folding out of human evolution which was to be challenged by the findings of the geneticists. And the fallout from such an effort was to be far more serious than the past upheavals experienced by the paleoanthropological profession, extending to all corners of the globe, even finally coming to rest at the University of Tokyo.

The geneticist assault was concentrated on the very rungs of the paleoanthropological ladder. And everybody knows, obviously, a rungless ladder heads nowhere. The preliminary attack, which was ultimately confirmed as a successful hit, targeted the bottom rung. Paleoanthropologists were stung in the late 60s when molecular biologists Vincent Sarich and Allan Wilson of the University of California at Berkeley revealed through genetic-related studies of blood protein that man had diverged from the apes quite more recently than the previous fossil record had indicated. Sarich and Wilson put the split at some 5 million years ago and thereby demoted the 15-million-year fossil Ramapithecus from pre-hominid or pre-Australopithecus status to that of just another ape. The subsequent defense of Ramapithecus by paleoanthropology proved fruitless and the field, in general, finally yielded to the authority of the Sarich-Wilson date in the light of biochemical and new fossil evidence. Vincent Sarich heralded the team's discovery as a mortal blow to what he considered to be the old bones-and-stones school of thought. In patting himself on the shoulder, he exclaimed that he had found no need to talk to these paleoanthropological types since all that was necessary for arriving at a conclusion was to obtain blood samples.[10]

The main assault came in 1987 and was applied to the top of the ladder. Consequently, the paleoanthropological profession was confronted with a more critical reassessment of the value of paleoanthropological studies. For without a top rung, there could be no grand finale in man's progressive paleoanthropological climb through time, which would seem to make the collection of fossils quite an esoteric business. In addition, the failure of paleoanthropology to deliver the final word on evolution, i.e., when and where Homo sapiens sapiens evolved, placed in doubt the significance of all the other rungs in the ladder. As such, the paper presented in a scholarly journal by Allan Wilson and his colleagues Rebecca Cann and Mark

Stoneking would have the effect of driving establishment paleoanthropologists to the ramparts.[11]

Genetics in the 1980s was no longer dominated by the conventional view that natural selection—genetic-related adaptation in an organism in response to changing local environments—overwhelmed all other causes of molecular change. The first version of neutral theory had been formulated by the Japanese geneticist Motoo Kimura in 1968 who held that most of the mutant genes detected by chemical techniques were neither more or less advantageous than those that they had replaced. As such, he asserted that at the molecular level most evolutionary change resulted from random rather than deterministic selection. This randomness presented scientists with the opportunity to dive into living organisms' pre-history with mathematical precision.[12] As Stephen Jay Gould put it:

> If you wish to understand patterns of long historical sequences prayer for randomness. Ironically, nothing works so powerfully against resolution as conventional forms of determinism. If each event in a sequence has a definite cause, then, in a world of such complexity, we are lost.

> The beauty (and simplicity) of randomness lies in the absence of these maximally confusing properties. Coin flipping permits no distinctive personality to any time or moment; each toss can be treated in exactly the same way, whenever it occurs. We can date geological time with precision by radioactive decay because each atom has an equal probability of decaying in each instant.[13]

A random model therefore makes it easier for molecular variations to be regulated by rates of mutation deciphered by means of mathematical equations and molecular clocks of evolution. It was with such a molecular clock that Sarich and Wilson had approached the man-from-ape issue, although a phenotype version, since they relied on blood proteins to understand the genes that engineered them. Wilson, Cann and Stoneking went straight for the genotype—the genetic material itself—with their molecular clock to arrive at a common ancestor for modern man, the mother of us all, a 200,000-year-old African woman. It was understood that this ancestor wasn't a real person per se but a "mitochondrial Eve." Mitochondria are threadlike rods of organelles within a cell which turn chemicals into energy. The genetic engineering material (DNA) within the mitochondria was quite minute in comparison with that found in the nucleus of the cell and therefore simpler to analyze. Moreover, the mitochondria possessed two extraordinary qualities for molecular clockers, according to the mitochondrial gang: Firstly, the genetic material of the mitochondria was inherited only from the mother. There was no need to unravel male-female genetic recombinations as in the case of nucleus DNA and consequently, the mitochondria offered a clear link back through an unbroken mother-daughter-grandaughter chain. Also, in this regard, natural selection didn't really enter the picture. Phenotype studies are more susceptible to natural selection oversights than genotype studies. But in this case the benefit was just about perfect since the genes studied were largely neutral for selection. Secondly, mitochondrial ticked faster, i.e., they accumulated mutations at about 5 to 10 times the pace of their counterparts in the nucleus, thereby magnifying the passage of time and providing diverse human populations with individual signatures or variably sequenced genetic interfaces.[14]

By comparing these neutral signatures, the researchers could tell just how closely the sample of 134 individuals from different geographic populations were related. And what they discovered was that Africa was written all over the geneological tree of man's lineage. Moreover, it was postulated that the longer a population had been around, the greater the variability in the signatures of that group. And Africa was shown to be number one in mutations.[15]

With a swish of their mitochondrial sword, the Berkeley crew had banished a whole host of hominid fossils from the lineage of homo sapiens sapiens. Goodbye to homo sapiens in Europe and to Asian homo erectus/sapiens. They were cast into evolutionary oblivion. Homo erectus dates from about 1.6 million years ago, Peking man (Homo erectus) from about 500,000 years ago, homo sapiens from about 300,000 years ago. European Neanderthal (homo sapiens) from about 125,000 years ago, disappearing suddenly less than 100,000 years later. According to Berkeley, homo sapiens sapiens, which had evolved out of a select population related to African erectus began a trek out of Africa into Europe and Asia somewhere loosely in the vicinity of 100,000 years ago, replacing all the homo-types that came before them. There was no interbreeding with primitive natives. Homo sapiens sapiens were invaders, conquerors, rather than the keepers of the evolutionary heritage of the Eurasian descendents of homo erectus. The signatures of these contestants, according to Berkeley, were not contained in the birthday book of homo sapiens sapiens mitochondrial DNA.[16]

If establishment paleoanthropogists were shocked by the fact that the fossil kill rate was a little high, they were also concerned about the extensive encroachment of molecular biology on their territory – for not only were out-of-Africa homo sapiens sapiens non-mixers, but their discoverers tended to be somewhat overzealous themselves. Cann worded her criticism of the paleoanthropological method of origins in this way:

> Besides the likelihood that the most sought after bones never will materialize, there is the problem of identifying the fossils that are found. It is hard to know, by bone shape alone, whether a fossil represents a species already identified or whether it is different enough to represent a species of its own. Then there is the difficulty of knowing whether the fossil was left by a human ancestor or by a related primate that became extinct. All in all, it is too much to hope that the trickle of bones from the fossil beds of eastern Africa will, in itself, provide a clear picture of human evolution any time soon.[17]

For Cann, the inherent power of genetics over paleoanthropology in tackling evolutionary issues was undeniable. She threw down the gauntlet in the *American Review of Anthropology* when she asserted that although there is no evidence that any phenotype or genotype identified fossil left genes in modern man, geneticists "operate with 100% certainty" that genes in present populations can be traced back to real ancestors.[18]

Well, not exactly 100%. One point of vulnerability in the Eve model is that if Eve's homo sapiens sapiens arose as a group because of a population bottleneck or a founding population that was small in size, the bottleneck might have been related to mitochondrial DNA only rather than a whole new species. One analyst of the evolutionary debates, Roger Lewin, makes the case in this way:

> If, for example, speciation had occurred at 400,000 years ago, and the population suffered a severe bottleneck at 200,000 years ago, then the pattern of mitochondrial DNA would look just as it does now. Distinguishing between these various possibilities on the genetic evidence alone would depend upon looking for signs of population bottlenecks in mitochondrial DNA variability and comparing it with signs in nuclear DNA, which would be affected differently. So far this has not been done.[19]

This line of reasoning also leads to a second problem, i.e., until the whole genome is mapped, the verdict will always be less than conclusive. Finally, there's the matter of the workmanship of the Berkeley geneticists' molecular clock. This represents a main weakness in their offense. There is less than a consensus even among geneticists on whether the molecular clock ticks at a universally accepted, uniform standard. For instance, regarding the question of universality alone, famous geneticists, such as Masatoshi Nei, of the University of Texas, and Wes Brown, of the University of California at San Francisco, believe that the rate of mutation is slower than the Berkeley figures. A slower rate means an older Mitochondrial Eve, perhaps one that isn't a Homo sapiens sapiens at all. Maybe, a late erectus![20]

In view of these soft spots in the Eve theory, the tryst between supporters of out-of-Africa invaders and those of the multi-regional body builders began in earnest. In the 1988 *Newsweek* cover story on "The Search for Adam and Eve," one paleoanthropologist was heartened by this division in the ranks of the geneticists over the reliability of the Eve data, stating that "we may be bumbling fools, but we are not any more bumbling than they are."[21]

It as within this combustible atmosphere that the University of Tokyo Symposium invited papers with titles such as "The Facial Evidence for Regionalism in the Far East," "The Near Eastern Hominids and the Origin of Modern Humans in Eurasia," "Genetic Expansions in Asia," "The Acheulian Site of Gesher Benot Ya'Agov – An Asian or an African Entity." and "The

Origins of Modern Asians: By Regional Evolution or By Replacement?". The latter paper underlined the potential volatility of the subject matter of the meeting since the presenter, Gunter Brauer of the University of Hamburg, of the Federal Republic of Germany, opened his analysis by referring to an American popular science magazine article on the paleoanthropology-genetics battle by James Shreeve who had written the inside story with Donald Johanson on the Lucy wars. Specifically, reference was made to a conference in Yugoslavia in which the mainstream paleoanthropologist Milford Wolpoff, of the University of Michigan, who questions even the value of genetic trees and divergences for population studies,[22] and the turncoat pro-Eve paleoanthropologist Chris Stringer of the Natural History Museum of London crossed swords. The article put it this way:

[At a recent conference in Zagreb, Yugoslavia, ...Wolpoff was scheduled to speak after Stringer. When the British scientist finished his arguments, Wolpoff took the podium and asked for the first slide. It was a *National Enquirer* headline breaking the news that Adam and Eve were actually aliens. His second slide was of Piltdown man, the infamous human fossil find that duped the English anthropological establishment for 40 years, until 1953, when it was finally proved to be a fraud.

"The British Museum has a long history of contributions to paleoanthropology," said Wolpoff, his voice heavy with sarcasm. "Next slide, please."][23]

Brauer, in his abbreviated version of the sparring, noted that he was chairing the session in which Piltdown man was brought back from the dead, and he explained that it was difficult to deal with the problem of regional development or replacement and be in the middle ground in view of such a polarization of views. However, the University of Tokyo Symposium turned out to be such a middle ground. There was no electricity in the atmosphere. Paper followed paper without let up in Japanese conference fashion. Discussion came at the end of the day tucked between the coffee break and a dinner party or the arrival of the bus back to the hotel. Everybody, despite their disagreements, remained on good terms throughout the three days. Paleoanthropologists, pro and con, and geneticists, all got together on the last day for the traditional Japanese group photo which was mailed to each participant at the end of the conference with a thank you letter from the organizers. It was as if, for the Western participants at least, Tokyo was far removed from the war theatre, the conference offering an opportunity to regroup one's forces, reevaluate information and positions. Or perhaps the reason for the calm in the proceedings was the absence of the more, stridently vocal or catalytical members of the establishment and the opposition. Absent were Wolpoff, Stringer, Wilson and Cann. Wolpoff wrote a letter to Akazawa protesting his exclusion from the conference. Akazawa told the *AERA* reporter covering the symposium that the failure to provide Wolpoff with an invitation was a mere oversight of the organizing committee.[24] True or not, whether the organizers of the conference had succeeded in brewing an academic meeting without any bitter aftertaste or whether, for the Westerners, the University of Tokyo just didn't seem to be the right place for personalized academic missiles, Brauer's implicit positioning of Wolpoff's stance in the wastebasket of extremism didn't result in anybody jumping to the podium to object.

Brauer's position wasn't very much middle of the road either, more patronizing than conciliatory, more replacement than continuous evolution in his perspective. Brauer based his paper on his own Afro-European sapiens hypothesis of 1982 "which referred to Africa, Europe and West Asia and suggested a complex variable replacement and hybridization process between the modern humans of African origin and the Neanderthals [homo sapiens]." He explained:

> Since this model assumes gene flow between Neanderthals and modern populations, the indications pointing to some degree of continuity across the Neanderthal/modern boundary in Europe and West Asia are in total agreement with this less extreme replacement model.[25]

Regarding the hominids of East Asia, although Brauer tended to believe that indications were pointing in a similar direction, he referred to the paucity of evidence and the relative obscurity of the fossil record in China and Australasia.[26]

Though no sparks flew when replacement innuendos were voiced, the symposium was evenly balanced on the out-of-Africa issue. Geoffrey Pope, of the University of Illinois, an East Asian paleoanthropologist and a friend of Wolpoff, believed that there was already sufficient evidence in Asia to refute replacement, even of the less extreme Brauer-kind. He asserted:

> The totality of the paleoanthropological evidence from the Far East is squarely at odds with the replacement model for the origin of anatomically modern *Homo Sapiens* favored by the results of some Mitochondrial DNA studies. Neither the archaeological record nor the morphology of the known fossil hominids supports a geologically recent, extra Asian origin of modern Mongoloid (Asian and Native American) populations. No evidence of the introduction of superior technological change, nor of non-Asian skeletal morphology (particularly of the Asian face) is evident in the Asian paleoanthropological data. Instead, both the archaeological and fossil evidence indicate that modern Asians are the product of a long process of regional evolution in which both isolation and gene flow helped to shape present geographic populations.[27]

Pope, who felt that if Brauer and other European specialists could read Chinese literature, they would be less inclined to file Asia under obscure, emphasized the need for more serious consideration of Asian finds. He even claimed that there was good evidence for a counterclockwise, vis-à-vis Africa, genetic flow to explain the dispersal of Asian traits into modern populations.[28]

Another authority who presented evidence in support of regional evolution was Christy Turner, of Arizona State University, an authority on dental anthropology and prehistory in Asia and the Americas. In the past, based on an idea formulated some 15 years earlier, he had postulated two migratory flows of Mongoloid-dental-type peoples in Asia, one coming to Japan over 10,000 years ago, the Jomon people, and originating in southeastern Asia and a second arriving from northern Asia, about 2,000 years ago.[29] At the symposium, he presented a new hypothesis that Southeast Asian dental patterns "could have been ancestral to all known anatomically modern Eurasians." He explained that in spite of the evidence favoring an out-of-Africa origin hypothesis, modern world dental variation could have more easily evolved out of the Southeast Asian pattern than out of the highly divergent patterns of Africa, north Asia-Americas or Europe. Although he conceded that the deficiencies in fossil evidence prevented a firm verdict on his plea, he also made it a point to note that the jury was still out on the value of mitochondrial DNA as well.[30]

The only quake at the symposium, which measured so low in intensity that hardly an eyebrow was raised among the participants, involved the country-gentleman-dental-expert Turner in an exchange with the patrician-geneticist Luigi Cavalli-Sforza, of Stanford University, one of the early pioneers in applying genetics to human ancestry. This very low-keyed debate, with some light, esoteric jabs, was in the phenotype-genotype mode and therefore not very personal at all. The impression left with this participant was that although the jury might still be out on mitochondrial DNA, the position of one geneticist was that the future lay with increased and improved measurements of genetic distances of the entire DNA spectrum, not just mitochondrial DNA, to neutralize interference from environmental forces and natural selection and allow the molecular clock to tick-tock off copious comparable data verifying when populations split and genetic expansions occurred. While Turner awaited new fossil evidence, Cavalli-Sforza looked forward to synchronized time travel through the human body's inner space.

These relative nondramatic performances of the Western actors were complemented by the neutrality of the Japanese participants, adding to the lack of electricity in the air of the conference hall. Although Akazawa had indicated his intention of tying the twain between Eastern and Western origins' perspectives by means of the Tokyo University Symposium, the Japanese papers were non-Eve presentations and centered more or less on Japanese anthropological events which were not much later than 30,000 years ago. In addition, Japanese scholars refrained from involving themselves in the Eve issue during the discussion period. One might raise a number of reasons for such Japanese aloofness, including language problems (the absence of language interpreters), the large number of Western participants which precluded time allotments for more Japanese presentations and the respect of the hosts for the international status of their guests. However, the reason which stands out is the traditional organization of a national educational project which is not structurally oriented toward a particular exchange of views at a specific place. The purpose of a symposium of the Tokyo University type is to establish a focal point for stimulating discussions within the project's study groups, thereby broadening the research horizons of the individual members.

This perspective must have been foremost in Akazawa's mind. For instance, one month prior to the symposium, a special seminar was held for project members to consider the relationship of "Out of Africa" within the context of other project issues. The exchange among the discussants highlighted a much stronger interest of Japanese scholars on the issue than one could gather from the symposium. The discussants included Akazawa, Bin Yamaguchi, director of anthropological studies at the National Science Museum, Keiichi Omoto, professor of Tokyo University, Naruya Saito, associate professor of the National Genetics Research Center, Hajime Ishida, lecturer at Sapporo Medical University, and Katsushi Tokunaga, assistant of Tokyo Medical University. Tokunaga and Ishida presented papers at the symposium in association with their colleagues, but neither of these papers touched on the Eve question.[31]

This discussion on how far back one could trace the appearance of the Mongoloid population was begun by Yamaguchi whose observations would have brought a smile to Rebecca Cann's face. He began by referring to an early authoritative assessment in the 1930s linking the remains, bones and teeth of Peking man, the some 500,000-years-old Homo erectus, to modern Chinese. The evaluation was done by the famous German anatomist, Franz Weidenreich, and was later confirmed by the analyses of Chinese scholars such as Xinzhi Wu, thereby integrating Chinese thought on origins into Western considerations of the multi-regional variety.

Wu, of the Chinese Academy of Sciences in Beijing, was a presenter of a paper at the symposium which hailed the major role of Peking man in the evolution of man. In a rather detailed examination, he explained:

> All of the anatomically modern human fossils found in China have some common features: the antero-lateral surface of the zygomatic process faces more forward than that of Neanderthals, the characteristic contour of the lower margin of the zygomatic process of the maxillary bone, the more obtuse zygomaxillary angle...and the shovelling of upper incisors. All of these features can also be seen in the early Homo sapiens and Homo erectus of China more frequently than those of Europe and Africa. Detailed studies of the fossils, combined with a series of chronometric and relative dates for them, suggest a continuous evolutionary lineage of humankind in China. These facts support the hypothesis that the anatomically modern humans in China originated from the indigenous earlier inhabitants instead of being migrants from other parts of the world.[32]

In Yamaguchi's estimation, Chinese scholarship on the Mongoloid character of Peking man was far from convincing. He noted that certain important bone-and teeth features picked up by these scholars were also found in nonMongoloid populations. In response to a question by Saito, Yamaguchi indicated that it was not sufficient to merely pick up some features and trace relations among the various populations to determine descent from Peking man. He observed that Mongoloid was defined by the shape of the face and asserted that since Peking man didn't have a flat face, it didn't qualify as Mongoloid.

Now, Wu, if he had been present at the seminar, would have disagreed with Yamaguchi on the flatness of the face of Peking man while Johan Kamminga, of Australian National University, another presenter at the symposium, would have found himself in agreement with Yamaguchi on difficulties of arriving at the general significance of specified Mongoloid attributes and their relative frequencies worldwide.[33] But Akazawa didn't want the evolution issue to turn merely on the face of Peking man and quickly shifted the discussion to a more distant disembarkation. He agreed that Peking man didn't have that Mongoloid look, but in order to discover its real identity, he asked the discussants to please talk about the Eve hypothesis and imagine that Peking man wasn't our direct ancestor. Ishida countered with the question of whether a single origin theory such as Eve could be easily accepted. Omoto concurred and stated that he couldn't decide on whether to become a follower of Becky Cann or not. Tokunaga, a geneticist, indicated his serious doubts about the single evolution theory. Tokunaga's ongoing origins' study centered on an evaluation of the human leucocyte antigen (HLA) system of polymorphic marker genes which play an important role in immune response, disease susceptibility and histocompatibility.[34] He explained that when one tries to determine when populations separated based on HLA studies, one discovers alleles as old as 30 million years. He held that in order to preserve such old alleles – at least 30 sets – down to modern times, when Homo became human, initially quite a few of them had to exist within the population and there should have been no drastic change after separation. Herein, Omoto interpolated a confirmative question to the effect that what Tokunaga meant was that at the point of separation, the number shouldn't be so small. Tokunaga responded with "that's right," explaining that since the sets of HLA included in Mongoloid peoples were quite large today, a great deal of heterogeneity must have existed from the first and there must have been enough numbers to maintain them to the present. To Akazawa's demand for some conclusion on the Eve hypothesis, Tokunaga set forth these points: (1) Mitochondrial DNA certainly could be traced back to a woman who lived 200,000 years ago; (2) although mitochondrial DNA might start from there, it didn't guarantee anything about the genes in nuclear DNA which number as many as 100,000 (mtDNA consists of only thirty-seven genes); (3) all of these could not be connected back to genes of 200,000 years ago. Saito then jumped back into the discussion with the idea that the linkage of genetics with the categorization Mongoloid might be inappropriate in view of the findings reached by Cavalli-Sforza in his present research. Cavalli-Sforza, according to Saito, had found that the south China or southeast Asia group of Mongoloid were completely different from northern Mongoloid, including the Japanese, and the southern

Mongoloid were rather near to Caucasoid, meaning that Caucasoid came into the Mongoloid group too. "So, perhaps," Saito remarked, "we can't use Mongoloid anymore." However, he did explain that Cavalli-Sforza's original data was not yet available for close scrutiny and therefore there was no certainty in this regard. To all this, Omoto merely set back and laughed while exclaiming that who knows, the Ainu (a minority people currently located in Hokkaido)-Caucasian (previously believed to be Caucasoid) Theory might come into fashion again.

The discussants also considered what should be done with all the fossil evidence which conflicted with the Eve hypothesis. Reasons voiced for setting aside past findings ranged from nonmingling since Eve's children had language and archaics didn't to the failure of the archaics to adapt to harsh environmental conditions during the temperature fluctuations of the Ice Age, resulting in their disappearance prior to the arrival of homo sapiens sapiens. Still, Omoto felt that it was very strange to say everyone disappeared all over the world all of a sudden, including the Neanderthals of Europe, especially since nobody really knew the reason why. Tokunaga also didn't see any reason for dismissing Homo erectus and the archaics. He thought that it was dangerous to look at just one kind of gene and universalize it. In his estimation, one kind, regardless of its information value, could not be almighty and, therefore, there was a need to undertake more extensive studies to arrive at similar results before engaging in a prognosis concerning the fate of fossil man.

This particular seminar, by taking up many of the points which were to be raised by many of the nonJapanese symposium participants, represented an interface for integrating Western time on origins with Japan time, for globalizing Japanese academic thinking on race. In this respect, Akazawa and the members of his project group, regardless of their pro or con views on the Eve hypothesis, could escape to a degree from popular cultural restraints to engage in academic intellectual pursuits which crisscrossed national cultural boundaries and mythohistories. In so doing, they, perhaps, provided themselves with a counterparadigm of Western/Asian/Japanese racial affinities. In any event, in view of the liveliness of the exchange among the seminar discussants, the effort of Akazawa in organizing the symposium was highly effective in fostering dissonance or food for thought in Japanese studies of Mongoloid dispersals.

In contrast, the mass media could find no escape. For example, although *AERA*, the Asahi Shimbun's national weekly news magazine, provided its readers with a feature article on the symposium, *AERA*, in its coverage, couldn't find in the event as a totality a story which was supercharged with questions pertaining to Japanese racial identity and instead fastened on to a pastime of Japanese journalism, i.e., how Westerners, in this case, scholars, differed from Japanese behaviorally. For the *AERA* reporter, a Western academic meeting was as different from a Japanese one as a Broadway show was from "Kabuki." The story began around an illustration of a caveman on a rock scratching his head and looking at an African dressed in traditional costume sitting on a wooden stool. All Broadway! And the billing read:

> I wonder if our ancestor who lived 200,000 years ago is an African. Where did we come from? New theory is that Homo sapiens sapiens whose birthplace is centered in Africa dispersed worldwide destroying Peking man and Neanderthal to become modern man. So, the anthropological field is now in turmoil since some scholars strongly insist on this. And this controversy has come to Tokyo too.[35]

From the introduction, it is clear that the coming-to-Tokyo lead-in was to be as important as or more so than the theme of out of Africa. The reporter did relate the basis for the controversy, but he emphasized more the manners of the actors rather than the pertinence of the play for his reading public. In this sense, the reporter became himself a kind of anthropologist, describing the strange ways in which foreign academics communicate among themselves. Too many foreign languages, too many rising voices, too much animation were the revelations which punctuated this reporter's review of the symposium. The reporter opened his story not with the beginning of the symposium but the end, more precisely, with the farewell party where he noted one out of two were foreigners and English was going on and French as well. He included a statement from Pope on how calm (but according to the reporter, more active than the usual Japanese event) this conference had been in relation to a recent boisterous American Anthropological Association meeting in New Orleans and the reporter noted that Wolpoff, who played a pivotal role at that high-pitched meeting and "who is known for his loud voice," was not invited to the Tokyo symposium. The reporter quoted one of the people (no name given) at the symposium who said that the Wolpoff-Pope continuous evolution group "are just like salesmen who insist upon their sales line again and again until the customer is worn down and signs on the dotted line." The *AERA* article then went on to relate that even though the discussion about ancestry was very exciting, one still had the choice of relying on fossils or genes for formulating a conclusion or of being swayed by "people with loud voices." In the article, loud voices had a persistent ring. In fact, the article concluded on such a note when asking once again the question of where did we come from. The writer responded that with the Eve theory in full retreat, the answer is wrapped in fog and until the fog lifts, the air of authority will be filled by the loud voices.[36] One should mention that in terms of Japanese culture, raising one's voice or overly insisting on one's opinion is considered rather childish and eventually self-defeating.

But *AERA* divided the issue of the Western origins' debate from Japanese concerns not merely by stressing the alien character of the performance, but also by failing to concern itself with the relevance of the display for Japanese racial origins. The article not only provided subjective confirmation for the readership of distinct Western-Japanese boundaries on human origins by indirectly ignoring the reasons why the Prehistoric Mongoloid Dispersals Project had organized the symposium, but also directly drew the line with the inclusion of a colorful and high-profile map depicting the movements of mankind and the main places where fossil man had been found. The map compared a first wave of dispersal out of Africa of some one million years ago (Homo erectus) with a second wave of 75,000 years ago. Of course, by taking the 75,000 year point in time for dispersal rather than an interval of, let's say, 75,000 to 30,000 years ago, the destination arrows extended just about everywhere but Japan.[37]

AERA's parent publication, the *Asahi Shimbun*, one of Japan's big three nationally distributed newspapers, distinguished the relevance of the symposium for its readers in a somewhat different manner than *AERA* but with the same overall impact. The *Asahi Shimbun* separated Western from Japan time unequivocally by focusing on two papers which were given at the symposium rather than on the symposium as a whole: one focused on about 300 B.C. to 300 A.D. in Japan; the other on 100,000 years ago in Europe. The relevance divide was further widened by including Japan-time in the main morning edition and Western-time in the supplemental evening edition two days later. Nevertheless, the important point here is how distant in time the two articles were from one another and how the newspaper made no effort to consider linkages within the context of the symposium between the two time zones. From the editor's or reporter's vantage point, each scholarly presentation existed within in its own universe, with its own unique appeal for the Asahi audience.

The Japan-time article was entitled "Yayoi People in Northern Kyushu Are the Origin of the Modern Japanese" and described the position of Yukio Dodo (the senior author), Hajime Ishida and Naruya Saito of Sapporo Medical University on a cranial nonmetric approach to the population history of Japan. Considering the highly esoteric character of the paper, it would seem that it was more suitable for a paleoanthropological journal than a national newspaper. However, the conclusions which the article picked up reflected a central focus within Japanese popular mythohistory and therefore it was not a bad editorial choice in terms of readership attractiveness to report on the symposium by describing the results from the measurements of over 100 craniums. The first appealing conclusion was that there was a population discontinuity between Jomon and Yayoi. The second was that northern Kyushu Yayoi were more closely related to historic Japanese than extreme western Honshu Yayoi. The third was that the northern Kyushu Yayoi type eventually genetically triumphed over all other genetic types in protohistoric Japan. In all, the idea of a cranial tidal wave sweeping over Japan from a point in northern Kyushu during the Yayoi period conformed to the mythohistorical framework of invasion from the continent of a new breed of people, the founders of the Japanese race.[38]

The Western-time newsline heralded western Asia as the place of humankind evolution, with the subheadline explaining that 100,000 years ago Cro-magnon man (Homo sapiens sapiens) co-existed with Neanderthal man. The author of the paper covered in the article was the French scholar, Bernard Vandermeersch. The article centered on Vandermeersch's analysis of the discoveries of hominids in the Israeli caves of Qafzeh and Skul in the Levant which he identified as ancestral to Cro-magnon man of Europe. Vandermeersch postulated progressive replacement of Neanderthal populations by Eve's children. What was the connection between these two replacement events: Neanderthal/Cro-magnon and Jomon/Yayoi? How did Eve change the way one should look at the Japanese cradle? Should race be thought of in universal rather than just Japanese terms? How did western mythical concerns compare with Japanese? No effort was made by the *Asahi Shimbun* to reflect upon the implications of Vandermeersch's findings for the Dodo imperative. European racial questions and Japanese were indeed distinct in terms of optimum mass media consumption and were packaged as such. The former was a matter of curiosity; the latter of national identity.[39]

The difference between Japan-time and Western-time on racial issues was evident in the presentation and media response to the 110th anniversary of Tokyo's National Science Museum's exhibition of the origins of the Japanese titled "Where the Japanese Came from." The museum exerted itself dramatically in the exhibition to bridge Japan-time and Western-time in the traditional paleoanthropological approach to determining ancestry, but the museum's approach contained too many glaring inconsistencies, resulting from the lack of unequivocal evidence. The ambiguities inherent in the early man exhibits provided the opportunity for media coverage to escape from a distant past, which said nothing definite or special about Japanese origins.

and reach out for a more congenial story in the more mythically infused post-Jomon times.

The focal point of the museum's effort to evolutionize the origins of the Japanese was the remains of Minatogawa man, who was proclaimed by the exhibitors as being "Our Ancestor." Minatogawa man is the name given to the fossilized bones of early homo sapiens sapiens found in southern Okinawa Prefecture in the area of Minatogawa in the late 1960s. According to the museum, the remains were 16,000 to 18,000 years old, which is close to a recent laboratory test which provided a date of 19,000 B.P. Minatogawa man was discovered in a limestone quarry, an alkalic, nonacidic resting place. In the main islands of Japan, since the soil is very acidic, bones readily dissolve and few fossilized remains dating from about 10,000 to 30,000 years ago (Japan's old stone age) have been discovered. Only a few bones have turned up since 1960 and nothing resembling the outline of a skeleton, a complete skull or even the facial framework has yet been found. At the exhibition, one could find Mikkabi man and Hamakita man from Shizuoka and Hijiridake man from Oita – all faceless, nonidentifiable men. All of these pieces of bones together, according to the organizers of the exhibition, could be placed in a school child's backpack. In contrast, Minatogawa man finds from the middle 60s included an almost complete skeleton of a 153 cm male and a quite detailed skeleton of a 143 cm female. In all, there are 5 to 10 bodies, i.e., at least, four individual bodies and one complete skull, plus 20 odd bones.[40]

With the initial focus of the exhibition centering on Minatogawa man, suppositions radiated backward in time to early homo sapiens sapiens in China and forward in time to the Jomon people. In fact, the exhibition extended even further back than paleolithic China and there was a section on human beings as a member of the primate family, the visitor being informed that the biggest difference between man and ape was bipedalism. The evolution of the hominid line was illustrated in detail. Stuffed apes and a primate classification chart appeared. A chart was provided with an evolutionary tree for man and ape, with the latter branching off from an ape ancestor into the orangutan, gorilla and chimp families and the hominid line separating off and giving rise to the usual homo arrays – a very conservative, Western-time museum presentation. There was even a time chart which layered hominids block by block on top of the ape block. However, the eye-catching feature of the ancestral tree was at the summit in a bounded layer in which Cro-magnon man, the early homo sapiens sapiens of China, Minatogawa man and Jomon man were bunched together.[41]

The evolutionary developments leading to the appearance of Minatogawa man or the ancestor of the Japanese were further underlined in the relating of the story of the discovery of fossil humans, which included tales of Neanderthal man, Dart's Taung child and Lucy. The exhibition was indeed proceeding in Western museum fashion. A timetable of human evolution was superimposed on a chronological table of the fossil bones shown at the exhibition. And an explanation was given:

> When we chase back in time the origin and evolution of life we call human beings, how far back can we go? Let's think about the direct evidence, the bones of the ancient people. In Japan, we found the body of Jomon man which is several thousands of years old and which is exhibited. The excavated remains of Minatogawa man and Mikkabi man belong to the paleolithic period of more than 10,000 years ago. And if we check details, there is some difference between old and new but all belong to homo sapiens sapiens in terms of the stages of human being evolution. we haven't found anything older in Japan but in China, we have discovered homo sapiens like Dali man who possesses a strong browridge and who goes back further. A group of Homo erectus does appear: Peking man and Java man. But in Asia ancient man went back no farther than this. Fossils of more than one million years have only been found in Africa.[42]

The exhibition then offered a map of the main human fossil remains being displayed. And the visitor learned that "when we think of the origins of the Japanese, the most important thing to study about is modern man and ancient fossil mankind living in geographical proximity in East Asia."[43] The museum explained that the closest that Asia comes to Australopithecus is the Javanese fossil Meganthropus which is the oldest fossil in East Asia – about one million years – and whose shape, in the museum's view, is quite primitive as a Homo erectus.

With the display of the rather crushed skull of Meganthropus, the exhibition moved on to the Homo erectus cranial remains of Java man (600,000 to one million years ago) and Solo man (also, from Java and dating to more than 200,000 years ago). As the exhibition shifted to Sarawak in Malaysia, human progress in terms of the ancestral line of the Japanese entered the gray territory of spurious supposition. Displayed were the some 40,000-years-old cranial remains of Niah man, Southeast Asia's oldest Homo sapiens sapiens and it was indicated that Niah man was related to early man in Tasmania in South Australia on the basis of studies of fossils and the skulls of modern people. But the exhibition drew lines as well to early Homo sapiens sapiens in southern China at Liujiang and to Minatogawa man, indicating that there were some similarities. It was even noted that there was the possibility of Niah man being related to old stone age man of the main islands of Japan – an interesting association since Japan's old stone age man was unidentifiable. The organizers did however qualify their creativity in anthropology by referring to the relationship as indirect.[44]

The next stop was fossil man in China. The story of fossil man in China, as already noted, usually begins with Peking man and the exhibition was no exception. The caves of Zhoukoudian (Choukoutien) located about 50 km southwest of Beijing have yielded up abundant human fossils. And in one of the caves rested Peking man, the oldest, confirmed fossil man of China, dating from 500,000 to 200,000 years ago. The cave was opened in the early 1930s. All of the early discoveries were lost during World War II and only casts of these remains exist today. The pre-war finds included four complete skulls and more than 40 bodies. After the war, a fifth skull was found along with some teeth and pieces of arm and leg bones. Prior to Zhoukoudian becoming an anthropological treasure house, the cave area which is known as Dragon-bone Hill was for centuries mined by peasants who ground up fossil bones taken from the hill to make dragon-bone potions for medicinal purposes. So, much had probably been lost even prior to the original excavation. Nevertheless, Peking man remains one of the two most famous representatives of the hominid group which originally left the African cradle and from the Japanese point of view, more significant than Java man because Zhoukoudian is just down the road in a sense. Such an important evolutionary thoroughfare was not to be ignored by the exhibitors in their chase into time, but once again they had to stretch those inferences even further than in the case of the Niah man-Japanese nexus since there is not even a hint of domestic production of dragon bone liquor in Japan.[45]

The organizers, however, were not intimidated by the enormity of the jump in the intersect with Route Peking Man and asserted that part of these Chinese Homo erectus "might have come across to the Japanese islands." And they related that "fossils of Homo erectus haven't been found in Japan as yet, but some possibility exists."[46] Their reasoning was based on the findings at Zhoukoudian of numerous animal fossils and the fact that similar fossils had been found in Japan. In the museum's estimation, since the thinking was that these animals came to Japan at the time of Peking man, there was nothing strange about inferring that people came with them, i.e., following the herds.

The excavations of the 30s uncovered not only Peking man's cave but also an Upper Cave housing the remains of Homo sapiens sapiens or Upper Cave man. As in the case of Peking man, the war left the museum world with primarily only casts to display of the specimens. None of the original three well-preserved crania survived. One of the eight bodies was that of an old man of 174 cm, which, according to the museum, was similar to Cro-magnon man in some respects as well as to Mongoloid in East Asia and dated from 10,000 to 20,000 years ago. The organizers referred to Xinzhi Wu's findings in describing the significance of the three crania. According to the description, the crania were closer to that of American Indian than modern East Asian Mongoloid and could be categorized as old-type Mongoloid.[47]

This assumption of two types of Mongoloid people in East Asia is a double-edged sword. It cuts Japanese ancestry, i.e., Minatogawa-Jomon lineage, into Western-time appraisals and at the same time, it provides a line along which Japan-time accounts can be easily detached and separately investigated. Such an interpretation serves itself up quite easily to mythohistorical interpolations. The Japan-time paradigm of old and new Mongoloid types or southern, with features of a warm-climate-adapted populations, and northern Mongoloid, with cold-climate adaptations, lends itself to distinctions between Jomon (of about 10,000 years ago) and Yayoi (of some 2,300 years ago) people, resulting in the replacement of the former by the latter. In this respect, the museum's effort to integrate ancestry into the Western fold through categorization was more than an attempt to cement inference, but a gamble, although not recognized as such, in revealing only one side of the cutting edge. Would mass culture, in terms of the exhibition's mass audience, or the mass media find a signal in the old-new dichotomy for disregarding, except from the curiosity vantage point, the strands of Japanese ancestry in early human evolution in favor of a later, singular, Japanese revolution?

It is noteworthy that since the museum was following a traditional approach to paleoanthropolgy in Asia, the old-new rather than a-just-plain-different or isolated-population formula in the Mongoloid or nonMongoloid sense, was perhaps unavoidable in considerations of early Homo sapiens sapiens in East Asia. Kamminga writes about the historical dictates in the paleoanthropological profession which call forth such an analytical framework.[48] He explains:

> When the human remains from the Upper Cave were first described they were thought to be of Late Pleistocene age. One of the reasons for this assumption was that the site was part of a cave network from which the largest collection of *Homo erectus* fossils in the world had been unearthed. A second reason is that the Upper Cave remains were not particularly like those of the Neolithic population of north China, which are modern Mongoloid in appearance, and scholars had already accepted the view that the *erectus* remains from the Locality 1 [Peking man] site were ancestral to the modern Mongoloids. The most commonly expressed opinion has been that the Upper Cave people are "primitive", "proto" or "archaic" Mongoloid, and that they are directly ancestral to modern northeast Asian Mongoloids and to Amerindians.[49]

Another representative of early Homo sapiens sapiens in China or old-type Mongoloids at the exhibition was the cranial remains of Ziyang man, with disparate dates of 37,000 years ago (39,000 BP, according to Wu) and 7,000 years ago. Ziyang man, whose remains were found some distance inland in the center of China, would seem to be far removed geographically from events in Japan, and, therefore, not surprisingly, the Upper Cave man's rival at the exhibition for line of descent from Minatogawa within the category of old and southern Mongoloid was Liujiang man of Guangzi in southern China, not Ziyang man. The geographical distance between Liujiang and Minatogawa is shorter, although slightly, than between the Upper Cave and Minatogawa. However, the Upper Cave remains definitely win out in terms of proximity in time to Minatogawa man.[50]

The display of the skull of Luijiang man carried the explanation that the exact date was unknown but it was older than the cranial remains of the Upper Cave, with some people saying that it was 40,000 years old (Wu, 67,000 BP). It was also indicated that Liujiang man, in terms of height, about 150 cm, was in the same league as Minatogawa man, both of whom did not compare well with the tall Upper Cave man nor, for that matter, with modern Chinese. The same conclusion as to the better match came from cranial measurements, with Liujiang outpointing the Upper Cave. Moreover, in an effort to tie things together for both an old and southern Mongoloid approach to Minatokawa man's ancestral inheritance, the close relationship between Niah man and Liujiang man was noted once again.[51]

If the organizers had wished to bias the display in terms of a Liujiang-Minatogawa linkage to Japanese ancestry, they certainly shouldn't have included a Russian section, which challenged the 100 percent paternity of the lineage. The museum's examination of fossil mankind in Russia, especially Siberia, yielded up no discoveries of fossil man east of Lake Baikal, but the survey did bring out the fact that the stone tools found in eastern Siberia were similar to the cultural complexes found in northeastern (Tohoku) Japan, which in turn differed from the complexes of southwestern Japan. Since no bones had been discovered in eastern Siberia or in northern Japan, the Russian exhibits placed a huge question mark over Japan's evolutionary land bridge. However, the Russian section was necessary to dispel a much larger cloud hanging over this chase through time, i.e., the paleoanthropological disparities between Jomon man and fossil mankind in East Asia.[52]

In this respect, the Russian journey was intended as a search through time for new or northern Mongoloid fossil man. West of Lake Baikal along the left bank of the Yenisei River, the remains of Afontova Mountain man, dating perhaps as far back as 25,000 years, were discovered in 1923. Although the visitor might have had some difficulty imagining the facial look of Afontova Mountain man from the part of the forehead shown, he was informed that "it has really flat features just like [just like?] Mongoloid [Was it really Mongoloid?] which adapted to a cold environment."[53] Much nearer to Lake Baikal, 85 km west of Irkutsk, in 1929, the remains of Malta man dating from 15,000 to 25,000 years ago were found, consisting of teeth and pieces of bone. The museum presented the finds, especially the teeth, as indicating that Malta man was Mongoloid. In addition, small, carved bone statues of females were offered as evidence of the racial affinity of Malta man, since certain of these Venus figurines, which were quite realistic in expression, were said to resemble modern-day Siberian people as to the shape of face, eyes and cheekbones.[54]

In a sense, the organizers were opening up a question on the significance of Liujiang man to fill in a blank in the link between Minatogawa and Jomon, the entrant – although not conclusively confirmed – being new or northern Mongoloid. In concentrating on the relationship between Asian fossil mankind and Jomon man, the museum made the point that head and face characteristics as well as a tendency for the upper body to be thin and the lower part to be well built had carried over from fossil human beings to Jomon people. Also, the explanation was given that the height of fossil mankind was passed on to Jomon man. The visitor was reminded while completing this final act of the exhibition's search for the Paleolithic roots that Minatokawa man, Mikkabi man and Hamakita man were quite small and although Upper Cave man was tall, he was the exception to the fossil human being rule exemplified by Liujiang man. However, the museum admitted that a great deal more had to be known about the parts of the body of fossil man in East Asia before it could be said that Liujiang-Minatogawa lineage evolved directly into Joman man. It was pointed out that certain strong tendencies in the Jomon population, such as the flat character of arm and leg bones and the long size of the forearm and lower leg, were absent in Japanese fossil human beings. Consequently, the organizers qualified their conclusion to "Our Ancestor" by confessing their inability to assert fully in view of the body evidence that fossil mankind evolved directly into Jomon man. Still, such a conclusion was put forward and the Russian display with its new or northern Mongoloid theme buoyed the Minatogawa line of descent.[55]

The visitor was assured that "Our Ancestor" lived in south China and moved to Japan during the land bridge period. After the disappearance of the land bridge, he was told that the thinking is "Our Ancestor" evolved into Jomon people while concomitantly retaining south Chinese people's features and receiving some changes. The cause of these changes was unknown, according to the museum, but among the possibilities mentioned, including changing life styles or changes in the natural environment, the coming of a new people was emphasized and the Russian-supported, new-Mongoloid theme replayed.[56]

The exhibition was divided into two sections, the first titled fossil mankind and old stone age culture and the second, Jomon period and the Japanese people after that. The division didn't represent a break in the exhibition's chase through time or a starting anew in Part II with a Japan-time, mythohistorically bound paradigm. Instead, whereas the first section had chased Minatogawa roots back into the past, the second stage followed Japanese lineage forward in time. The Jomon-Minatogawa-Liujiang line was reaffirmed and focus was placed on how this line adapted to future conditions. Since the Jomon period lasted for perhaps as long as 10,000 years or more, naturally, differences in physical features occurred. However, the displays bore witness to the highly significant dissimilarities which

58

occurred in the Yayoi period (from about 300 B.C. to 300 A.D.). Because Yayoi bones were not buried in alkalic shell mounds, there were fewer remains than in the Jomon period. But excavations in northern Kyushu and Yamaguchi Prefecture had uncovered many Yayoi bones and these differed from those of eastern Japan and northwestern and southern Kyushu. The exhibits displayed bones from the latter area as "Jomon-kei" Yayoi and those from the former sites as "Torai-kei" Yayoi. While the Torai-kei label might imply foreign-type or at least non-native-type bones, the museum did not refer to an invasion or migration to Japan in the Yayoi period in making the distinction. Instead, the Jomon-kei label was applied by the museum to designate remains with Jomon features while the Torai-kei category included bones with similarities to those people of the new stone age, the metal age, modern Korea, or modern China.[57]

In comparing the features of Jomon-kei and Torai-kei Yayoi bones with those of Kofun or Tomb period people (from about 300 A.D. to 700 A.D.) and those who came after, the exhibition through specimens, charts and diagrams underlined the pull of sociocultural forces by proceeding in the following fashion: revealing the strong effect of Torai-kei Yayoi on Kofun period people in western Japan, but evincing Jomon-kei as well as Torai-kei influences on the characteristics of the people of eastern Japan; assessing people in Kofun period as being quite different from those of Jomon times; comparing Jomon, Kofun and modern Japanese features and arriving at the position that such an approach yielded a continuum in which the middle range in the development of traits resided in the Kofun period; always emphasizing that the Jomon-Yayoi-Kofun-Modern progression should be understood in terms of man's gradual adaption to changes in his environment, i.e., the impact of metal tools and rice cultivation which altered man's working and living habits and provided him with a more stable and perhaps a more nutritious and bountiful food supply.[58]

At the end of the second section, the museum presented the various past and present academic theories on Japanese roots to give the visitor the opportunity to contemplate what they had experienced at the exhibition in terms of what others had said on the questions posed. It's an interesting footnote to the preoccupation of Japanese culture in terms of man's origins that such a presentation fell into the Jomon and after phase of the exhibition. Nevertheless, the museum's evaluation of the various Japan-time academic "origins" theories confirmed the general objective of the exhibition since one of the schools acknowledged was highly compatible with the drift of the museum's presentation. Perhaps, in waiting to the end of the exhibition to touch on the various theories, the museum was intentionally loading the dice in favor of this theory of continuous change.[59]

The name much associated with the theory of continuous change is Hisashi Suzuki, formerly Professor of Anthropology at the University of Tokyo. This school of thought held the following based on the study of a great many human skeletal remains in Japan: (1) There were no large-scale migrations adding to the racial mixture of the Japanese after the Jomon period; (2) The changes in the physical characteristics of the Jomon population through Yayoi, Kamakura, Muromachi and Edo periods and down to the present were the result of environmental forces, primarily sociocultural, and regional geographical specializations. Although the museum made no reference to this theory's view on the place of Minatogawa man in the scheme of things, it's interesting how close the museum's conceptualization and Suzuki's analysis were on the matter. For Suzuki, if Minatogawa man was not "Our Ancestor," he might be considered to be "Our Far Ancestor." In addition, Suzuki held that Minatogawa man was more blood-tied to Liujiang man and Jomon people than to Upper Cave man.[60]

The other two theories related were rather inimical to the exhibition's perspective on Japanese origins. If the museum had followed their precepts, human evolution would have been a moot point and analysis would have centered in the realm in which mythical waves swept the landscape. One was the mixture theory which apparently, from the museum's point of view, had superseded the proto-Japanese theory, an old approach which dated back to the end of the 19th century. According to proto-Japanese theorists, the Japanese people were a mixed race formed in the Jomon period from a proto-Japanese, a compound of ancestral Ainu, Malay-Indonesian types, Mongolians, Chinese and Koreans. This original hypothesis, at least in its time focus and in its mesh of possible old (Ainu nowadays are considered to be Mongoloid but a number of scholars view them as old Mongoloid) and new Mongoloid types, was not antithetical to more Western-time evolutionary inquiries. In contrast, the new mixed race theory, presented at the exhibition, was less than compatible, holding that during the Yayoi to Kofun period, people from the Asian continent came to Japan from Korea, mixed with the Jomon people and established the foundation of the modern Japanese race. In this case, there would seem to be very little motive to seek out Minatogawa man, especially if the mixture was dominated by the later arrivals.[61]

The final theory presented maintained that Japan was invaded by a continental people who just about destroyed the native inhabitants or pushed them into the boondocks, and occupied most of the country. The antecedent in this case was the confronting school of thought in which the Jomon people were Ainu and the Yayoi people were the ancestors of the present Japanese. The history of replacement thinking can be traced back to the observations first made by a Dutchman, Philipp Franz von Siebold, in 1823.[62] The post-World War II exposition postulating the coming of a nomadic, horseriding people to Japan in the Kofun period represents a variation on this old theme.

The museum's perspective on the tale which the exhibition was to tell – evolution/continuous change – didn't carry over so well to the story published by the event's sponsor, the *Yomiuri Shimbun*, Japan's leading national newspaper. In a series prior to the opening of the exhibition on July 16, *Yomiuri* endeavored to attract popular interest in a manner which contrasted emphatically with the museum's vision of what the visitor was to take home with him. The series consisted of five articles and ran consecutively from July 11 to 15.[63] The writer, who also had represented *Yomiuri* as a member of the exhibition's writing staff, found it exceedingly difficult to create an appealing story out of a quest for Japanese origins which was so nebulous: the connecting points being so far apart in time or correspondence and the ultimate destination or reason for the undertaking being relatively unclear. Reading between the lines, one could almost grasp a mythical refrain querying why do we have to go back so far and why do we need to associate the Japanese cradle with events which are inspiring for Western-time believers. The reporter didn't even relate the possibility of a Peking Man in Japan nor did he seek to capture reader's enthusiasm with a headline proclaiming: "Minatogawa Man Is Our Ancestor." In fact, the first article in the series focused not on the Okinawa connection or for that matter, on skeletal remains, but on Jomon people and Jomon culture. Instead of human evolution, the reader learned that if he came to the museum, he would get the opportunity to view the recently discovered Jomon Venus with its overly rounded posterior. No, it wasn't a cutout from the Jomon edition of *Playboy*. It was an example of a "dogū," a female stone figurine probably related to rites of birth and agricultural production, recently excavated in Nagano Prefecture. The second and third articles in the series sustained the Jomon-Minatogawa-Liujiang line of descent but the author didn't gloss over some of the difficulties with such an approach, relating for instance that approximately 20,000 years separated Minatogawa man from Liujiang man and the Liujiang to Okinawa crossing of fossil mankind was but a possibility. In any event, the Jomon-Yayoi-Kofun nexus was to shine more brightly cradlewise in the pages of the *Yomiuri* than in the halls of the museum. As the series moved closer to the day of the opening, the writer moved away from the continuous change theme of the exhibition and centered his attention and that of his readers, on foreign migration or invasion. The fourth article was entitled "Toraijin" or foreign visitors and set forth the theory of Kazuro Hanihara, who followed Suzuki as Professor of Anthropology at Tokyo University. Hanihara had recently put forward the hypothesis that, in the 1,000 years from 300 B.C. to 700 A.D., one million foreigners came to Japan.[64] Although the theory was not presented uncritically, the toraijin hook, from the reporter's vantage point, seemed to be too important for catching an audience to leave as in the case of the exhibition gameplan to a background rather than a center stage role.

Naturally, Hanihara, with his un-Suzuki-like posturing, was not featured at the exhibition, but Hideo Matsumoto was. Matsumoto, a professor at Osaka Medical College, specializing in the study of genetic markers of human immunoglobulins, held that the origin of the Japanese race was in Siberia, most likely in the Lake Baikal area, and his viewpoint was presented in an exhibit on tracing Japanese roots through molecular biological analysis.[65] Therefore, the *Yomiuri*'s emphasis on Matsumoto's conclusions in the final article coincided with the museum's, except for one crucial aspect, i.e., time of occurrence. Whereas the fourth article raised the curtain on a foreign influx into Japan, the fifth was intended to dramatize this happening by locating the source. However, in this instance, the writer had to shift gears somewhat. Without mentioning that Matsumoto's Lake Baikal theory was anchored in the dawn of the Jomon period in line with the museum's injection of a northern Mongoloid catalyst in the change from Liujiang-Minatogawa to Jomon, the reporter eased Matsumoto's viewpoint into a categorical framework of southern and northern routes. The southern route was taken by people similar to Liujiang man and became Jomon man. The northern route witnessed northeast Asians coming to Japan from late Jomon to Kofun period. According to *Yomiuri*, these northerners had a big influence on the formation of the characteristics of the modern Japanese.

The frailty inherent in the museum's Liujiang-Minatogawa-Jomon paradigm worked against media promotion of the exhibition in terms of an evolutionary-continuous change approach to Japanese origins. From a readership attractiveness vantage point, there were just too many informational/credibility deserts for Japanese popular culture to pass through in order to reach an unmarked oasis of racial identity. The process was too mentally laborious, with too many qualified rationalizations. And the ending was left unresolved. What was the next stop in the ride back after Liujiang man and what did it hold in store with regard to an identity benefit? Could Japan share the bastion in the Asian sector of multiregional evolution currently occupied by China? Besides the articles in the *Yomiuri*, *Newton*, a popular graphic science magazine, reflected on the contents of the exhibition in a special issue on "The Origins of the Japanese" or "Where We Came From." Although the *Newton* issue appeared 16 months after the museum event, it covered the same territory as the exhibition had (from Australopithecus to Kofun Japanese), stated its objective in a similar manner (chasing Japanese roots back through time) and took into consideration the expert opinion of staff members of the museum (consulting with two ranking officers of the museum in the course of the project).[66] Instead of showing specimens, *Newton* simulated the exhibition's chronology entirely in double- and triple-page and take-out, poster-style graphic representations.

Newton made an effort like the *Yomiuri* to link up the chain of events in the pre-Jomon period. It even went so far as to give Peking Man his due, although unlike the exhibition there was no attempt to include the Japanese land mass in the territorial domain of Homo erectus. The heading read: "Peking Man, Maybe the Roots of the Japanese." Newton explained that the very old fossil humankind who evolved out of Peking Man possibly came to Japan since, even though no skeletal remains had been found, stone tools had been excavated which dated back 40,000 years. However, the problem with this line of representation was that the image drawn of Peking Man related to a Western-time intersect with Chinese rather than Japanese anthropological history. The picture was not Japanese passport size. In addition, *Newton* provided faceless descriptions for these pre-Liujiang fossil Mongoloid arrivals, an invention not exactly in keeping with its graphically illustrated chronology.[67]

Newton also attempted to sure up the time and characteristic discrepancies between Liujiang man and Upper Caveman in China and fossil humankind in Japan, including Minatogawa man, through the catch-all explanation that they all belonged to old-Mongoloid-type rootstock. A group of these old fossil human beings were pictured on a hill in Korea overlooking a land bridge to Japan. The headline read: "People in Old Stone Age Came to Japan Across a Land Bridge During the Ice Age." But even *Newton* had to concede that Jomon man only seemed to be a descendent of these people.[68]

Nevertheless, the magazine's efforts in the Western-time zone were not crucial to the message that it was trying to relay to its readers. There really was no need to tie up all the loose ends from Peking man to Jomon man. In fact, ambiguity served the magazine's intent in the issue. Since the Liujiang-Minatogawa-Jomon line lacked a strong personality to warrant a strong attachment in its readers, it was easy to dispense with the lineage at the proper moment for all significant genetic purposes. And this cataclysm was associated with the beginning of the Yayoi period.

The first graphic to be displayed within the pages of the origins of the Japanese was not fossil humankind or Jomon people, but a reconstructed rendering of the Toro ruins of 200 B.C. in Shizuoka. Raised storehouses, dwellings and irrigated rice fields were illustrated against a backdrop of a bellowing Mt. Fuji. The copy informed the reader that wet-rice cultivation was high technology in those days and new tools, especially those made of metal, were introduced alongside this innovation.[69]

This opening display made the excursion which followed down fossil mankind lane a prelude to Yayoi. And when the curtain went up on Yayoi once again, it went down on old Mongoloid with an explosive finality. An undersea volcano of the Kikai Caldera located 30 kilometers off the shore of southern Kyushu erupting, dark, gaseous smoke billowing skywards, tidal wave forming, people along the beach running from their boats, all these elements were pictured under the heading "Volcanic Eruption Devastates Jomon Population of Kyushu." According to the magazine, this climactic event took place 6,300 years ago (mid-Jomon) at a time when Jomon population was declining. A chart showing Jomon population figures taken from the evaluation of Jomon ruins by Shuzo Koyama, of the National Museum of Ethnology, was colorfully reproduced. The chart revealed that Jomon population had slid to 75,000 at the outset of the Yayoi period from a pinnacle of about 260,000 in mid-Jomon.[70]

On the following page, a calm sea with a long boat of the type inferred from Kofun period "haniwa" (miniature clay statues) closing in on the Japanese shore and a huge portrait of a "henpei" or flat-faced toraijin rising in the foreground provided the visual for "Ancestor of Yayoi Were the New Mongoloid Who Came Across the Sea."[71] The flat-faced features of the new Mongoloid contrasted with the "horigafukai" or sculptured face of old Mongoloid of the previous pages. Incised characteristics are considered to be more appropriate for living in a warm environment, according to those who use climate as the standard for differentiating Mongoloid populations. Precisely etched contours jut out into the cold resulting in susceptibility to frost bite because of poor blood circulation and accompanying heat loss.[72] From the *Newton*-ian perspective, Yayoi people and Yayoi culture filled a human void in Japan, eventually assimilating the loose remnants of the native people. At the end of the display, *Newton* assembled portraits of Jomon, Yayoi and Kofun people and concluded that the blood of the toraijin after the Yayoi period became "mainstream" Japanese. An interesting footnote to Newtonian graphics was the inclusion of a double page illustration of Yoshinogari, a fortified Yayoi village in Kyushu, to fortify the "mainstream" image. Yoshinogari gained fame after the museum's exhibition through a media blitz and became associated in the popular mind with the coming of the toraijin and the establishment of a unified Japanese country. The graphics showed a heavily guarded, fenced-in village and the copy proclaimed power to the toraijin.[73]

Media coverage of the University of Tokyo symposium and the National Science Museum exhibition revealed the relative impotency of images generated by educational instruments within the milieu of mass media communication and reflected the strength of the mythical paradigm within Japanese popular culture. The media's response also attested to its tendency to tick off developments or events according to two separate ways of telling time, Western and Japanese, which was bolstered by unresolvable limitations to the sculpting out of Western-time appraisals a strong and concise racial identity image with which to captivate its audience.

With the media locked into the mythohistorical period of Japanese origins and the borders of the mythical paradigm secured, modernization of the myth can proceed uncontested. Through the creativity of the media acting upon the dramatic outlines of the myth, new information which falls within or touches upon the paradigmatic boundaries of the modernizing myth can serve as a vehicle for reappraisal or review of the main story line and for the development of affirmative images. One should keep in mind that diverse media enterprises are highly competitive, always looking for new themes and images to gather up their share of the viewing or reading audience. As such, free market competition within the field of mass communications provides the modernizing mythical paradigm with great momentum and with enhanced strength of impact on the information which is input and processed. The state of Japanese mythohistory resembles a highly-valued and high-grade consumer product in an inflexible market in media terms. The media must differentiate to compete.

CHAPTER III

RESURRECTION

Two years ago, Yoshinogari, an important 3rd century excavated ruins with huge watchtowers in Northern Kyushu, encountered the mythical origins of the Japanese race and was transformed by the mass power of this myth exercised through the instrumentality of the mass media. At first, Yoshinogari became the play within which a modernized, academic-tinted rendering of past retellings could be performed to satisfy an up-to-the-minute news and commentary oriented mass audience interested in reaffirming its roots. The myth surrounded and absorbed Yoshinogari in the months that followed, displacing it from its historical moorings. By the end of 1989, Yoshinogari had become a symbol of the myth and the media could refer to Yoshinogari to awaken a conditioned reflex in the audience as to the credibility of mythohistory. There was a short revival of Yoshinogari as an historical entity and a revised mythohistorical drama was briefly reenacted. However, by 1990, Yoshinogari–although the most powerful signaling station–had joined some sixty established sites possessing the innate potential for communicating a symbolic message capable of integrating diverse images into a distinct pattern of cause and effect. From 1989-1991, tourists, popular readers and the TV viewing audience made the journey to Yoshinogari to relive their births, racially speaking, and trace their bloodlines to superheroes in fantastic times. The true believer didn't have to

68

relive every mythohistorical moment of Yoshinogari; a momentary basking – literally or figuratively – in the light through the watchtower would suffice.

The rite of passage of Yoshinogari offers not only an insight into the strength of the modernizing mythical paradigm within mass culture but also reveals strains of racialism/racism. The Western myth of origins has its deviant forms as already noted. It is not surprising that superheroes sometimes falter as well. In Japan, perhaps, racialism rather than racism best fits the offense since color, white or black, is not a priority discriminator. In fact, the tangent of discrimination within the Japanese context is along Japanese-nonJapanese lines. But more to the point, Japanese racialism is more inner directed than other directed in that it doesn't require disparagement of other people's capabilities. In conceptualizing the nature of their uniqueness, blood and soil are mixed to produce a nation of the most vital and energetic people, able, like the phoenix, to rise from the ashes to heights of worldwide recognition in all fields of endeavor. The racialism associated with Yoshinogari fuses diverse elements, including singularity and unity of race, domination, aggressiveness and flexibility, to create a crescendo emanating from within the confines of an old and glorious kingdom, the predecessor and progenitor of the Japanese state. The media orchestrates the sound to the point where it resembles the distant drumming of hundreds or thousands of mercilessly driven horses beating the path of the sun.

Media coverage of this old and glorious kingdom of Yoshinogari began in February of 1989 with a news article reporting the discovery of a 3rd century "kangō shūraku" or fortified village ringed with moats in Saga Prefecture, northern Kyushu. The story was scooped by the *Asahi Shimbun* and resulted in a rush in popular interest in the site. This scoop is credited with rescuing the 3-year Yoshinogari excavation in Saga from being turned into an industrial park, which was scheduled to begin on March 10.[1] Also, the scoop made Yoshinogari, by and large, a story of *Asahi Shimbun* and its associated publications, according to a custom of Japanese journalism. Although in 1989 *Yomiuri Shimbun*, the nation's number one newspaper in terms of circulation, would run some 60 pages of articles on Yoshinogari, number two *Asahi Shimbun* would carry more than 70 pages. Moreover, generally, *Yomiuri Shimbun*'s articles would be short, matter of fact descriptions of the excavation while *Asahi Shimbun*'s would be long and extensive (even a full page), quite sensational and very colorful (in terms of language and color photos). Even *AERA* took up the story, providing two-page coverage with pictures and maps of the ruins on March 21.[2] Still, just in terms of sheer amount of newsprint dedicated to Yoshinogari, one can understand the significance of such an archaeological discovery for Japanese mass identity. It's hard to envision a Western discovery which would generate an equivalent media response.

The February 23 article observed that Yoshinogari would provide big clues for solving the mystery of the ancient Japanese kingdom of Yamatai, relating a remark by Sahara to the effect that he could imagine from the findings just what the ancient record of the Wei Kingdom in China was talking about, which is not necessarily a Yamatai allusion, but....[3] A few months later, Sahara, in his own series of articles, would maintain that Yoshinogari would never show where Yamataikoku was.[4] As noted in the last chapter, the *Wei Chronicle*, which was compiled toward the end of the 3rd century, is the only source material, although not necessarily a wholly credible one, on the seat of authority ruled by a female shaman, Queen Himiko.

Recognizing the shortcomings of the Wei record, Seicho Matsumoto, a well-known writer and a highly regarded popular historian, in an *AERA* article on June 13, 1989 on the historical and geographical distance separating Yamatai from Yoshinogari, wrote that the compilers certainly had never been to Japan since they had failed to reflect upon the natural scenery. Now, the Chinese weren't interested in Japan per se, being more concerned with illuminating their own perceptions and values on a Japanese canvas. Such a disposition would not only account for the lack of scenic description and problems concerning directions, but would raise much more damaging questions of credibility. Such queries Matsumoto avoided. And the editors of *AERA* would continue to avoid. For instance, in the following week's issue, *AERA* ran an article on an excavation in Nara and pounced on how it might help to solve the riddle of the Yamatai controversy. All told, both Matsumoto and *AERA* were pursuing a proven marketing formula by thrusting forth the idea of a Queen-centered Yamatai Kingdom as a tasty tidbit for popular consumption. Whereas Matsumoto is an advocate of a Kinki location for Yamatai, the Yoshinogari excavation has strengthened the hand of the Kyushu advocates since previously a major failing of the position had been the absence of a large shūraku of queendom proportions.[5]

Aside from being the largest shūraku ever found in Kyushu, Yoshinogari's initial claim to preeminence rested on these features: Firstly, it was the only shūraku ever discovered with watchtowers, as recorded in the *Wei Chronicle*. Secondly, the tomb mound of a powerful person (or persons), measuring 40 m from north to south, had been discovered.[6] But there were deficiencies. In addition to the reservations already set forth, there had been no discovery of Wei dynasty mirrors, of a large tomb mound in which, according to the *Wei Chronicle*, Himiko was buried with over one hundred human sacrifices and of a place in the vicinity with a name resembling Yamatai. Also, as Kyotari Tsuboi, the former Director-General of the Nara Research Institute of Cultural Properties, pointed out, it would not take the one month specified in the chronicle to cross the mountains between Yoshinogari and the coast.[7]

Yet, in spite of the lack of conclusive evidence, the veil of Himiko held tight to Yoshinogari from February to May of 1989, with the media providing the allure of a solution to the origins of the Japanese people and kindling more than enough attention to attract hundreds and thousands of "source" pilgrims to a rather barren-looking and isolated archaeological excavation. A special magazine published by *Saga Shimbun* in March[8] was widely circulated throughout Japan, with the aim of keeping the fires burning. The magazine featured dramatic page-size pictures and illustrations as well as bold-print, eye-catching headlines. The cover, with a picture of the sun rising over the site, carried the title, "Yoshinogari Kingdom," with an overhead subtitle proclaiming the following: "From here, Yamatai can be seen." Inside the message of revelation that the unearthing of Yoshinogari placed Yamatai in Kyushu was reinforced with an aerial photo of the ruling elite burial mound and the caption: "From the darkness of history, Yoshinogari Kingdom popped out." The query of "who was buried here?" appeared with a close-up of the royal burial mound. Under the headline of a "gigantic burial mound, symbol of power," there appeared an account of how powerful the person buried in the tomb was, being either a king or a chief of a clan. On the following page, the contents of the central urn – blue glass beads and a bronze dagger – were heralded as further evidence of the kingdom's wide power and great authority. If the reader missed the intention of tying history and archeology to an unprovable assumption of power and unity, a two-page illustrated reconstruction of Yoshinogari was presented, with Queen Himiko rising from beyond the outer moat, her hands molded above her head in a gesture of authority. All told, the publication circumvented questions of the nature and extent of the power and unity described. How much power was centered at Yoshinogari? How far did it extend? The words in the *Saga Shimbun* resembled idols rather than analytical tools; they were to be worshipped rather than explained.

On May 2, the anchor of NTV (Nippon Television) night news was in Fukuoka, a major city in relatively close proximity to Yoshinogari, for a special broadcast on the site. His coanchor in Fukuoka was dressed as Himiko, i.e., clothed in a white dress worn by slipping the head through an opening in the center. In this instance, in addition to the slipover white dress, the coanchor wore a bluebead necklace and a crown. The visual association of Himiko with Yoshinogari was emphasized at the outset of this special news clip, but the newsworthiness of Yoshinogari was underscored by the theme of how and why a roped-off, bare ruins, which could only be viewed from a distance, was attracting such a large number of visitors during Japan's Golden Week vacation period (from April 29th for one week), about 25,000 visitors a day.

For instance, in presenting to the viewers a model of Yoshinogari in the Yayoi period, the queen-for-a-day commentator observed that maybe one of the houses in the village was occupied by Himiko's ancestor. Takayuki Matsushita, an Associate Professor at Nagasaki University's medical department, was interviewed on the difference in skulls found in Kyushu at the time and he set forth the hypothesis that two types of people were living side by side: descendants of early period people or Jomon people and new arrivals from Korea or Yayoi people. The impression tendered of the presence of two distinct population groups—an implicit blood-soil, invasion-domination scenario—was reinforced by an ensuing segment in which the Yamatai-Yayoi skull was examined by a computerized police laboratory identikit and proclaimed to be quite similar to that of the modern Japanese. Coincidently, an article appeared on the same day in *AERA* on the Yoshinogari tourist boom. *AERA* had already introduced Matsushita's hypothesis in its article on the ruins in March, although not as dramatically.[9]

The sensationalism of Yoshinogari—one million visitors within a matter of several weeks—carried over from commercial media presentations to public television in May when NHK-G (Japan Broadcasting, General channel) scheduled a 3-part, prime-time hourly program on consecutive nights. The series' slant was evident in its title: "The Resurrection of Yamatai Country." The focus was to be on the appearance of a powerful kingdom in Kyushu and the significance of it all for Japanese history. The main quest of Part 1 of the "Resurrection" was Yoshinogari's chief excavator, Juhei Takashima, an official of the education department of Saga Prefecture. In his presentation and the accompanying footage, the emphasis was on how well Yoshinogari conformed to *Wei Chronicle*'s specifications: double moat, fence, watchtower, hill mound and palace. When he was asked by the program's host to explain why Yoshinogari had caused such a big sensation, Takashima replied that the size and chronicle-type character of the shūraku, especially the hill mound, had caused the stir. In Takashima's estimation, Yoshinogari and ruins in the surrounding area made up the country of Minu (described in the chronicle as being under the dominion of Yamatai and Queen Himiko).

Part 2 of the "Resurrection" was both a look beyond the king's tomb and a look back to a period predating Yamatai. From the very beginning of the program, one had the suspicion that myth rather than historical reality was gaining control of the program's story and Yoshinogari was to be more a symbolic offering to the shrine of the origins of the Japanese than a credible analytical survey. As the camera surveyed the ruins once again, the viewer was told that the king's tomb was actually the tomb of the king and his family – perhaps a concession to the other bodies found in the mound. But this was just an initial hint of unexplained divergence from part 1. From the other burial urns excavated at the site, the viewer was informed that Yoshinogari existed in an era of fluidity and conflict rather than one of consolidation and unity since evidence had been uncovered of bodies marked by the ravages of war and of instruments of death.

If Himiko was to be associated with the end of turmoil, how could a turbulent Yoshinogari be related to Minu country? Nevertheless, myth has a mobility and flexibility which historical facts lack and to answer this question, the director of the series merely had to shift chronological gears and "time-machine" the viewer to another century. Consequently, Yoshinogari could represent both the road to unity as well as its existence in terms of the resurrection of Yamatai.

The swift departure from the 3rd century to the late 2nd century was done with the rapid movement of the camera's eye to twelve larger than man-size poster boards stretched across a stage. This herculean presentation was necessary since as already noted the Japanese section of the chronicle was peripheral rather than central and therefore consisted of only some 2,000 characters. So in order to present the viewer with its greatness or authoritativeness, there was a need for some theatrics. The theatrics also served as a distraction since the camera focused on that part of the Japan section which described the period prior to the rise of Yamatai.

Henceforth, the program took on a air of conformity to the ancient folklore of the founding of the Japanese state by emphasizing a forward power surge of a consolidating force. Suddenly, the audience's attention was shifted from Yoshinogari to a shūraku in Osaka dating from the late 2nd century. The announcer explained that quite a number of ruins with defensive installations had been uncovered from this period. This was followed by a map of Japan showing more than 200 Yayoi sites of the type indicated.

This thesis being rendered was that excavations of this period revealed that war existed throughout Japan at this time and that the forces of consolidation, following a sudden mysterious but unexplained population explosion in Kyushu would move from victory to victory until arrival in Kinki and the establishment of Yamatai. In view of Japanese traditional thinking on the matter, the most likely implication for the viewers of such a population increase would be an invasion from the continent of a new breed of people, the ancestors of the modern Japanese people. Among the authoritative, academic-vested findings presented were population studies supporting a concentration/movement scenario, weaponry alterations revealing a change from hunting to killing objectives, the existence of many "kōchi sei shūraku" or hill-top outposts where people could take refuge or engage in combat, the establishment of "noroshi" or early warning networks of kōchi sei shūraku, especially a very extensive one in the Osaka-Yodogawa River area, the concentration of Wei-style mirrors of the type supposedly presented by the Wei Emperor to Himiko in the Kinki area, the findings of an excavation in Okayama pointing to an alliance in the 3rd century of Kibi and Kinki and the program's closing sequence of a search for Yamatai in Nara at the recent Makimuku Ishizuka tomb excavation.

The final chapter of the "Resurrection," i.e., part 3, represented merely a return to part 1, a rehash of the debate on where Yamatai was actually located. In a sense, it is almost as if part 2 never really happened; there had never been any departure of Yoshinogari from the 3rd century – another instance of the triumph of myth over historical reality.

By the summer of 1989, the media had fashioned Yoshinogari into a double-double image. In media terms, Yoshinogari had the authority to exist in either the 2nd or 3rd centuries and in both invasion-conflict and consolidation-unity phases. In the fall, at the time that Yoshinogari was reopened to the public once again, one of these double images was already evolving into a vision of relative timelessness within a 700 to 800 year period to accommodate an emphasis on the invasion aspect of the conflict-consolidation-unity continuum.

In November, both NTV and NHK-G broadcast programs on the age of the Yoshinogari ruins. NTV focused on Yoshinogari and the "Japanese Madonna" (Himiko), on imagery of the virgin birth of a new people. NHK-G correlated the birth of a new people with the coming of the toraijin, who would supplant or genetically overwhelm the indigenous population, and establish the foundation of the modern-day Japanese race and culture. In view of the chronological ambivalence surrounding academic studies on this matter, toraijin stories can be merged in various ways to reinforce the basic tenet of a single origin paradigm. And the program took advantage of this time warp in linking toraijin to Yoshinogari.

At the beginning of the NHK-G show, the announcer climbed one of the two twelve-meter-high reconstructed watchtowers at Yoshinogari and explained that from this vantage point, a lookout would have a view of the cultivated fields, the sea and the arrival of the toraijin. When Yoshinogari reopened in October, the idea of Saga Prefecture was to commercialize further upon this proven tourist attraction by reconstructing on part of the site moats, fences, watchtowers, granaries and dwellings and by opening an exhibition hall. The reconstruction of Yoshinogari provided a formidable backdrop for further mass media publicity. And the NHK-G announcer was given a high-rise pulpit to expound upon the toraijin and to set forth on a journey to track down the man who was to herald the beginning of the toraijin era, Jofuku – no matter if this character existed in the 3rd century B.C. and Yoshinogari 2nd or 3rd century A.D. According to the Han Dynasty (prior to the Wei) records, Jofuku, a Tao magician, was sent overseas by the Chin Emperor to search for the elixir of eternal life. Although there is no real proof that Jofuku ever came to Japan, legends or traditions abound in this respect and the program assumed that he did. In addition, the program provided the magician with a very respectable and highly honorable image. He was cast as a man of great learning who had the enormous energy to travel widely throughout Japan dispersing his knowledge of Chinese culture and science. Special attention was given to his role in introducing rice field irrigation techniques in Japan.[10]

An *AERA* article which appeared shortly before the airing of the NHK-G program provided a more formidable costume for the toraijin, more in keeping with a mythical line dating back to 8th century Japanese political treatises, i.e., the idea of an invasion of a warlike people who established a colonial spearhead in Kyushu from which they exacted tribute from the surrounding native population before extending their imperial rule over the eastern regions. The basis for this imagery was the assertion that the few hundred bones already uncovered from the graveyard of the common people and from that of the ruling elite in Yoshinogari appeared to be different from the other people living in the vicinity. Also, the article explained that the defense-consciousness of the toraijin of Yoshinogari, who came from Korea because Japan was highly suitable for rice cultivation, reflected a state of continuing conflict with the native population and the need for extreme vigilance. Finally, the analogy made in the article to the era of Rome and Carthage had the effect of conjuring up naval excursions and imperial legions with armed men on horseback. In fact, the whole article riveted up an image associated with the modern-day "horserider theory" of the origins of the Japanese. The idea that the Japanese people can trace their descent to a vibrant, aggressive people, is an inherent aspect of the modernizing mythical paradigm and represents, as noted at the outset, a very popular point of view. And the *AERA* editors drew upon this popular disposition to gain the readers acquiescence in the thesis that Yoshinogari could be correlated with the toraijin. Once again, Yoshinogari transcended the flow of time – no matter if the academic issue of whether galloping invaders came to Japan is centered in the 4th and 5th and not in the 2nd and 3rd centuries.[11]

The horserider theory is a more factually based mythical presentation than the one which dates back to the World War II state-propaganda period and to the *Kojiki* and *Nihon Shoki*. The legend of the eastward movement of the imperial forces under the sun goddess' descendant from Kyushu to dominion is rather passé nowadays. The modernized myth, whose primary author is Namio Egami, Professor Emeritus of Tokyo University, offers a similar concept of the coming of an imperial race but packages it in historical and archaeological evidence, which would seem to contradict the mythical label except for the transformative quality of the evidence when confronted with paradigm dissonance. The horserider theory is a roller coaster moving around and around between aggression and nonaggression, conquest and cooptation, dominance and assimilation within an arena of chronological ambivalence and a lack of direct historical sources. Gari Ledyard, an authority on horseriding theory, notes that Egami is ambiguous on many matters, including the roots of these North Asian people who first conquered a portion of southern Korea, their ethnic relationship to other Korean tribal groupings, the political character of their rule – magical or baronial – and the "loss of memory" in Korea or Japan of an invading force crossing the Tsushima Straits.[12]

An objection might be raised that Ledyard's comments are based in the 1970s and that things must have changed somewhat to promote this continued focus of attention on the horserider theory – new documentation or substantiation perhaps. For instance, the NHK-G Jofuku program presented Hanihara as one of its toraijin authorities and he expounded the idea that the origins of the Japanese can be considered in terms of separate continental movements of old or southern Mongoloid peoples and new or northern Mongoloid peoples. In the program, Hanihara was shown as asserting that Yayoi people genetically swamped the earlier Jomon people. Although the appearance of this information on a program about Jofuku represented an implicit message of invasion and domination, there was no reference on

Hanihara's part to conquest nor was there any dating of this swamping action to any specific time period. In fact, Hanihara is usually associated with analyses concerning the break between Jomon and Yayoi rather than later events. In all, academics today, no less than in the 70s, who involve themselves in early continental movements tend to disagree on when, from where and how people moved from the continent to Japan.

More to the point is a Yoshinogari-inspired book for the general reading public. This book, *Horseriding People: Did They or Didn't They Come?*, is in the form of a dialogue between Sahara and Egami, with the former standing in opposition to horserider theory. Sahara draws strength for his assault from the evidence garnered from Yoshinogari, reinforcing the view that Yayoi was not a peaceful farming period as postulated by Egami but a period of widespread conflict. However, when Egami answers that, of course, there was some fighting in some areas, but generally the Yayoi period was a peaceful one, a new transformational defense enters into the paradigm which tends to make any attack on the peace-conflict, early-late chronological division of the horserider theory irrelevant and immaterial. Egami's original warlike, baronial horseriders who came to Japan are no longer portrayed as being so warlike or baronial but instead they are pictured as being witting and cunning, better in using their brains than their weapons. According to Egami, although the horseriders invaded Japan with weapons, they didn't have to fight to establish their dominion, but instead, they used their wits to cement alliances. In fact, as Sahara observes somewhat ironically, Egami's horseriders are Ieyasu-planner rather than Nobunaga-fighter types and weapons found in the late-period tombs are nothing more than accessories. Sahara sardonically reviews Egami's stated position in the following manner: (1) The horseriders came to Korea from Northeast Asia and assimilated to Korean ways, giving up their own customs. (2) Even though they had weapons, they didn't fight when they came to the northern part of Kyushu. (3) They then moved on to the Osaka area – all peacefully – to plant their kingdom. In all, Sahara concludes that Egami's nomadic horseriders would seem to be no different from farming people with horses, since they had given up their nomadic talents and foresaken fighting. Egami replies that even though they left fighting behind, they kept their feudal ("hōkenteki") way of structuring power and continued to retain the attributes associated with high prestige when horserider culture faded in the 7th and 8th centuries.[13]

As can be seen, toraijin invaders/horseriders continued to ride through popular perspectives on early history in 1989 without being grounded in origin, time or character. Heavily laden with a transformational profile, the invasion concept was easily linked with Yoshinogari, already cut adrift by the swift current of mythohistory. Such a result was perhaps inevitable in terms of mass media presentations. The conflict and consolidation myths surrounding Yoshinogari invited a more dramatic portrayal of Japan's "special and unique" origins, especially one which was ambivalent regarding precise comings and goings and contained values for which the media could find a ready audience. Moreover, the linkage was inevitable since the horserider element was an established and integral step in the process of modernizing the original myth of the birth of Japan.

Through the firm addition of foreign conquest, Yoshinogari mythohistory moved transparently into the theatre of racial identity. In all, the failure of Yoshinogari to immunize or separate itself from the Yamatai and toraijin myths reflected the media's immersion in the modernizing mythical paradigm.

The implications of Yoshinogari's mythical journey in terms of the unique racial identity of the Japanese became even more evident in 1990-1991 when the excavation's current events status had begun to wane, leaving the media waiting in the wings for the appearance of a "new idol of the ruins" to celebrate in mythohistory. The media didn't abandon Yoshinogari under the circumstances but increasingly approached the excavation in a more refined fashion, finding value in Yoshinogari's romanumental or monumental-with-romantic-feeling stature ("roman" meaning romantic feeling in Japanese). The passage of Yoshinogari through a modernizing mythical paradigm had processed the contents of the excavation into a byproduct of free-association symbolic imagery which could be applied without reference to an historical paradigm of verification and credibility. Already, as 1989 moved into 1990,[14] mythohistorical media treatment was trending away from such transformation of Yoshinogari evidence to the transformation of Yoshinogari itself. Yoshinogari was being media-designated to become more a corporate-identity-style emblem for internal as well as external mythohistorical liaisons. At first, however, the external or romanumental would predominate.

Perhaps, one could date Yoshinogari's alteration in status to New Year's day 1990 when Japanese preparing or returning from their January 1st visit to the shrines to prayer for personal and national prosperity, etc., found the cover page of the special New Year section of the *Asahi Shimbun* sporting an article on the resurrection of ancient times, with a half-page color photo of reconstructed Yoshinogari. From the article, readers learned a little about what was discovered in Yoshinogari and a great deal about hearing "the beat of ancient times." The writer Sugimoto Sonoko presented her view that history should be based on systematic proof, but she noted that the Yoshinogari boom was not like that and lots of amateurs were coming forward with fantastic theories. Still, she found Yoshinogari so exciting that she was willing to overlook discrepancies and distortions. Sugimoto wrote that she felt her spirit being buoyed by the overexcitement and that she herself wanted to experience the rising sun over Ariake Bay from the heights of the Yoshinogari watchtower and feel like a Yayoi person. She closed her article on this triumphant note on, in her own words, the "pull of the past" for the Japanese people: "When we ask ourselves who we are, from where we came and how we are here, our eyes go further and further ahead of us. History is not just here opening the door to the past but is also the key to the future."[15]

For over 60 days after this special edition, the *Asahi Shimbun* could extract no news item from Yoshinogari, which had previously offered at least one story a month. All was quiet from the Saga front. When Yoshinogari returned in March, it settled into the newspaper's pages as a romanumental cutout to be associated with an issue external to the excavation itself. Yoshinogari was about to be served up by the media as a central course in a campaign to preserve historical excavations, the aroma of Yamatai spreading beyond its mythohistorical boundaries to draw popular attention to the need for action as well as underline the potential for monetary gain. In the March 26 article, Yoshinogari was presented as exemplifying how greatly rewarding it could be to relive the past. Emphasis was placed on how Yoshinogari was a lucky ruins, having been rescued from industrial development reburial by the Yamataikoku debate, the implication being that other ruins had not been so fortunate. Readers were informed that almost all scholars now believed that Yoshinogari was Yamatai. And the article expounded upon how Yoshinogari was in the process of providing an economic benefit to the locality far superior to industrialization, the premise being that the allure of Yamatai was too inviting to be ignored by the "origins'" consumer. In this regard, the newspaper related that millions of sightseers had been attracted to the site, with 24,000 visitors arriving on March 25 alone. Reference was made to the potential for future commercialization of the area, although, as yet, money hadn't been invested in the area, no restaurants, large shops, etc., to exploit this escalating tourist boom and coincide with the political pressure to have the ruins declared a national park. The article estimated that publicity for the locality alone generated by the site came to some 10 billion yen.[16]

Four days later, in an *Asahi Shimbun* editorial, Yoshinogari was more specifically linked to the issue of the general preservation of ruins. The central government's decision to designate Yoshinogari as a national cultural property was applauded and the government's positioning to establish Yoshinogari as a national park welcomed These efforts were portrayed as taking place within the context of past neglect of historic ruins, resulting in the damage and destruction of the nation's heritage. In referring to the original plan to develop the area enclosing Yoshinogari into an industrial park, the editor explained about the recent surge in the number of excavations of cultural properties nationwide, more than three times that of

10 years ago, and how almost 90% were related to infrastructure development projects, which created the need for emergency research and recovery of properties and artifacts. Noting that infrastructure-related sites were destined to be lost to posterity, the editorial lamented on the lack of national government funding to preserve archaeological sites, amounting only to 12 billion yen, a mere 20% budget increase over 10 years ago. Economic pressure from owners of excavated sites usually prevented historical preservation and local governing bodies usually relented in such efforts even if the site equaled in importance that of Yoshinogari, according to the newspaper. Also, the problem of too many sites and too few official experts to perform the necessary procedures and paperwork was related. Under these circumstances, the editor concluded as earlier reported that Yoshinogari was a lucky ruins and greater efforts should be made to preserve other important sites. He also wrote that the national government should support Saga Prefecture's plan to rebuild the Yayoi world in Yoshinogari by proclaiming Yoshinogari to be the nation's second national historical park (Asuka Mura in Nara being the only one in 1990). At the end of the editorial, the intention to romanticize Yoshinogari to enhance the appeal being made, not only for Yoshinogari but for all ruins, through saturating the general message with images of Yamatai and racial origins was explicitly evident in the wording: We want the national government "to preserve the ruins in which the roman of Yamataikoku could be expanded...."[17]

From October to December, it appeared that Yoshinogari might escape that romantic feeling and slip back into history or at least center-stage mythohistory. New findings or conclusions relating to the excavation of the site offered the opportunity for the development of a new program presentation concept for the mass audience, one pertaining to historical evolution. There was the possibility that Yoshinogari could be marketed as a microcosm for understanding the evolution of Japanese culture and efforts were made by the media in this regard. Consequently, at the end of 1990, mass media attention seemed to waver between a substantive handling of Yoshinogari and the creation of a more symbolic representation. In other words, two directions in the way in which the media were blowing could be noted, i.e., toward a more Yoshinogari-style story format or toward the symbolic linkage of the site to an associated tale in which the mythohistory of Yoshinogari was not the main course being served.

Yoshinogari's split media or, more precisely, mythical personality, was evident in print and on TV. In December, the *Asahi Shimbun* ran two Yoshinogari articles; one in the preservation mold; the other stressing cultural evolution, although the preservation theme was present. The former was almost a three-quarter page spread. The banner headline proclaimed "Discovery of the Ancients: Many New Findings This Year," and subheadlines read "Use Restoration of Ruins for Revitalizing the Locality" and "Restoration of Yayoi: 2.15 Million People Went to Yoshinogari [by October 1990]." A great deal was made in the story which followed of reconstructed Yoshinogari's commercial success and how other localities are proceeding in a similar fashion to preserve their ruins as a "sightseeing resource." But the overall approach was not merely commercial. Tucked within the contours under the banner was a related article headed "Excavations Which Can Bring to Light the Roots of an Economically Big Country." The interesting point here is that there was no relationship between title and article. The heading was a cross reference to the Yoshinogari-Yayoi subheadings to romanumentalize the appeal to the readers and to extend the image of the birth of a people or the unification of a state in the Yayoi period to cover a range of chronologically unrelated ruins of castle walls, Tomb Period burial mounds, temples, shell mounds, etc., which also appeared in more detail in a map accompanying the text. The article related that the government would give money for the restoration of ruins to eight places every year for two years and that 16 places already had been so designated.[18]

The more cultural-evolution-oriented article received much less space. Bannered "Yoshinogari Ruins" and subheaded "Area a Great as 40 Hectares" and "Boundary Survey Almost Finished," the article proceeded to weave a mythohistorical pattern within the context of a broader versed historical framework than before.[19]   Since the information presented emphasized continuity of developments within a highly tense environment, mythohistory was confronted with a difficult course to follow. Continuity creates dissonance for a mythical paradigm of the type which requires definitive breaks in the story of ancient times. For instance, if tension is continuous, how can the pre-Himiko, Himiko and post-Himiko eras as related in the *Wei Chronicle* be differentiated for popular consumption on the basis of the Yoshinogari excavation. Also, if continuous social tension is reflected in the long history of this kangō shūraku, then, where do the "kiba minzoku" or toraijin fit in as conquerors of earlier populations.

The article placed emphasis on recent findings of the Prefectural Education Committee which consisted of the following: (1) the area of Yoshinogari was much larger than originally thought – 40 hectares rather than 22; (2) marshland as well as moats contributed to the defense of Yoshinogari, "sakamogi" (a wooden fence which slants outward and is sharpened at the top) being present in the marsh section and dating from the middle Yayoi period (100 B.C.-50 A.D.); (3) from the late Yayoi period (50 A.D.-300 A.D.), an artificial cliff extending down to the marshes and cut more than 2.5 meters at the bottom served as a defensive installation. The article not only offered a structure for continuity in the defensive character of Yoshinogari, but also provided ammunition for consideration of the ruins in political evolutionary terms. It was explained that rice cultivation and the raising of livestock were practiced in the surroundings of Yoshinogari from the beginning of the early period (from 300 B.C.), providing a possible source of economic wealth, and that a center of power possibly appeared in Yoshinogari quite early within a 4 hectare area surrounded by a moat. The establishment of a bronze-making factory (based on the discovery of tin material and molds) was associated with an emerging politically powerful group at the beginning of middle Yayoi and the gigantic mound was dated to about 50 B.C. – goodbye to Himiko's Tomb or even a Minu royal family burial place. Actually, when the mound was originally discovered, it was dated to the 1st century B.C., but, in the clamor that followed, the date was misplaced. Also, the mutilated bodies and bodies pierced with arrowheads as well as the glass beads, etc., were provided with a similar time frame – goodbye to Egami's horseriders. The reporter referred to the education committee's conclusions and related that the society of Yoshinogari in this period featured a person who prayed to the gods, craftsmen and an excellent leader, the place resembling more and more a "clandom."

However, such continuity was to be short-lived once the article entered the domain of the Gishiwajinden. At this point, the article made a swerve into the "Rome or Carthage" territory of mythohistorical modernization, failing to consider the full ramifications of the information presented and introducing the requisite discontinuity into the evaluative framework. The article's interpretative analysis was not to be centered on the early or middle period but on the late period and the interpreter took great pains to move Himiko's tomb and the ghosts of the toraijin to Gishiwajinden-Yoshinogari and to picture Yoshinogari as a center of great wealth and power. Suddenly, the article catapulted Yoshinogari from shūraku to city-state status. Besides the usual cited attributes of power, such as the watchtower and the palace, special attention was given to an increase in the number of iron products, including axes, hoes sickles and spades and to the discovery of a mirror as indicative of a power concentration. The mirror was not a Wei mirror, however, i.e., a triangular-edged one with designs of deities and animals. Also, much was made of the raised storehouses being number one in the world at that time in size and number. All of these elements were enlisted to sever Yoshinogari from the umbilical cord of its historical past, leaving only the gigantic mound which could not be described in view of its date as the resting place of a powerful person of a city-state. However, the gigantic mound could serve as evidence of a big power by being pictured as a grand temple. In this way, a source of dissonance could become a source of affirmation. And so it followed. The article explained that the gigantic mound of the early middle period, having lost its graveyard function, became a sacred place, a magnificent sanctuary in the late Yayoi period.

There was also the matter, as the article noted, that a second gigantic tomb dating from the same period and about similar in length had been found in the southern section of the excavation. One wonders how the 1989 TV programs, given their time focus, would have dealt with two Himiko-style gigantic mounds. Could Yoshinogari's power have been divided or dispersed among a power elite rather than concentrated in the hands of a queen or a king? Consequently, could internal politics explain the evidence of social tension? A few weeks prior to this article, a two-paragraph report on the discovery of the second mound had raised the possibility of two families ruling the place.[20] The December article, however, circumvented the question of who was buried in the second mound by equalizing without cause the status of all those buried in the northern mound and offering a nonburial-related interpretation of the significance of the southern find. The writer explained that the contents of the mound in the northern section had revealed the graves of more than 10 people together with gorgeous objects while in the new find only one grave had been discovered and the body had not been buried in a jar together with fine accessories. As such, the reporter surmised that (1) the graveyard of kings was located in the northern part, and (2) the southern mound was an early place of worship. In other words, two sanctuaries appeared to be better than one since the existence of a possible earlier shrine supported the concept of graveyards as sanctuaries. And the presence of two sanctuaries strengthened the suggestion of a great power concentration and was in accordance with a city-state interpretation. In this regard, the article compared the 40-hectare Yoshinogari with two famous bronze-age city states in Palestine and found Yoshinogari to be bigger in scale. As if to channel the contents of his report into an even clearer image for the mass audience, the reporter ended with a statement by Egami. The infusion of the story with the mythical message was therefore implicitly completed. In other words, the horseriders had entered the city state. Egami's appearance also had the effect of firmly putting the article within the newspaper's editorial fold of preservation of important ruins. Given a single line of space, Egami, who had become chief of the Ancient Orient Museum in Tokyo, was quoted as saying: "The wide-ranging conservation of Yoshinogari is a national responsibility to preserve for posterity the opportunity to think about the importance of the information which the ruins holds."[21]

The weaving of discontinuity within a theatre of continuity when executed by television could be accomplished through visual denotations distinct from the spoken storybook. This rather interesting hybrid was shown on TV Tokyo on October 26, 1990 on the program "Coming to the Core II," which was aired for close to thirty minutes in the 7:30 PM weekday time slot. This particular presentation was called "The Period of Yamataikoku: Yoshinogari and Yayoi Culture." The storybook progressed along the following lines.

[visual of Jomon site and pottery]
Voiceover: From 10,000 years ago to 300 B.C., during the Jomon period, the economy of Japan was centered in food gathering and Japan possessed its own earthenware culture. In view of late-Jomon agricultural evidence from Itatsuke ruins, the belief that wet-rice cultivation was a Yayoi innovation can no longer be maintained. Nevertheless, when the curtain rises on the Yayoi period, with its firm agricultural base, 8,000 years of people's lives are *drastically changed*.

> [visual notation: With the voiceover of ...drastically changed, Jomon rope-patterned pottery is "salvoed" to the ground, shattering explosively – a visual of cleavage rather than evolution in the movement of Jomon to Yayoi culture, an emphatic treatment which is not evident in the narration.]

[visual of Yoshinogari]
Voiceover: What was discovered at Yoshinogari matches with the account of Japan in the Gishiwajinden and this has caused a great sensation in terms of the debate on the location of Yamatai country. Moreover, the excavation has brought to light a lot of important clues for understanding Yayoi culture which is rich in internationalism.

[visual of Fukuoka coastline]

Voiceover: The sea was an important road for combining the cultures of Japan, China and Korea, a corridor for the passage of Yayoi culture into Northern Kyushu. It was along the coast of the Genkai Sea that agriculture began in late Jomon. At the beginning of Yayoi, the area was the site of the height of Yayoi culture. A small clan country developed there. Around there, Yoshitake Takagi ruins dating from 1 B.C. can be found and the things excavated from the site vividly portray for us society in those days.

[visual of sword, mirror and "magatama"]

Voiceover: Chinese-style bronze swords produced in Korea were imported. These are really sharp and can be used for actual warfare. Regarding this Korean mirror, Jomon people must have been very surprised when they first laid eyes on an instrument such as this one. As for the magatama or curved jewel, this was handed down from Jomon to Yayoi. The sword, mirror and jewel were the three symbols of authority of the clan chief and provide insight into the nature of the chief's power.

[sea background]

Professor Jiro Sugiyama, Nagaoka Technical and Science University (Commentator): The government of the Late Han in China controlled large areas through the use of iron and weaponry. Korea, which was colonized by Han China, became an important source of iron for Yayoi Japan to be used for weapons and farming equipment, such as the iron axe.

[visual of abundance of rice harvest]

Voiceover: In fact, iron was the moving force in the development of Yayoi culture and agriculture.

[visual of modern-day restaging of the bronze-making process]

Voiceover: While iron was starting to be imported, bronze was beginning to be produced domestically. A bronze halberd was made using this stone mold. Soon, bronze instruments became large in size and ceremonial in nature. So even with the arrival of iron, bronze continued to be used as common ceremonial artifacts in Northern Kyushu.

[visual of "dōtaku" or bronze bell]

Voiceover: The hypothesis that dotaku were never used in Kyushu collapsed when a mode for producing the bell was found there. Initially a musical instrument, dōtaku became a ceremonial artifact. The designs on this dōtaku are representative of animals found in rice fields. Therefore, we can see a relationship of the dōtaku with cultivation.

[visual of Yoshinogari]

Voiceover: The Yoshinogari burial mound dates to the first century B.C. and is the biggest in Japan. Kings have been sleeping here for two thousand years.

[visual of artifacts from Yoshinogari burial mound site]

Voiceover: Considering the international character of the artifacts found in Yoshinogari, we have a ceremonial sword made from one mold which may have come from Korea and we have glass beads made from Western material, which was formed by utilizing Chinese techniques and produced in Korea. The beads tell us that Japan had a route to the West even before the advent of Christ. Since glass was more precious than ordinary jewelry and very expensive, it was impossible for the common people to be the possessors of glass objects.

[visual of iron weapons]

Voiceover: By the first century A.D., Japan was drifting into turmoil and by the second century, war was endemic. Iron killing weaponry multiplied and iron made and broke kingdoms. In this atmosphere, fortress countries or "kuni" surrounded by fences appeared.

[visual of reconstructed Yoshinogari]

Voiceover: Here we have the Yoshinogari kangō shūraku dating from the beginning of the second century A.D. During the turmoil, perhaps, Yoshinogari's relations with other countries became quite tense. With this development at Yoshinogari, for the first time, we can step outside of the pages of the Gishiwajinden and gain a visual understanding of the description of the kangō shūraku mentioned in the *Wei Chronicle*. Yoshinogari possesses the attributes imparted by the chroniclers to their account of a Yayoi country.

[visual of Yoshinogari watchtower sector or a beach background]

Voiceover: In the third century, when leagues of clans were engaged in warfare, Yamatai country under the rule of Himiko appeared. By this time, already, Han China had fallen into ruin and chaos had spread throughout East Asia. In Korea, the power vacuum spurred wars of independence. In this environment, Himiko sent a mission to the Wei Kingdom, one of the three kingdoms which had succeeded the Han, and received a gold seal and mirrors in recognition of Yamatai's right to rule. By late Yayoi, the Wei mirrors had replaced bronze weaponry and the bell as symbols of a clan chieftain's authority to rule.

[visual notation: During this part of the narration, the camera focuses on the Yoshinogari watchtower and fence and the picture shakes back and forth and up and down as if the camera is riding on horseback. The sounds of horses' hoofs can be heard. Suddenly arrows fly and pierce the wooden fence under the watchtower. These are followed by flaming arrows. Then, with waves hitting the beach, horses, in their lower extremities, are captured racing forward with the incoming tide. In this way, the rise of Yamatai is visually associated with discontinuity, an invasion of horseriders from East Asia, but the evolutionary continuity inherent in the narration is never broken.]

[visual of key-shaped burial tombs]

Voiceover: After Himiko's death, a new power era was initiated which resulted in the unification of all of Japan. The Kofun period (of Japanese history) witnessed the building of huge key-shaped grave mounds by powerful chiefs. The wealth and knowhow which precipitated the foundations which gave rise to these large tombs were cultivated in the Yayoi period. Such antecedents led to the birth of a unified political state.

[visual of sunrise over Yoshinogari]

Voiceover: In the Yayoi period, the flow of iron and rice spread swiftly to embrace Japan and awaken it from a long sleep. The culture flowers opened just like the Yayoi of March. (An old meaning for Yayoi in Japanese is March.)

The latter part of 1990 presented the media with a renewed mythohistorical opportunity to dramatize the Yoshinogari story. The academic raw material for renewal was there: a chronological reconsideration of the development of Yoshinogari, a broader understanding of Yoshinogari as a bronze-making center and the discovery of a second burial mound. Evidence could be embroidered or transformed within a structure of discontinuity, if not within a double-double image scenario. But the original flame of popular interest had grown weaker and the new findings didn't have the power to rekindle the fire of the initial excavation announcements. There was to be no escape for Yoshinogari from the romanumentalization process by which Yoshinogari would sink further into the quicksand of imagery, becoming more and more a marketing symbol for the myth. As noted, the *Asahi Shimbun* "preservation" campaign did detour somewhat and return to historical Yoshinogari and TV Tokyo did do an aboutface. Nevertheless, the December article included the theme of preservation of the national heritage and the TV Tokyo broadcast was just a little less than a half-an-hour early evening, school-age rather than mass-audience program. The *Asahi Shimbun* never reworked the "Rome and Carthage" legend by itself alone, nor for that matter did its weekly news magazine, *AERA*, which removed Yoshinogari from its feature news coverage in 1990. Previously, *AERA* ran two major articles featuring Yoshinogari in the November and December issues of 1989, but they were in the romanumental, preservation vogue.[22] Moreover, these new findings on Yoshinogari didn't spawn any three-day, prime-time special broadcasts or extended TV news features.

In fact, to find after 9 PM TV programming on Yoshinogari in 1990 in the Tokyo metropolitan area, one had to turn to local broadcasting and UHF. And the one channel, a Yokohama station, which ran such a program spotlighted preservation rather than historical progression. The 30-minute program appeared on a Saturday night in mid-November at 10:30 PM on the series "Compass U." Its listing in the TV guide was revealingly in terms of what has been already related on the changing media perspective on Yoshinogari, the title of the show being "Using the Ancient Romance ("roman") to Fulfill an Area Dream." And its featured guest was none other than the Poirot of the Ancient Japanese texts, Biten Yasumoto. Yasumoto was introduced on the program as the expert who held that Yamatai country was in the vicinity of Yoshinogari and that Himiko was Amaterasu. And the viewer watched Yasumoto explain that the Emperor Jimmu arrived too late, 280 to 290 A.D. in his interpretation, on the *Nihon Shoki/Kojiki* scene to be associated with Yamatai and that Amaterasu's period coincided with Himiko's. On the location of Yamatai country, Yasumoto related that in the Amaterasu-Himiko period, there was a Yasu-no-kawa, a heavenly river. He noted that such a river could be found today in the Yoshinogari area and that there were many place names in the vicinity which corresponded to those mentioned in the ancient texts. The director of the program visually underlined Yasumoto's points by positioning the young female announcer in front of the Yasukawa and by showing a map with the similar sounding place names encircled. According to the announcer, the place names conformed to the texts not only in terms of sound but also in terms of relative location. Later on in the program, Yasumoto admitted that there were similar place names in the Kansai as well, but he assured the viewers that people when they went from Kyushu to Kansai took the old names with them.

Nevertheless, the theme of the broadcast was the development of historical sites for culture and profit. Focus was on the efforts of the Yoshinogari preservation committee and commercial ventures surrounding Yoshinogari. A souvenir vendor at the Yoshinogari pavilion was interviewed and her comment that everyday, 126 big tourist/school excursion buses arrived at the site was edited into the story. Other areas with ancient ruins in Kyushu were reported upon in terms of those communities' preservation-commercialization activities. When the camera returned to Yasumoto, he was heard to say that it is a very good thing to have a Himiko beauty contest and a Himiko festival in the Yoshinogari area. He also thought that signs and pictures should be placed around excavations in general to inform the public of the value of these sites. Regarding Yoshinogari in particular, he applauded the local chamber of commerce's plan to build a Disneyland-style Himikoland nearby. In his estimation, such undertakings "mean that Japanese will come to excavations and think about what they were like in the past."

As Yoshinogari passed from 1990 media accounts to new opportunities for coverage in 1991, there was no fanfare in the *Asahi Shimbun*, no special New Year's section. However, *Shūkan Asahi*, the newspaper's weekly news commentary and analysis and special features' magazine, ran a four-part series (later expanded into a longer and varied series) which begot the pull of ancient times during the New Year's holidays and which featured Yoshinogari in a cameo role. The first issue was on the stands in late December and the articles continued into February. Gulf Crisis coverage preempted other stories in the magazine and resulted in the series' nonsequential appearance. The magazine's cover, which earlier had been bedecked with women of aristocratic bearing dressed in various national costumes pictured against Chinese, Italian, etc., textured designs of high art, was suddenly called to war. A girl's face was hidden behind a gas mask. Bush and Hussein were superimposed against a black, foreboding background. Somehow, this abrupt change in the tempo of the magazine seemed appropriate for the unfolding of a very different tale of conflict. The movement from relative calm to Desert Shield/Storm, with great repercussions for the natural environment and human life, echoed the coming of the toraijin hundreds of years ago in Japan as described in the nonGulf pages of the magazine. Of the four articles in the series, the second and third bore directly upon the Yayoi period and the third referred specifically to Yayoi and included a picture of Yoshinogari.

It was under this series' heading of "Japanese Roots Through the Use of High Tech" that the imaging of Yoshinogari entered the final stage of complete metamorphosis. The romanumental application had revealed the power of Yoshinogari to evoke a set of mythical images which could be linked to an issue divorced from mythohistory. In this respect, Yoshinogari achieved a standing in the media and in the myth as an issue-external activating symbol "to break the barrier of an individual's indifference," in Ellulian terminology.[23]   Therefore, it was not without ageing that Yoshinogari achieved robustness and came to be employed by the media and the myth as an issue-internal activating symbol. Such an integrative imaging conditioner could be called up in the telling of the tale in such a way as to interact with diverse archaeological discoveries and social and natural scientific inputs to modernize the telling of the origins of the Japanese and make the average man caught up in the "Future Wave" more secure in his primal identity.

One issue which mythohistory has persistently addressed to maintain the viability of its paradigm is what caused so many toraijin to swoop down upon Japan. Could one blame it on the weather? Perhaps, one could. At least, the second article wanted the reader to consider this high-tech possibility in view of the lack of any overriding alternative. The article said to the reader: "Consider these past forecasts and their effects based upon the findings of a host of Japanese experts." And the reader learned ...

During the late Jomon period, the forecast was for much colder weather and Jomon sites decreased throughout Japan. Decreasing sun spot activity anticipated a cold spell, which resulted in diminishing food supply for the inhabitants of the islands. Nuts couldn't grow well. Icy water conditions affected the collection of shell fish since too much soil was being deposited along the shore. While people were dying in the Jomon population centers of eastern Japan, reducing the total number to a fraction of what it was 2,000 years earlier, Yayoi people came to the warmer, low lying damper areas of western Japan and brought with them wet rice cultivation. Some 2,800 years ago, in the Yoshinogari area, people were growing rice as well as red beans, russet, gourds, melon and millet. Population and Yayoi culture concentrated in western Japan at first and then dispersed outward. Jomon people were probably dumbfounded by the activities of the Yayoi people, unable to understand how they could live in such a low, dampy mosquito infested place.[24]

Apparently, (the reader must have wondered if Japanese immigration officials kept such good statistics in those days) about one million toraijin, about 1,000 people per year, came to live in Japan. (Hanihara's hypothesis, once again!) From 300 B.C. to 700 A.D., the population increased by some 5 million people over that of late Jomon. Confirmation of this population movement existed in the Chinese record in the context of Jofuku's imperial journey in search of immortality. Population in China at the time of Jofuku (Jofuku certainly did live a long life – from 300 B.C. to 700 A.D.) centered around the Yellow River or the mouth of the river and there was constant pressure upon these centers from outside populations. Consequently, whenever there was war or famine, a lot of people took to boats and it was these people who came to Japan attracted by the excellent conditions for rice cultivation.[25]

The second forecast related to all of East Asia, including Japan, and pertained to a severe change in climatic conditions for the 2nd and 3rd centuries A.D. In the wake of this small ice age, with its much colder summers, drought spread throughout East Asia with dire consequences: famine, disease, peasant revolts and large migrations. Populations battled for the possession of crops which were in short supply. And it was in this period of turmoil in China, Korea and Japan that Himiko sought to establish the authority of Yamatai country and bring an end to the anarchy which had enveloped her land.[26]

This article in the series focused on climate – not Yoshinogari – to picture Japanese roots in the Yayoi period. However, the invasion and domination aspect of the mythical paradigm was evident in transforming the evidence of the adverse effect of climate on Jomon populations into a scenario for a large invasion of the warmer, low-lying areas of Kyushu by boat people. Nevertheless, the problem remained that the postulated time of the invasion was too early for a Gishiwajinden sequential interpolation. Moreover, there was the matter, with regard to the transformation of evidence, that the big chill was being used not merely to explain the outset of turmoil, but also its end. Since climate is evidence which is quite general and all pervasive, not necessarily localized location or event specific, it lacks the inherent persuasiveness of Yamatai associated images, e.g., Yoshinogari artifacts, to bolster the plausibility of a U-turn in consequences. If climate is the cause of both disunity and unity, then, climate is not a cause at all but merely the general environment in which various causes operate to bring about results. In logic, such a postulation would be considered as a distinct fallacy of composition in which a part of the whole is held to be the cause of all circumstances merely because of its distinctive presence. In all, climate provides weak support for a blatant mythohistorical movement as the one noted.

A follow-up article on general weather conditions was therefore required to reinforce climate factor believability as well as bridge the time warp. It was in this third article in the series that Yoshinogari's strong image was invoked to carry the author's arguments. Although the written reference to Yoshinogari was quite terse, both of the concrete visuals (photos) were of Yoshinogari and one of these visuals was inserted partially into an illustration of Himiko's palace, which extended across the front two pages of the article. This photographic visual had a model dressed up as Himiko in the foreground and in the background there was a Japan Railway's poster of the Yoshinogari excavation headlined "Dream of a Legend, Saga." The photo caption read: "Was there a Queen Like Himiko Even in Yoshinogari Ruins?" Within the article's inner pages, a second photograph offered an overview of the area in the vicinity of the Yoshinogari watchtower. The content of the article was definitely being overexposed to a strong dose of the evocative image of the Yoshinogari myth to support its scientific theme and interpolate the Gishiwajinden.[27]

In terms of written content, the beginning of the third article was all weather and a little Yoshinogari. The writer focused on the findings from the study of Kochi field in Osaka where it was discovered why in late Yayoi many large shūraku disappeared or became smaller in size. In so doing, the writer returned to the theme of conflict and turmoil brought about by climatic change, the nature of the field itself revealing the impact of adverse weather conditions which severely affected farming in the area. But herein a jump had to be made to an assertion that climate and the deteriorating conditions in the land – the cold period lasting to the Kofun period – triggered a movement toward unification, toward the concentration of wealth and power. Confronted with a precarious leap, the writer grasped for symbolic trigger support, i.e., Yoshinogari, the reader's attention being drawn to that huge kangō shūraku, that gigantic burial mound and those war-scarred corpses. Textually activated, the image of Yoshinogari was utilized by the writer to provide the overture for the entrance of Queen Himiko, the stage for which had already been set through the article's visuals. The article didn't dwell on Yoshinogari, but merely mentioned it matter of factly. Having meshed climate with unity through imagery, the writer turned to the question of why a female was chosen as the ruler of Yamatai, a topic which was to be treated in such a way as to be in line with the high-tech aspirations of the series. And although it's difficult to understand the logic behind it all, the pursuit of the answer to the question led to a date for the coming of the toraijin which paralleled the formulated image of climate, Himiko and Yoshinogari.[28]

Herein, the article rattled off a host of animal studies in combination with *Kojiki* interpretations and archaeological evidence to explain that sexual charm was the reason for selecting a female. The animal behavioral studies which were selected related to the sexual habits of monkeys, i.e., the showing of the female sex skin or the performance of an act of seduction by the female in the midst of turmoil to calm the aggressive behavior of male combatants. The writer wondered whether even in ancient Japan this kind of animal behavior could be applied and noted that there were certain examples in the *Kojiki* to give food for thought, referring to a striptease dance by a goddess to entice Amaterasu out of a cave and let the light shine through and to the baring of breasts by the same goddess to a male god to gain safety of passage from heaven to earth of the August Grandchild. In addition, according to the writer, artistic representations, such as the dogū figurine with its big bust and clearly drawn sexual organ, indicated that people believed that the female symbol had some power to drive malaise away.[29]

However, what was most interesting at this point in the article as it flowed from monkeys to dogū, to Himiko, was that the toraijin imagery associated with Yoshinogari appeared to slip into the story, although the coming of the toraijin had been emphasized in the previous article as preceding the onset of the turmoil. It was almost as if the writer himself could not escape the impact of the visual concept of his article. Relying in part on the interpretation of the Gishiwajinden by a foremost scholar of Japanese ethnology, Taryo Obayashi, of Tokyo Women's University, the writer reported on Himiko's sacred female role (as a symbol of sacred sexuality) in the consolidation of Yamatai power and how political prerogatives came to rest in the hands of a brother-king. In Obayashi's estimation, Himiko's reclusive behavior, her failure to show herself in public, was intended to heighten her sacred character. According to this scholar, Yamatai was a sacred royal country enmeshed in agricultural-related ceremonies, with the performer of royal power rites being Himiko, the political actor being a brother-king. And the writer related Obayashi's understanding that the sacred tradition of "ōken" (royal power) as manifested in the "inasaku" (rice harvest) ceremony could still be seen today in the daijo-sai, a rite performed on the enthronement of a new emperor. Building on Obayashi's comments, the writer pushed forward in formulating the conclusion to the article by setting forth the opinions of two other scholars on the meaning of ōken in the Gishiwajinden to the effect that the sacredness of Himiko reflected old-style Japanese spiritual power and this symbolism was combined with political methods derived from knowledge brought from China by a new ruling or powerful class of people. In other words, the article ended with Yamatai, if not an enclave of Yoshinogari horseriders, at least, as a country under foreign control, thereby synchronizing the invasion with the Yoshinogari activated images.[30]

In the *Shūkan Asahi* articles, the metamorphosis of Yoshinogari into a mythical paradigmatic image was evident in the manner in which Yoshinogari was positioned in the story. Yoshinogari functioned to evoke images for circumventing a fallacy in the logical flow of the contents (unity-disunity), for associating a structural element of the paradigm (consolidation-unification in the person of Himiko) with archaeological discovery and for bringing a paradigmatic sequence (invasion) into sync with the occurrence of other paradigmatic events. More generally, Yoshinogari glued mythical formations to scientific information to enable the presentation of a highly modernized version of the tale of Japanese origins.

In the month following the *Shūkan Asahi* series, evidence of Yoshinogari performing the evocative role of an internal image could be garnered from television as well. The program, a special, approximately ninety-minute, national holiday broadcast on TV Tokyo, focused on ancient Kibi (Okayama-Hiroshima area). However, a prelude journey to Yoshinogari was undertaken to evoke an image of the development of great power centers in Japan beginning in the late Yayoi period, the narrator explaining that the Yoshinogari excavation had refueled a debate on the character of Yamatai country which had been dormant for many years.

A map of Japan followed a tour-like visit to the reconstructed kangō shurakū. A video photo of the main Yoshinogari watchtower was superimposed on northern Kyushu while a still of Japan's largest key-shaped tomb in Osaka was placed upon Yamato in Kinki. Thereafter, a visual of Kibi zoomed out between the two, the voiceover relating that emerging from between these two great centers of power during the late Yayoi-early Kofun period was a third great force. To support the idea that Kibi in the early 5th century was exceedingly powerful, perhaps even stronger than Kinki, the program noted that 150 key-shaped tombs had been discovered in the area and that 365-meter-long Tsukuriyama Tomb was not only Japan's fourth largest, but the largest of its time, dating to the beginning of the 5th century. To gain the viewer's attention on how powerful was powerful, various grand key-shaped tombs were shown; information on how it took some 1,500,000 people to build Tsukuriyama Tomb was passed along; and an interpretation was given of how a huge key-shaped tomb was not just a burial ground but represented, through its construction and the performance of the funeral ceremony which followed, the handing down of royal power from one generation to another. What was quite revealing in the imaging of Yoshinogari in the early scenes vis-à-vis Kibi was that a village was equated with the power represented by a key-shaped tomb which required the efforts of so many to complete. Yoshinogari never contained very much more than one-thousand people and one of its gigantic mounds, if it had been shown in the program, would have been no more than a mole on the face of Tsukuriyama, although both Yoshinogari mounds compared well with late Yayoi mounds.

The program never returned to Yoshinogari or for that matter Kyushu after the initial segment until a sequence of a few seconds at the very end of the documentary. Instead, the program staged a consolidation-unification scenario within the precincts of the main island, the invasion-conflict paradigm apparently being left to whatever connotations the audience wished to draw from the image radiating out of the Yoshinogari-watchtower snapshot. As such, the relationship of Kibi power to the origin of the Japanese state was considered within a Kinki framework and the development of the character of the key-shaped mound in the Kibi area was argued as confirming Kibi as an independent and competitive power center until the end of the Kofun period. The voiceover related that 3rd century Tatetsuki Tomb in Okayama which was excavated 15 years ago represented in terms of its shape – a circular mound with projections jutting out from the northeastern and southwestern sides – the source for the independent evolution of the key-shaped tomb in Kibi. The narration, overlooking the possibility that Yamato in dispensing its royal prerogatives had granted Kibi the right to construct Yamato-style burials, concluded that just as Kibi traveled its own route on the road to the key-shaped tomb, it also went its own way, apart from Yamato, in building up its power and culture.[31]

The final segment of the program focused on how Kibi's strength and prosperity was substantially based on its great iron-producing capabilities, the program relating that recent archaeological discoveries reveal Kibi as possessing the oldest iron furnace/iron works (Kubokiyakushi ruins, 5th century) in Japan as well as a very old iron-smith village for shaping the iron into weapons and agricultural tools. Katsuhito Katsuhara, of the Ancient Kibi Culture Center, explained that iron weapons and tools were very important in raising Kibi's strength and productivity. Without iron to secure materials from the hard mountain earth, the viewers learned that Tsukuriyama Tomb could never have been built to its present scale. Then, suddenly, edited in between iron-making ruins and key-shaped tombs, for just a few seconds, the watchtower was resurrected, with an actor walking below in ancient dress and the camera focusing on his sword – i.e., an image of power through iron, a borrowing from one past to create another. The voiceover responded: "It's quite ironical that Kibi which became prosperous because of iron-making was, we can say, ruined by iron." By "ruined by iron," the narration was referring to Yamato's subjugation of Kibi. Katsuhara had earlier put forward the supposition based on a reading of the *Nihon Shoki* that Yamato coveted the iron-producing strengths of Kibi.

From 1989-1991, Yoshinogari was processed by mythohistory to the point where it was completely metamorphosed into an image integrated within the mythohistorical structure itself. The prospect of motion reversal of the process, of Yoshinogari slipping back into the garb of 1989-style resurrection within a significant timeframe, appears highly unlikely unless a glamorous discovery from the media vantage point, such as Himiko mirrors or a gold seal, can be recovered from the site. Also, it should be kept in mind that Yoshinogari is but one image of a host of images available to the media to activate mythohistorical associations. Perhaps, with time or the heralding of a new resurrection, for instance, at 3rd century Makimuku Ishizuka Tomb in Nara, which the TV Tokyo program cited as the root of the key-shaped tomb in Yamato, Yoshinogari's star will dim, its appearance in the media diminishing in frequency.

Toward the end of the TV Tokyo broadcast, a poem from antiquity was read. The "roaring of an iron flame" in the verse was explained as an aside to Kibi as Iron Country. In Japanese poetry, such usage is called "makura kotaba" or pillow words. In Japanese society, "who we are" is primarily explained in nihonjinron terms, but implanted in nihonjinron is a racial perspective or a set of pillow images reflected in the interaction of the modernizing mythical paradigm of racial origins and the media. Consequently, the lesson of Yoshinogari is twofold. One is the manifold power of the mythical format in Japanese society. Two is the emphatic presence of prejudicial racial values in mass culture. Dower, in his study of racial imagery associated with World War II relates the existence of a certain legacy of residual racialism in the post-war period in the representation of Japanese businessmen as being different from all other races in the same profit-making endeavors. He asserts that it is not only nonJapanese who dwell on "myths of extraordinary singularity" but many Japanese as well "attribute their massive accomplishments to the unique and ineffable spirit of the Yamato race."[32] In this regard, it should be noted that Egami was not just looking backward in time. In an NTV special sponsored by Matsushita Electric (National/Panasonic) in 1985, which was emphatic in associating Japanese racial origins with modern-day characteristics, Egami appeared to set forth his ideas that Japanese who take to business and politics have inherited the characteristic of kiba minzoku, i.e., being self-assertive, aggressive and dominant.

CHAPTER IV

SCIENTIFIC IMMUNITY

Whereas the media's idol of Japanese mythical origins in the late '80s and early '90s was archaeologically based, the mid-'80s, lacking such an antique jewel as Yoshinogari witnessed the rise of a scientific star within the mythical format. At first glance at the particulars of this contestant, one wouldn't think that such an esoteric product would be able to contribute more than an informative article in a series on racial origins. One would perhaps be taken aback to find that a highly technical and erudite thesis could drive the myth and provide symbolic imagery for audio-visual consumption. But such was the case with regard to the TV debut of a blood-group system, the genetic markers of human immunoglobulins. In considering the early history and development of the system, one would find nothing to intimate its future on television in spite of its relevance for mythical digestion.

The primary function of man's immune system is the production of protein molecules, immunoglobulins or antibodies, which are found in the blood and which serve as the main line of defense against invading foreign proteins or bacteria. These molecular ninjas within our bodies swoop down upon our enemies, which are called antigens because they precipitate the antibody response. The antibodies neutralize the antigens by binding to them. There are five major classes of immunoglobulins, each with its distinct structure and functions. For instance, the IgG class of antibodies, are highly fine-tuned molecules which allow for precision rather than clustered assaults on the antigen's multiple binding sites. An immunoglobulin molecule consists of two identical heavy (H) or large-size chains and two identical light (L) chains, each attached to one another and each ending in a variable offensive team of about 110 amino acids, the building links of protein strands. In all other respects, the H or L chains for a given type of antibody are made up of nonvariables or constant regions. It's the variety in the amino acid sequences within the variable region of the body's antibodies that allows for the rapid mobilization of special teams specially tailored to blanket targeted invaders when the antigen alarm is sounded.[1]

Nevertheless, for the purpose of zeroing in on racial origins, it's the constant regions, specifically those of the H chain of the IgG class, which are of interest to population geneticists. Structural differences within this theatre result in distinct antigenic determinants which can be identified serologically. These differences form a series of genetic markers or Gm markers mirroring genetically controlled polymorphisms. One of the pioneering names in the field of Gm studies is that of Matsumoto, of Osaka Medical College.[2] Matsumoto's interest in Gm dates back at least to the early 1960s when, in his mid-30s, he traveled to the United States to horn his skills in legal medicine. Matsumoto's initial research was not concerned with race per se, but with a kind of genetic fingerprinting to determine the legal father of a child. In the U.S., he undertook Gm-related research at Western Reserve University with Arthur G. Steinberg. He subsequently discovered that Gm was superior to other blood group systems in determining parenthood. Moreover, on returning to Japan, he became caught up in research into Japanese origins as he hit upon what he considered to be Gm's high potential for differentiating racial groupings.[3]

Gm population studies are actually phenotype-based since the researcher is looking at the molecular structure of immunoglobulin rather than at the genes which produce the antibodies. However, since such structural differences are inherited, they are designated as allotypes or genetic markers, each marker being associated with an H-chain domain. These markers are the result of genetic mutation, meaning the substitution of a single amino acid within a sequence. Allotypes, such as Gm (a), (x), (s), etc., as they are so labeled, appear in immunoglobulin in fixed combinations designated as Gm haplotypes. Those Gm haplotypes common to Mongoloid populations are Gm ag, axg, ab3st, and afb1b3; Caucasoids, Gm ag, axg, and fb1b3; and Negroids, Gm ab1b3, ab1c, ab3s. As such, Mongoloids show Gm ab3st and afb1b3 haplotypes and Caucasoids Gm fb1b3. Negroids reveal nothing in common with Caucasoids or Mongoloids.[4]

Matsumoto's research contributed significantly to these findings. And thus he was able by the 1980s to exclaim that the Gm system provided markers unparalleled in studies of human genetics, particularly in identifying a major racial grouping or a local variation.[5] Matsumoto's enthusiasm was shared by his fellow researcher, Steinberg, at least with regard to major races. Steinberg heralded Gm as the system of blood group systems in characterizing major divisions. In a co-authored work, he wrote:

> The difference among the human races for all polymorphic systems other than the Gm system are *quantitative*; i.e., with rare exceptions, the antigens are polymorphic in all races. As will be shown later, the difference among races in the Gm system are *qualitative*; i.e., some haplotypes are absent from or confined to certain races.[6]

Nevertheless, Matsumoto's primary focus or cause for enthusiasm was on the pertinence of Gm for distinguishing ethnic variation caused by the flow of genetic material between breeding populations or the drift of genetic material out of a small population through the measurement of variance in Gm haplotype frequencies.[7] In his 1987 scholarly article on Mongoloid populations, Matsumoto underlined the value of Gm frequency analyses by referring to data from Haifa University on Jewish populations. The Haifa data included the frequencies of eight Gm haplotypes. On the basis of the frequencies, Matsumoto noted that Jewish populations could best be described "as basically Caucasoid with slight Mongoloid admixture but with considerable similarity to Negroids."[8]

Regarding his own investigations, since 1962, Matsumoto had been collecting data from a series of serum samples from Mongoloid, Southeast Asian, East Asian and North and South American populations. In his book in 1985 and in the article, he wrote that his findings were based on over 20 years of study.[9] His research team had discovered in 1966 the Gm ab3st haplotype characteristic of Mongoloid populations. According to Matsumoto, in terms of frequency distribution, the four Mongoloid haplotypes could be divided into northern and southern groups since the northern group showed a high frequency of Gm ab3st while the southern group was characterized by a high frequency of Gm afb1b3. The dispersal center for this northern haplotype was located among the Buryat people of Lake Baikal while southwestern China was designated as the frequency capital of the southern haplotype. A precipitous drop was noted for the northern factor along a line descending from mainland China to Taiwan and Southeast Asia and from North to South America.[10] However, the data revealed this haplotype to be very much evident in Korean, Japanese, Ainu and Eskimo populations. Matsumoto's overall conclusion was:

> The Japanese race belongs to northern Mongoloids and that the origin of the Japanese race was in Siberia, and most likely in the Baikal area of the Soviet Union.[11]

And it's right here, by locating the cradle in Lake Baikal, that Matsumoto's trek bridged the morass of specialized terminology and designations and entered into a visual associative universe. The old cliché that a picture can say a thousand words appears to be quite appropriate in this case, although it's more fitting to think of the picture in question as replacing those words. Allotypes and haplotypes are difficult words to swallow for most people and serum analysis is not a subject which can spark one's imagination, except for those specialists who possess certain vested interests in the outcomes. For the mass audience, the response to a complete dosage of Gm findings on TV would activate a host of boredom antibodies, resulting in agglutination, if it wasn't for the evocative power of the image of the Buryat people, i.e., nomadic horseriders, the descendants of the hordes who swept across Euro-Asia in the past in search of empire.

The TV special in 1985 which introduced the viewing audience to Hideo Matsumoto and blood genetics played heavily upon the horserider implication of Buryat Gm frequency, offering up another dramatic portrayal of the propagation of mythical symbolization. Such a presentation was indeed a mythical production since Matsumoto's theory of racial origins was a molecular biological treatise which said nothing about the culture of the Gm forefathers. Matsumoto's conclusion was that the source was northern Mongoloid, not horseriding Mongols. On race and culture, Matsumoto maintained the scientist's stance:

> Changes in the human race and its cultures do not necessarily go hand in hand.... The best comparison would be in terms of language, where phraseology is the core, vocabulary being selectively absorbed later on with cultural spread as human races interact.[12]

As a matter of fact, Matsumoto would have been at a loss to argue anything else since nomadism developed on the steppe from 1,200 to 500 B.C. as a result of increased aridity of the land and the decline of farming civilization.[13] The appearance of horseriding culture, therefore, is much more recent than the appearance and dispersal of Gm ab3st according to Matsumoto's calculations.

In addition, TV as well as mythologization required a less technical and more "I can identify with that" approach to the Buryat-Gm-Japanese relationship to insure that the mythical accent of roots traced in blood remained within the common man's range of message reception. Such was provided in the Gm TV debut, the basis for which could very well have been derived from the pages in Matsumoto's 1985 book concerning his journey to Russia in 1983. Herein, his pedestrian impressions of the people whom he believed to be situated at the center of the Japanese cradle were set forth. Matsumoto passed two days and three nights in the Baikal region, spending the rest of his 10-day tour in Moscow, primarily in discussions with scholars at the Russian Academy of Science.[14]   To quote some of Matsumoto's verbalized wanderings about the Buryat:

On a walk through a city park in the Baikal.... "In this central park, people who look like Japanese, Buryat, were strolling with innocent and happy looks upon their faces. There was such a resemblance to Japanese and I thought if I spoke to them in Japanese, we could communicate with each other. Their hair was black, eyes narrow and faces round."[15]

Upon addressing a meeting.... "At the beginning of my speech when I said 'what do you think I am, Japanese or Buryat?', everyone present burst into laughter." When I looked upon the faces of the researchers seated in the chairs, the atmosphere was such that I felt I was speaking in Japan and the words from my mouth came naturally and I got the impression that I could communicate in Japanese."[16]

While visiting a folk museum.... "I never expected that I would see things like these in such a place. This farm equipment really resembles those I saw in Japan when I was a child. It was astonishing to me when I realized that this equipment was used at such a distance and in olden times."[17]

Also at the museum.... "I was really surprised when my eyes fell on two very old storehouses which they said were brought from the Baikal. These buildings which had been made without a nail were exactly the same as 'azekura' in Nara."[18]

The television program which feasted on the Buryat image in terms of rootstock as well as physical resemblance was broadcast on NTV on November 4, 1985 in a prime-time slot. The sponsor, National/Matsushita Electric, was also engaged in 1985 in associating the implications of Japanese roots with its corporate identity through a display at the company's pavilion at Tsukuba Exposition in Tsukuba Science City outside of Tokyo. This science and technology exposition ran for 184 days, from May 17 to September 16, attracting a wide range of international and Japanese exhibitors and over 20 million visitors. According to Dentsu, Japan's leading advertising agency, it was the largest event in the history of international expositions.[19]   Aside from its emphasis on being Japanese down to the root with a display on the origins of the Japanese, National's pavilion featured the world's largest liquid crystal superscreen. Also popular was a portrait-drawing robot. If one missed the concept from the inside, there was always the stylized, ancient-burial-mound form of the pavilion itself to enlighten one that what the person was about to experience was an encounter between the distant past and the supermodern.[20]

National origins, the TV program, however, carried a very strong sense of the unique characteristics of Matshushita and the Japanese salaryman as being fated in blood. And the opening sequences of the show were a 1, 2, 3 composite consisting of first, the intent faces of Japan's business elite along a downtown street, secondly, a display map of Asia from Tsukuba Expo, with the camera focusing on an arrow designating men with horses riding through Korea to Japan, and finally, a multi-screen ensemble with the written characters appearing letter by letter on each screen and then gradually being replaced by horses. The characters read: "Where are you from? From a country which has horses!" The narrator related: "Where the Japanese came from is a puzzle, but now there is a very attractive theme." Suddenly, the viewer was in the midst of a group of brightly dressed Mongols on horseback galloping across the "endless" steppe right into the program's titles: "Ancient history special." "Did or didn't horseriding people come to Japan?" "Japanese Roots!" Within these initial frames, a small, unpresumptuous looking individual gowned in a white laboratory outfit and seated behind a desk was introduced and the diagnosis was pronounced. The man was Hideo Matsumoto and his conclusion was as already stated.

The program then took the viewer to Matsumoto's laboratory where serum was undergoing tests and a colorful chart was presented indicating the Gm frequencies throughout Asia. But this somewhat technical aspect of the Gm theme was given only a matter of minutes to engage the audience before transport for Matsumoto and his theoretical implications appeared and, by rail and sea, the viewers were taken for a ride along the banks of Russia's "Pearl of Siberia," Lake Baikal, on route to the city of Ulan Ude.

As the broadcast weaved through the streets of this Baikal city and the neighboring metropolis of Irkutsh, the history and culture of the Buryat were unfurled. The Russianization of the region was related. The Buryat people, numbering about one million, according to the narration, had become a minority in their own land, with the 300,000 or more Buryat in Ulan Ude representing only 30% of the city and Irkutsh being known as the Paris of Siberia. As if prompted by Matsumoto himself, the camera's eye toured these cities in search of Japanese-looking faces, especially those of the cuter sex. The narrator indicated that such sightseeing represented a search for people with the Japanese Gm gene in their blood. If the viewer had some difficulty in differentiating a Japanese-looking from a Mongolian or Korean-looking face along the avenues, the camera's eye also pursued Japanese-looking faces within an elementary school, finally capturing a girl, which the narrator explained resembled strikingly the character of a highly popular Japanese TV drama (the NHK drama "Oshin") of the time.

When the program returned to Matsumoto again, he was seen visiting the Buryat branch of the Russian Academy of Science and speaking with a Russian scholar who expressed great interest in Matsumoto's findings. However, it was after this particular sequence, when Matsumoto was walking along the lake, about to provide his thoughts on how such a grand landscape seemed to be so suitable for being a gene center, that the narrator inserted Matsumoto's non-horseriding, 8,000 B.C. date for the coming of the Japanese-looking faces to the Japanese islands.

Although a discordant note, the visual strength of the theme was sufficiently strong to permit the director and the viewing audience (I have replayed the program every year for six years in my class and none of my several hundred students have ever noticed the incongruity) to turn a deaf ear to Matsumoto's indicated time of arrival. Three or four authenticating words proved powerless against iconographic persuasion. As a matter of fact, in the following segment of the "Ancient History Special," the director marched the time of invasion into the Yayoi period in line with the mythical supposition.

Herein, the guests were Yoshiatsu Naito, of Nagasaki University, and Hanihara. Naito compared the bones of Jomon and Yayoi people noting the differences in height and shape. In considering the influences, environmental, etc., behind these differences, Naito emphasized that he couldn't help thinking the Yayoi remains revealed the infusion of north Asian traits which came to Japan via Korea. He added a little political humor to his comparison of Jomon and Yayoi skulls by associating one with a leading LDP member and the other with a former Japanese prime minister. This emphasis on facial rather than Gm marker identification was reinforced by Hanihara's appearance on the program and the presentation of his thoughts on the relationship between looks and living in an extremely cold environment. In this regard, he explained that in the Yayoi and Kofun periods, cold-area people, such as the Siberian-Baikal Mongoloids, with characteristic flat-faced features inundated Western Japan and moved eastward to Kinki where they founded the Japanese "öken." A Flintstone-style cartoon representation followed which contrasted the strong nose of the Jomon face with the almost nonexistent nasal relief of the Yayoi caricature. This segment ended with an above shot of a huge key-shaped tomb and the narrator relating that the people who came from the north were destined to establish Japan's first "kokka" called the Yamato Imperial Court.

Subsequently, another time slip took place although not as steep as the initial fall. The cause of the slide was the appearance of Egami on the program. With a repeat visual lead-in of present-day Mongol horseriders, the viewer was introduced to Egami through a computergraphic presentation of the progress of an invasion from northeast Asia via Korea to northern Kyushu and then to Yamato from the 4th and 5th centuries, according to Egami's horserider theory, and through an archaeological escapade from Okinoshima, an island between Korea and Kyushu, across Japan, picturing horse trappings, haniwa horses and murals of horserider motifs, including a horse on a boat, taken from various ruins and tombs. The narrator explained that according to Egami the 4th century burials offered findings associated with farming, the 5th century with horseriding people. It was also noted that both Japanese and Buryat mythology featured an august grandson descending from heaven to bring order to the world below. In all, the audience had been taken for a ride from 8,000 B.C., to the Yayoi period, to the latter part of the Kofun period. It was in this broadcast that, as indicated previously, Egami expounded on Japanese politicians and businessmen as inheritors of the socio-political attributes of their nomadic ancestors – a slant which also inadvertently or intentionally merged the sponsor's or Matsushita's corporate image as a company of elite salarymen with Japanese racial root-values. The closing segment reproduced approximately the Gm dispersal path through sequential pictures of faces in Ulan Ude (Buryat), Manchuria, Northeast China, Seoul.... Finally, the camera made the crossing to the faces of Japan's "kiba"-businessmen. According to the narration, the blood of the conquerors of the Baikal region, a really active and brave people, ran through Japanese veins.

In July of 1988, this original program was revised and updated with new information and observations. Footage from the original show was recycled. The showing formed the basis of not only another National/Matsushita Electric "Ancient History Special" but also a special broadcast to commemorate NTV's 30th anniversary. As before, the opening included the following: a scan of Japanese businessmen's faces; a trip to Baikal on the old footage to catch the faces of the Buryat in Ulan Ude and revel in the old horseriding culture; and observations on facial appearances and racial affinity. The updated keynote of this special was the sensational fiberscope investigation of the stone sarcophagus of Fujinoki Tomb, a 6th century grave site in Nara, which was receiving extensive mass media coverage at the time. Already, a number of horse-trappings had been recovered from the tomb and the narrator expressed the expectation that soon Japanese would come face-to-face with their "toraikei" ancestor. One should perhaps note here that when the lid of the sacophagus was finally removed in the fall of 1988, cultural influence from Korea rather than nomadic horseriding invaders rose from the dead.[21]

This ancient history special was entitled "The Birth of the Toraijin Islands." And therefore, not surprisingly, the first commentator was Hanihara, explaining that the toraijin created the Japanese people and Japanese culture and presenting his assumptions and data on the one-million-human tidal wave which engulfed the dwindling Jomon population in a one-thousand year period from the outset of Yayoi to the 7th century. Consequently, when the narrator followed and exhaled the question of when and where the Japanese came from, the pursuit of the "when" answer appeared to be rhetorical and such an understanding was confirmed when Matsumoto appeared as the second commentator to center the "where" in Siberia by expounding upon Gm frequencies. In this new version of the National special, there was no follow-up in the narration as to Matsumoto's 8,000 B.C. date for the arrival in the islands of Gm Japanese, the Hanihara argument being given complete immunity from dissonance in the Gm-horserider-toraijin chain of events and Gm, Lake Baikal, Buryat, toraijin and Yayoi-Kofun being meshed into a finely knit embroidery of Japanese origins.

Well, not so finely, perhaps! To elaborate on Hanihara's cold-etchings of the toraijin physique and draw a concrete line between Siberia and Japan, the program introduced recent ruins along the Okhotsk coastal area of northeastern Hokkaido, especially Tokoro ruins. As a result, the time link in the chain was broken for an interval before being reset to Hanihara time. The narrator began the breach by noting how some people were drawing upon an old stone age culture in the Northern Sea area to gain some understanding of where Japanese came from. A pot from the finds was shown and observations were rendered on the high quality of the material, the high temperature of the firing and the elegant patterns on the surface. The narrator related that Jomon and Yayoi wares didn't have such designs. In addition, he noted that in view of these patterns, one could picture Okhotsh culture as a seafaring one, the people living off the sea and its riches, catching fish and hunting seals and sea lions, for instance. The micro-blade stone tools of the Okhotsh culture were indicated as being representative of Siberian technocomplexes. The foremost authority on the

Okhotsh-Siberian paleolithic, the archaeologist Shinpei Kato, of Chiba University, was interviewed on the dispersal of Siberian technoculture. According to Kato's studies, Siberian microblade culture originated in the Lake Baikal area and then spread north to Alaska and east and south to Mongolia, Korea, North China and Hokkaido-Honshu Japan. Recent excavations have further detailed the dispersal of this culture to the Niigata area and the middle Kanto, regions previously associated with the older Siberian knife stone tool tradition.[22] However, on the program, Kato was seen talking about how the micro-blade culture originally came to Hokkaido's Okhotsh coast, referring to the strong current between Sakhalin and Hokkaido. There is always the problem of when land bridges disappear in Japanese accounts of migrations and Kato more or less went with the flow rather than with a bridge. But whatever the relationship was between Siberia, Okhotsh culture and Japanese origins, the program's story was out of sync with its Yayoi-Kofun characterization. In fact, whereas the first special deviated with regard to the statement of a date, this revised one strayed while reporting on a whole cultural complex. Still, such a long contradictory passage was not edited out by the director since what was significant was the strength of the mythical imagery in which cold Siberia was enmeshed rather than the time make-up of Okhotsk culture.

It is also interesting that the Okhotsk culture segment represented a missed opportunity to pursue a different storybook, one based on Matsumoto time and set in non-nomadic terms. In his 1985 book and in the first TV special, Matsumoto had placed the arrival of the Gm Japanese at about 8,000 B.C., calculating on the basis of a random-model molecular clock. According to Matsumoto, the genetic structural counterpart of the Gm antibody had evolved by gene duplication and point mutation from a common primordial gene, with an average rate of change calculated at 32 PAMs (accepted point mutations per 100 links of an immunoglobulin amino acid chain) in one billion years, assuming a mammalian radiation dating to 75 million years ago.[23] As such, Matsumoto's original date was a laboratory one in the Sarich, Wilson and Cann tradition. However, he felt the need to calibrate it against all aspects of the ethnological record and he did just this prior to the second broadcast. One can just about imagine what a "Wolpoff-ian" reaction would be in this instance, perhaps one to the effect that "those darn genetic clocks just don't work so well."

In view of his belief that culture followed race, Matsumoto stretched his date of 8,000 B.C. to take the origins of the Japanese race back to the end of the world's last glacial period. In line with his thinking of culture following race, he wrote:

> Recent archaeological surveys have provided considerable evidence that substantial populations have lived in Siberia, Korea and Japan since ancient times. Archeological materials collected from northern Asia suggest that a 'micro-blade culture,' which was born in the Baikal area about 30,000 years ago, gradually dispersed to the east and arrived at the northeastern part of Japan approximately 13,000 years ago. Thus it is very likely that the carriers of the micro-blade culture played an important role in the formation of the proto-Japanese islanders. The Islands of Japan are narrow in width from north to south and have two entrances, to the Asian continents, one at the northern end and one at the southern, the cultural exchanges with the continent always having been made through these two entrances.[24]

In this respect, Okhotsh culture would appear to be highly appropriate for a program with a Gm-Siberia concept, but such a production would have had to have been situated in the ice age – an era way too frigid for National and its consumers, both of which required a warmer, more human image, not one made of stone.

Aside from unveiling Gm implications within Yayoi packaging, TV also introduced a double-playing Gm. To maintain a horserider theme, a double coming was entered with the input of Matsumoto's findings: first, Gm ab3st arrived in Japan very early; Second, Gm ab3st came again after several thousand years. Such a paradigm defense was observed at first on Japanese Broadcasting's educational TV or NHK-E. NHK-E, unlike its sister station, NHK-G, mainly targets its programing for segmented populations rather than for general consumption. Daily programing consists of senior high school correspondence lectures, language conversation classes, public school coursework, nursery school classes, calligraphy instruction, etc. As such, NHK-E doesn't qualify as a "mass" media. However, in one time slot, in particular, 8 to 8:45 PM, NHK-E emerges on week nights from its high-starch cocoon in search of a greater and more diversified audience within a commercially-oriented market. Consequently, NHK-E becomes less instructional and more intent on developing material that would be attractive to TV's prime-time viewers. At 8 PM, NHK-E and NHK-G share a common objective which emanates from representing the wealthiest public TV corporation in the world, one which secures its operating fees from obligatory subscriptions from some 32 million homes with TVs.[25] Such an operating budget entails continual justification of the organization's existence partially by remaining responsive to the social tastes of the viewing audience. In a book published by the Japan Association of Broadcasting Art, one of the main points emphasized is that "the development of television broadcasting has been enhanced by the terrific competition between NHK and the commercial stations, and among the commercial stations themselves."[26] Although NHK-E's 8 PM entree is not NHK-G exactly since it has a one-dimensional, lecture/symposium-style quality to it, the topics tend to be similar to those more vividly portrayed on the other channels. Therefore, the productions, although more detailed and scholarly, are in tune with what people are watching. The current 8 PM program reflects this aim in its name, "Modern Journal." This need to attract a wider audience and keep them glued to NHK-E for 45 minutes in spite of all those professors and the high lecture content makes NHK-E's 8 PM just as susceptible to mythical digestion as TV broadcasting in general through the selectivity inherent in the concept and through the presentation and editing of the information. Who and what will appear and in what order is by no means a textbook decision.

The double play was first served up on NHK-E's ETV8 program on "Japanese Roots" on February 11, 1987. The program was hosted by an NHK announcer and Hanihara. The stated objective of the broadcast was to gather Hanihara's thoughts on recent findings concerning Japanese roots. In view of Hanihara's leanings on the matter, the observations and conclusions were obvious from the outset. Therefore, his selection as co-host and commentator provided an attractive and thematic toraijin note to a series of separate episodes on rather esoteric experiments with rocks, plants, blood and bones. Hanihara's status as senior professor of anthropology at Japan's most prestigious university was also an attractive ingredient, but his board and dynamic viewpoint provided the program with a rather secure, mass-appeal anchorage for an NHK-E show. Nevertheless, in spite of the rather predestined nature of the program, Hanihara decided to deviate from his usual structure of origins to weave a new web around Matsumoto and Gm frequencies, the double playing Gm. There really didn't appear to be any need to do so since Matsumoto was securely positioned by the program's director within Hanihara's double layer structure of old Mongoloid/Jomon and new Mongoloid/Yayoi. Matsumoto's appearance was preceded and followed by presentations confirming the validity of such a structural emphasis. One might even suggest that Matsumoto was already collared.

In the preceding sequence, the viewer was presented with a study of Japanese dogs' blood types. Yuichi Tanabe, of Gifu University, related his analysis of the blood relationships among the various Japanese dog breeds and set forth his findings on the distinction between Hokkaido and Honshu breeds. According to Tanabe, the Hokkaido dog's ancestry was very old and was related to breeds in Taiwan and southern Asia while Honshu breeds revealed a close affinity to the Jindo breed in Korea. On the basis of the oldest dog bone found in Japan of 10,000 years and his thinking on human migrations, Tanabe put the origin of the Hokkaido breed in the Jomon period and that of the Honshu hybrids in the Yayoi period, the Hokkaido dog being a non-mingler.

Tanabe's Jomon and Yayoi distinctions were made to order for Hanihara who maintained that humans in Japan showed a similar distribution, with people in isolated areas of Japan having more Jomon-like characteristics. Hanihara even shaped Tanabe's conclusion into a tautology by indicating that since the dog was man's best friend, Tanabe's study offered further evidence of human migration during the Yayoi period from the Korean peninsula. To heighten the significance of the implications from Tanabe's research, Hanihara referred to a study of mouse mitochondrial DNA which revealed a north-south, Asian-origin split in Japan's west-east mouse population distribution.

The segment which followed Matsumoto also fit into Hanihara's double-structured-layer assessment. Herein, the history of the ATL virus or Adult T-cell Leukemia virus was documented by Yorio Hinuma, of Kyoto University, one of the pioneers of ATL studies involving the detection of antibodies to antigens in human sera and the application of the results to the geographic distribution of the disease. An important route of the transmission of this particular cause of malignancy is from mother to child by breast feeding. Although the virus is carried forever by the infected person, the chance of the individual succumbing to leukemia is not very strong.[27] Hinuma noted that ATL virus carriers still could be found among Negroids in Africa and in isolated areas of Japan (as well as among the native people of Papua New Guinea and Australia and among Caribbean people brought to the new world as slaves from Africa). He related that when modern humans first appeared in western Asia, 50,000 to 100,000 years ago, there must have been many ATL virus carriers within the original Mongoloid populations but the subsequent mingling of carriers and noncarriers led to this attribute's disappearance. In other words, the implication was that two populations came to Japan, old and new Mongoloid groups.

In all, Gm had been positioned by the organization of the material and the Hanihara structure to conform to a particular perspective. And the edited-in Matsumoto sequence would have created no dissonance whatsoever except that Hanihara decided to expand on what the viewers had seen. Matsumoto, in the broadcast, said nothing pertaining to the date of arrival of the Mongoloids from the North and therefore there was no explicit contradiction of the double layer structure inherent in the sequence. Even the NHK announcer in asking for the comment of Hanihara on Matsumoto's presentation emphasized how Gm northerners would probably have come to

Japan after the migration from southern Asia had taken place. However, although it all appeared to be made to order, Hanihara chose to digress. He explained that Gm doesn't necessarily match with the double-structured layer since, according to Matsumoto, it dated back to the old stone age. He, therefore, thought that perhaps a triple-structured layer with a double playing Gm was appropriate, i.e., northern, Gm ab3st Mongoloid in the first layer, southern Mongoloid in the Jomon layer and northern, Gm ab3st Mongoloid again in the Yayoi layer.

When Hanihara and Matsumoto again faced the cameras together on ETV8 some three years later on September 4, 1990 on a program concerning the search for Japanese roots through human blood analysis, the triple-structured layer did not exactly resurface. However, there appeared a variant, one which merged the first two layers into one, thereby keeping the double playing Gm and continuing with Hanihara's usual double-layer structure. Once again, the broadcast focused on Hanihara who was presented minus the NHK announcer. Hanihara asked questions of three panelists – Matsumoto, Hinuma and Kimiyoshi Tsuji, of Tokai University's medical school – and provided commentary on what was said. Hinuma emphasized the very early arrival in Japan of the ATL virus, perhaps during the Jomon period. He found evidence for this in the distribution of carriers in coastal areas and on the very small islands of Japan as well as among the Ainu. Tsuji, who like Tokunaga at Tokyo University is studying HLA blood types, brought out the difference between the general population of Japan and Ainus and Okinawans. Matsumoto's opinion on Gm seemed to fit in somewhat with this line of reasoning in that Ainu and the people of Japan's southwestern islands offered a different pattern of Gm distribution among the populations of Japan, although the root of all three was viewed as north Asian from Matsumoto's vantage point.[28]

The dramatic compression of the first and second layers of the triple-layer structure came, however, with a video clip on Tobishima Island, an islet off the coast of Yamagata Prefecture. This isolated locale contained a population of 800, a slew of 1,000 year old bones of 27 bodies dating back to the Heian period, 6,000-year-old Jomon pottery of special type similar to those found only in Hokkaido ("entōgatafukabachi" type) and a tree called "tabunoki" found only in southern Japan. Hanihara was shown measuring one of the Tobishima skulls in the prefectural museum and considering how Jomon-like it was. As a matter of fact, in case, the viewer got lost perspective-wise on his tour of Tobishima, Hanihara had introduced the video clip with slides of the two distinct paleoanthropological faces of Japan, Jomon and Yayoi. Regarding Hanihara's final measurements of the Tobishima remains, the audience learned that these Heian islanders were more closely related to present-day Ainu and Jomon people than to the general Japanese population and toraikei people. Hinuma and Tsuji backed up Hanihara with their blood analyses of the present Tobishima inhabitants: a very high distribution of ATL carriers and a very different HLA pattern. (Tsuji admitted however that only 10 people had been tested for HLA.) Matsumoto's Gm tests were also confirmative. Although Matsumoto held fast to his north Asian origin position, even for the Tobishima islanders, he admitted that the Gm pattern in Tobishima differed from the usual distribution frequencies in Japan, an assessment which in terms of what Hanihara, Hinuma and Tsuji had presented added to rather than distracted from the implications of this island tale. As such, by filtering the contents of the broadcast, already containing a heavy dose of Hanihara, through a Tobishima Island vehicle, the impression was firmly offered of an old and southern Mongoloid race with some kind of northern (Gm) characteristic mix as the root of the Jomon population.

An October 20, 1988 NTV two-hour special in the 9 to 11 PM slot on a visit to Japanese origins presented a composite of the thematic and structural features of the National and ETV8 broadcasts. However, the packaging was quite different since the program was a much lighter, more romantic travelogue adventure along the "Far Away Japan Road." The travel reporters were three attractive females and focus was on their discoveries rather than on professorial concerns, although both Hanihara and Matsumoto as well as others made guest appearances. The special was sponsored by Nissay, Nippon Life Insurance Company, Japan's largest life insurance company,[29] and commemorated the 100th anniversary of the firm – once again, a corporation drawing on the image of origins to market a corporate identity.

Route One in the journey followed one of the female reporters from Hokkaido to Siberia to discover what conditions were as much as 20,000 years ago when, according to the narration, the sea level was 140 meters lower than today and Japan was connected to the Eurasian continent through Sakhalin, allowing prehistoric hunters access to the islands. After a look at the typical micro-blade culture of Okhotsk Hokkaido of 13,000 years ago, with thin-blade-like flakes crafted for insertion into wooden or bone spearheads, knives, etc., to provide a sharp cutting edge, the Route One traveler made her way to Russia where she joined a group of Japanese and foreign archaeologists who were about to pursue the roots of these micro-blades into Siberia. In the Altai Mountains, at Denisova Cave, the Russian archaeologist, Anatoly Derev'anko (who presented a paper at the Tokyo University symposium) offered the young lady a tour of quarters dating back 60,000 years to the ancient origins of stone tools. He explained that the people who went east from here, eventually dispersed as far as Japan, a thought in line with the idea that perhaps the propagation of northeastern Japan's stone knife culture of 20,000 years ago was the end result of such a population movement. Later, Shinpei Kato, who was a member of the expedition, related his thoughts to the reporter on a second wave of stone culture, referring to the spread of micro-blade culture from its center in the Baikal as far as middle Kanto. However, even in the Altai Mountains, the narrator reflected on Hanihara's ideas of cold climate adaptation and reminded the audience continually to look behind the tools to the faces that made them.

The transition from the stone age to a present-day Buryat village was authored by Matsumoto. Matsumoto's appearance took up a matter of seconds, enough time only to introduce the Baikal villagers as the closest blood relatives of the Japanese. No explanations followed of when this relationship developed nor how it survived. Instead, the narrator exclaimed enthusiastically that the faces of the villagers looked just like those seen on location in Hokkaido while shooting the program. Soon, the reporter remarked on how Japanese the Buryat were and how one individual looked just like her. Then, the villagers commented that during World War II when Japanese were first encountered, they were surprised to see faces just like their own. They also indicated how the NTV production crew were so very Buryat in their features. Subsequently, the reporter organized a name-that-face competition, giving the villagers an opportunity to determine the nationality of three famous faces, all of which were Japanese. One face received a unanimous vote as typically Buryat. The photo in question showed one of the most popular faces in the history of Japanese movies, that of Tora-san, a good-natured vagabond who continually experiences the pangs of unrequited marriage-type-love, played by Kiyoshi Atsumi. With the choice of such a theatrical example, the frame of the reporter with Tora-san's picture in hand was frozen and the live image of Hanihara was flashed on the screen. Hanihara found the selection to be very appealing, especially in view of his thoughts on Japanese origins. He explained that Tora-san's face was typical of human beings who had lived in very cold areas in the prehistoric past. He then proceeded to apply his cold adaptation theories to the eyes and cheeks of this beloved character: eyes small and narrow to protect against freezing winds and mammoth cheeks to warm icy cold air which could damage the lungs. Before the program returned to the female guide, an ancient Siberian dogū-style figurine with thin eye slits and big cheeks was shown and the narrator commented that old-stone-age Siberians who had faces like this, having adapted to severe weather conditions, came to Japan.

The following segment found the reporter on a boat somewhere between Russia and Hokkaido in the company of a Russian archaeologist, a specialist on paleolithic Siberian migrations. Here she listened to his explanation that improved hunting techniques provided for an increase in population in excess of local food supplies and led to groups of people leaving an area. In his opinion, such overpopulation and migration events happened repeatedly from place to place and perhaps it took 5,000 years to cover the distance to the coast of Hokkaido. As for the type of food which "the faces" were following, the reporter explained that around 13,000 years ago, Siberians chased salmon rather than mammoth, which was bordering on the edge of extinction.[30] (Actually, recent dating puts the origin of micro-blade culture in Japan between 14,000 and 15,000 years ago and its dispersal at 13,000 years ago. One wonders if, in the future, Matsumoto will have to reset his molecular clock once again.)[31] She noted that the appearance of Hokkaido's micro-blade culture coincided with this new specialization in food procurement, such tools being well-suited for the preparation of the fish. Clothing and shoes made of fish skins also became prevalent, according to the narrator.

At the end of Route One, Hanihara and Tora-san reappeared and the viewer was provided with a structure to analyse what had been shown along the way. The Gm double-playing, triple-structured layer popped up once again on television. A computerized portrait of Tora-san was altered to conform to the dimensions of the Minatogawa skull. On commenting on the distorted configuration which resulted, Hanihara explained that Minatogawa rather than stone-age Siberian man was most likely the ancestor of Jomon, though Jomon was a little more modern. Then, the computerized program drew Tora's image according to Jomon and modern-Japanese dimensions and the results were compared. Naturally, Kiyoshi and modern Japanese matched perfectly while Kiyoshi's Jomon mask appeared quite pushed together. The point was therefore effectively made that cold-adpated humans or Buryat types with high Gm ab3st frequency must have come to Japan once again after the Jomon period, thereby recirculating the blood of the modern Japanese people.

Routes Two and Three of this far Japanese road confirmed the dichotomy of pre-Jomon/Jomon and Yayoi/Kofun by associating Jomon more with Japanese culture rather than Japanese race, although relating how some people might have journeyed to Japan from the south at that time bringing these particular elements. Instead of face and blood, Route Two focused on the Jomon dogū. Interestingly, although the Siberian dogū was presented to exemplify racial features, the rationale for the Jomon figure never crossed paths with physical anthropology. The questions asked at the beginning of the passage were for what purpose was the dogū made and why did Jomon people break the figurine into pieces according to its body parts. The reporter for Route Two journeyed far afield from a central source of huge population dispersals such as Siberia to Flores, a small Indonesian island very close to Australia. In a village of 110 people, she discovered a mythical tradition similar to one in the *Kojiki* concerning a tale in which the death of a goddess brought forth from the various parts of her body rice, wheat, millet and red beans. She also encountered an ancient custom of breaking a fertility figurine into pieces and placing it at various locations in the cultivated field, the dogū substituting for animal sacrifice (i.e., small birds) to insure a good harvest.

Route Three also followed the cultural road to a point, but since it extended into the Yayoi period, it intersected with Hanihara's third layer. This final journey took the viewer to the heights of Yunnan Province in China, to where the roots of Asian rice cultivation might lie.[32] It was also explained that since the area offered access to two mighty rivers, the Mekong and the Yangtze, harvest traditions could easily flow south and east. Bronzeware from Yunnan dating back some 2,200 years which vividly portrayed with figurines ceremonial human sacrifice to insure a bountiful harvest was presented and associations were made between ancient Yunnan customs and those of Flores and Jomon Japan, the Mekong perhaps being the carrier of the former, the Yangtze that of the latter, according to the narrator. The program followed the Yangtze downstream to Hemudu ruins excavated in 1973 and dating to 7,000 years ago. The viewer learned that Hemudu people ate rice and that rice-centered Yangtze River culture was two thousand years older than millet-centered civilization along the Yellow River. The possibility of Yangtze River people being swept away by the warm, Tsushima current and traveling at as much as 3 knots an hour on the East China Sea to arrive in Jomon Japan and introduce rice cultivation 2,500 years ago was graphically represented on a map. Political turmoil in China was given as the reason for motivating rice farmers to wander afar.

When Route Three transversed the Yayoi period, its course swerved far north to Korea to uncover the influence of Chinese rice culture on Korean civilization. But there was another reason for this deviation in course. The source of Route Three's flow of events in the Yayoi period was not to lie in the south but in the north and the energizing current was to be predominantly racial rather than cultural. Hanihara was brought back to bring the search for Japanese roots to a conclusion. With his computerized pictures of Tora-san in the background continually being altered into Jomon, Yayoi and modern Japanese, Hanihara stated that many people with flat, long faces moved down from north Asia and came to Japan via Korea in the Yayoi period. He related that these people mingled with the Jomon people and became the ancestors of the modern Japanese. In this way, the second coming of "out of Siberia" was dramatized for the mass audience. In a sense, Matsumoto's "face" had been transformed into Hanihara's.

The suitability of a convoluted Gm double-playing, double-layer or triple-layer structure for mass consumption reflected the mythical framework within which the media was operating. But the articulation of the myth to include Matsumoto, Gm, Buryat Mongoloid and Siberia under a Yayoi roof was evident in not only what was pictured on the screen but also what was left out. Neither in the Nissay program nor in any of the other broadcasts did the producers seek to reveal the complete version of Matsumoto's thesis. If they had, then, it would have been impossible to return to north Asia in the Yayoi period for Japan's new Mongoloid ancestors. The whole story of Gm and the origins of the Japanese, according to Matsumoto, was centered in one time zone, the end of the Ice Age. Afterwards, these proto-Japanese were isolated from northern Mongoloid people on the Korean peninsula who were henceforth subjected to repeated invasions or migrations of the northern Chinese populations with different Gm haplotype frequencies and as a result the Korean populations developed a Gm pattern between that of the Japanese and the northern Chinese. There was some mixing of populations in Japan in Jomon, Asuka and Nara periods, but these new additions were small and were absorbed into the much larger proto-Japanese population. Consequently, the haplotype frequencies were not altered as significantly as in the case of the Korean populations. In Matsumoto's own words: "In fact, the Gm constitution characteristic of northern Mongoloid populations has clearly been maintained as it was in the present-day Japanese populations."[33] As for Hanihara's southern Mongoloid of the Jomon period, Matsumoto maintained that the majority of proto-Japanese had not migrated to Japan from southern Asia, although he conceded a strong cultural influence from that direction.[34]

The difficulty involved in integrating Matsumoto's total thinking on Gm with a Yayoi scenario is evident in terms of three conditions underlying his theoretical model. Firstly, the initial population would have to be large; otherwise, high haplotype frequencies, such as that of Gm ab3st, would not survive the infusion from later immigrants. Secondly, secondary migrations from southern Asia could not result in significant admixture since such a postulate would conflict with the calculation of frequency. Thirdly, the initial migration should take place earlier rather than later in time. To hold that migrants came in a steady stream from north Asia from Yayoi to Kofun via Korea, as Hanihara does, would mean that these people would have to pass through areas more heavily populated than in the Ice Age, mingling with populations, such as Koreans and Chinese, who possessed very different Gm patterns than themselves. Consequently, their haplotype frequencies would be greatly altered. In addition, they would confront existing populations in Japan, another variable which would have to be taken into account.

The degree of stringency in Matsumoto's approach, which was not brought out in the broadcasts aimed at structuring various findings on Japanese roots into a systematic totality, did surface in a solitary *Asahi Shimbun* article in October of 1989 on a singular scientific discovery. This news report posed the question of whether Jomon Japanese in the Kanto region and people of Southeast Asia (Malay-Indonesia) shared a common origin. The basis for the query rose out of an observation set forth by Satoshi

Horai of the National Institute of Genetics based upon an amplified sample of mitochondrial DNA extracted from an ancient Japanese skull of about 6,000 B.P. Horai had compared the sample with those of 107 modern humans in terms of genetic base sequences and found that it was identical with two Southeast Asians out of 16 nonJapanese Asians. Since Horai's research focused not only on archaeological samples but also on human population studies through the comparative examination of modern mitochondrial DNA, he was clearly of the opinion that the ancestors of modern Japanese fell into two distinct mitochondrial groups, with the Jomon skull representative of one of these groupings. Matsumoto's response to Horai's archaeological sample, as related in the article, was that it was too early to talk about origins in terms of base-sequence analysis since a well-established and systematic method had not as yet presented itself. Matsumoto held fast to his position that Gm analysis was the only way at present to pinpoint Japanese origins and that Japanese, with distinct northern-Mongoloid-from-Lake-Baikal haplotype patterns, could not be classified with Southeast Asians. He asserted that "Jomon are not so much different from modern people," an emphatic statement of his position and one which was never heard on any of the above TV broadcasts. He added that Horai's results with the Jomon skull were not impossible but he believed Horai had uncovered something out of the ordinary.[35]

Another quality of Matsumoto's approach to origins which the media conveniently overlooked was the centrality of the molecular clock in his chronological assumptions. Of course, there was good reason for this, as already noted, i.e., Matsumoto's dating conflicted with mythical time. There is also the matter that Matsumoto's assessment in this regard differed from experts, such as Hanihara, influenced by assumptions based on physical anthropological differences between Jomon and Yayoi people. A molecular clock, like Gm itself, was no substitute for a human face in the media's dramatic presentation. But even after saying all this, one cannot but wonder whether the media would have treated Matsumoto's calculations any differently if, in the 80s, the Western Eve and her molecular clock would have succeeded in raising the eyebrows of the Japanese public, thereby making the phenomenon of the molecular clock, both motochondrial DNA and Gm-related types, more attractive to the media. Would the Western-time/Japan-time perimeters of the mythical paradigm prevented such a media linkage in spite of this association of Eve and Buryat Mongoloid along a molecular date line? Would Gm's strong facial imagery within the mythical paradigm have thwarted the telling of Japan's ancient time along anything but facial lines in any event? Although there is no direct way to answer these questions, in November 1991, a media performance, which unfortunately was illustrated rather than televised and in which Matsumoto did not appear, offered up some strong hints on these questions.

The medium was *Newton* magazine; the article was entitled "The Human Race Was Born in Africa;" the story related the significance of telling time with a molecular clock. This molecular clock story in *Newton* provided informative written and visual coverage of the significance of the mitochondrial DNA timepiece for understanding man's origins. Focusing on an African birthday, the article touched on vital points which were still coming hot off the presses in the West. Under the heading that homo sapiens sapiens were born in Africa and dispatched throughout the world, the reader learned about Eve, Allan Wilson and Rebecca Cann. It was indicated that it was now known where and when homo sapiens sapiens appeared and dispersed.[36] Just prior to the November issue, the *International Herald Tribune* and other publications carried news of a recent finding of scientists from Allan Wilson's laboratory at Berkeley, Wilson having passed away that summer. The finding which appeared in the scholarly journal *Science* presented the results of an analysis of 189 people of diverse races, including African populations. The conclusions of the original study having been based on an American black mitochondrial DNA sample rather than an African one had engendered the criticism of whether American blacks were an authentic source of African mitochondrial DNA in view of the possibility of black-white genetic mixture. The new study not only addressed this issue but also confirmed the accuracy of the 1987 clocking of some 200,000 years ago of the appearance of a common female ancestor in Africa. Linda Vigilant, who helped to write the report was quoted as saying: "We feel this paper has made a major advance in firming up the placement of an ancestor in Africa."[37]

Also, fitting in nicely with recent Western media reporting were the pages on Cro-magnon vs. Neanderthal. Here, the heading posed the question of whether the Neanderthals were completely destroyed by Homo sapiens sapiens.[38] In September, the cover of the *U.S. News & World Report* flashed the picture of a black Cro-Magnon man of 36,000 years ago with the bold-lettered caption of "Early Man." Inside, the article revealed that out of Africa theory had received a major boost when researchers in Europe during the summer had succeeded in dating pieces of flint alongside a Neanderthal body to 36,000 years ago. This date confirmed the existence of Neanderthal several thousand years after modern human's postulated arrival in Europe and, as indicated in the article, contributed to the point of view of the Neanderthal line as being a dead end in human history. The date also provided another focal point for signifying the accuracy of the molecular clock.[39]

Nevertheless, the timeliness of the *Newton* article receded with the dispersal of the out-of-Africa population throughout the world. In the descriptions and illustrations which followed, mitochondrial DNA gave way to hot and cold faces and bodies and physical time replaced molecular time. The separation of the races was molecularly clocked down to some 50,000 years ago. However, this genetic distance also represented a convenient turning point for a divergence into physical anthropology. In the early 80s, in the West, blood and enzyme (protein) group analyses utilizing the molecular clock had preceded mitochondrial DNA studies in examining the genetic distance relationships among the major racial groups. Such analyses clearly indicated, according to one trained observer, that racial divergences were recent events in human evolution.[40] One conclusion was that "the genetic distance for protein loci between the Negroid and the Caucasoid-Mongoloid groups had been shown to correspond to a divergence time of about

$110,000 \pm 34,000$ years, whereas the distance between Caucasoid and Mongoloid corresponds to a divergence time of $41,000 \pm 15,000$ years, though these estimates depend on a large number of assumptions."[41]

Beyond the 50,000 year ago clocking, it was as if *Newton* had experienced a close encounter with Hanihara. Suddenly, the article was turned inside out. The cruelties of the passage of time were interpreted as etching telltale signs into the physical characteristics of human beings. The long, lanky, easy-to-cool physique of summer man with his distinctive facial features vs. the short-limbed, stocky and well-insulated character of winter man with his flat facial contours replaced genetic distances as the topic of dramatization.[42]   When *Newton* made the transition from Mongoloid dispersals to Japanese origins, one page was given over to illustrated portraits: a side view of a clean-shaven, weak-nosed Yayoi man overlapping that of a heavily bearded, strong-nosed Jomon man. The opposite page featured two dispersal diagrams. The one dated 20,000 to 10,000 years ago had arrows emanating from a circled area encompassing southern Asia and extending across land bridges to Japan and Okinawa. The dispersal center was labeled southern Mongoloid and included Upper Cave man and Liujiang man. Minatogawa man's home was also indicated on the map. The inclusion of Chinese fossil men in the diagram, a paleoanthropological linkage, heightened the separation between molecular and physical attributes, thereby reinforcing the traditional view of Japanese origins. The second diagram showed northern Mongoloid dispersals via Korea to Japan some 2,000 years ago. The accompanying text underlined the facial differences between northern and southern Mongoloids and explained that the non-cold-adaptive types could still be seen today in Hokkaido and Okinawa. Information was also given that Ainu and Okinawan people were characterized by wet-type earwax common to southern continental people in contrast to "Wajin" who had dry type – another cold-adaptive feature, perhaps. The editors concluded that the theory in which the Japanese were northern Mongoloid and Ainu and Okinawan people southern Mongoloid was kind of the definitive one.[43]

With genetic distances held to a descent of 50,000 years ago, all information was processed through a southern/northern Mongoloid, climatic filter. All the outcomes or faces of the ancient Japanese confronted one another across Jomon and Yayoi time periods. One could only think about how appropriate it would have been, especially in view of the recent divergence of the Mongoloid and Caucasoid races, to have offered up the archaeological record in Siberia and input Matsumoto's Gm molecular clocking to provide a more consistent and accommodating framework to a genetic analysis of who "WE" rather than "US" are. But then again, inputting Gm would probably have only output Buryat Mongoloid faces. As the *Newton* editors had pointed out, the southern (Jomon)-northern (Yayoi) Mongoloid approach to Japanese ancestry was the commonly accepted one. In the following month, *Newton* published a special issue on archaeology and ancient world cultures. At that time, *Newton* once again associated traditional anthropological views on evolution with Japanese roots by inserting without revision the article which appeared in its April 1990 issue (described in Chapter II). One might say that for *Newton*, at least, out of Africa and multiregional evolution were musical chairs but Japanese roots remained nailed to the floor. The strength of this Japanese fixture, in this case, was reinforced by the inclusion of a second insertion entitled "Yamatai Country Was in Kyushu" taken from the September 1989 issue and featuring Himiko, Yoshinogari and Gishiwajinden in big picture color.[44]

In the 1980s, Gm theory achieved idol status within the scientific category of myth modernization, an event which compared well with that of Yoshinogari in the historical mold. The transformation and symbolization of Matsumoto's approach to origins matched the process which unfolded around Yoshinogari, although, in the case of Gm, the processing by the media was quite instantaneous. The attraction of the mythical paradigm resulted in a facial image correlation especially in view of the association of the Gm distribution frequency findings with nomadic horseriding people, the Buryat. This in turn led to the virtual cooptation of Gm origins by the scientific-theoretical framework within which the myth resided in the media, i.e., a southern Mongoloid-northern Mongoloid confronting pattern occurring within a Jomon vs. Yayoi revolutionary genetic upheaval scenario, in spite of substantive incompatibilities. In this way, Gm beat the general path followed in the media's representation of the Yamatai resurrection surrounding the excavation of Yoshinogari. In the course of the media presentations, the boundary between Western-time and Japan-time remained unbroken. The mythical diaphragm remained intact.

With the 1990s, one might be catching a glimpse of a new science-media idol but then again its future is not so apparent. The prospective idol is Japan-group mitochondrial DNA which is currently undergoing continuing sequence analysis at Horai's laboratory at the Japanese National Institute of Genetics. Japan-group mitochondrial DNA fits quite nicely in certain respects into the mythical paradigm in terms of present findings. Although Horai's study is not based on a molecular clock analysis, it enjoys a close relationship with the highly modern Eve approach. Such an association would allow the paradigm to exploit an international scientific modernizing image without upsetting the prevailing boundaries between Japan-time and Western-time. Also, paradigmatically compatible is Horai's hypothesis of the existence of two distinct groups of Mongoloid mitochondrial DNA. Since Horai associates one of these groups with Jomon and Ainu people, the stage is set for a Jomon-Yayoi confrontation story.[45]

On the other hand, there are certain obstacles to media stardom. The matter of Horai's ambivalence on the arrival of a Japanese Yayoi Eve represents a significant weakness. At a conference in Kyoto in September 1990, Horai was quite specific on the Jomon origins of mitochondrial-DNA-group-II Japanese. But he held that "part of people who migrated from the continent during the period of two to three thousand years ago [which would put them in late Jomon or at the dawn of Yayoi] may be representative of the other group (group I) of the modern Japanese."[46] In the January 1992 issue of the *Kagaku Asahi*, a monthly journal of science in the *Scientific American* style, Horai maintained that Jomon and Ainu belong to group II and those who migrated to Japan after the Yayoi period "might" belong to modern

Japanese group I.[47] The reason why Horai seemed to be somewhat reticent on group I specifications became evident during the Ministry of Education's 6th University Science Symposium from January 24 to 25 of 1992. At that time, Horai explained his thinking regarding his conclusions in the following manner:

> The data on Jomon reveals that those people belong to quite a different cluster than modern Japanese. [Yamaguchi] Bin told us the story about the origin of the Japanese. One is the continuous change theory which is Jomon didn't mix so much. Without mingling so much, they gradually evolved into Modern Japanese. The second one is the torai theory. Most of the paleoanthopologists support this theory. Since we don't have data for Yayoi bones, we have *to guess* what kind of genetic background those people had.[48]

Another shortcoming which would appear to be the greatest obstacle to a career for Japan-group mitochondrial DNA equaling that of the Gm gene marker, i.e., to a presence around which the retelling of mythohistory could occur, is the lack of qualitative distinctiveness concerning group I mitochondrial DNA. Besides Japanese, this DNA type applies to Koreans, mainland Chinese, Chinese in Taiwan, Taiwanese and ancient native Americans and many Oceanian people, including Polynesians.[49] In other words, there is no small, singular founding group, like the Buryat, to which the mythical paradigm could be attached. In addition to the drawback of a blurred origins, there is nothing heroic in the mitochondrial telling. There is no specific relation to a north Asian steppes heritage and to nomadic horseriding people.

CHAPTER V

TWO KOREAS

There are two Koreas in the media's treatment of Japan's ancient international relations of the 4th and 5th centuries: Japanese mythical Korea and Japanese historical Korea. The role of Korea within the modernized mythical paradigm of origins is generally reflected in the media's fashioning of a Second Korea side by side with the general textbook version to allow for open, unimpeded transit from north Asia to Japan of an invading population. This Second Korea is usually a sketchy outline of its substantive self and, more often than not, it exists only to highlight an arrow whistling its way from the Asian grasslands to northern Kyushu. Japanese mythical Korea is nurtured by the fame and popularity of Egami and his horserider theory. Egami's theory centers on nomadism. Since nomads are people of passage who leave little behind for the consideration of future generations, the media can bypass Korean historical evolution because one can only expect to discover a few remaining odds and ends of these nomadic invaders. Also, since the nomadic world is one of continual, pulsating expansions and contractions, the media can be somewhat negligent of chronology in considering the arrival and departure from Korea of an invading population. In this respect, as seen in previous chapters, horseriding invaders can even escape back into the more distant past of the Yayoi period.

The media divide between the two Koreas is illustrated in the publicity generated by recent excavations of ancient burials in the vicinity of Pusan, which came to light in mid-1990.[1] Masao Okuno, in the summer of 1991, wrote in a featured section of articles in the scholarly journal *Higashi Ajia no Kodai Bunka* (Ancient Culture of East Asia) how surprised he was over the fact that these excavations which could be so enlightening about the coming of horseriding people to Japan had not kicked off a media stampede. Instead, he noted that coverage of the Taesung tomb group had been somewhat stingy: a newspaper article, two TV broadcasts and an article by Egami in the June 1991 issue of *Gekkan Asahi*.[2] Okuno didn't mention that following and supplementing Egami's article was a shorter piece, only three pages, on Taesung written by the chief excavator, Kyungcheol Shin, of Kyungsung University. Shin's article offered detailed archaeological documentation for Egami's main assertions and was more like a long footnote in this respect. It blended so well into Egami's copy that one could conceive of Okuno considering Shin's piece to be included in his reference to the citation. Actually, at the outset of Egami's article, a large photo was included showing Shin and Egami together. Shin did not, however, assert that horseriding people came to southern Korea in the 3rd century nor did he make any reference to horseriders subsequently coming to Japan. In fact, he explained that the horseriding finds at Taesung could be the result of either racial or cultural movements. Furthermore, with regard to Japan, he indicated that one should be very careful about what conclusion one drew about this subject.[3]

Okuno opened his article with a strong statement on the published account of the Sahara-Egami dialogue referred to in Chapter 3, particularly upon Sahara's unbending position after two days of discussions on the horserider issue. He explained that he thought Sahara's stand was strange and he wondered as to what were the conditions under which Japanese archaeology would be willing to acknowledge Egami's theory. He ruminated that perhaps Japanese archaeologists would never concede on this matter unless the same ruins or remains which were found in north Asia turned up in Japan. As for himself, he related that he agreed with the horserider argument. In his estimation, the enlightenment of the Korean finds would serve as a cultural bridge between the north Asian culture of the kiba minzoku and their lifestyle in Japan, confirming that northern culture entered Japan in the 4th or 5th century. He indicated his doubts on whether the life of the horserider could be exactly the same in north Asia as it was in Japan, holding that on the way to Japan new cultural elements would be assimilated, resulting in changes in the shape and quality of the original forms. He asserted that the same could be said about the northern Asian culture of the Taesung tomb group in the sense that one wouldn't expect it to appear exactly as it was originally.[4]

What was not apparent in Okuno's exposition regarding the media's lack of attention to the possibility of playing up the horserider theme was the absence of paradigmatic pressure acting on the media to highlight a Korean archaeological story in terms of the mythical dimension. Since, within the context of the origins of the Japanese, Korea plays a minor role of dispatcher, there is no reason for the media to build up the role. In fact, to do so could downgrade the heroic drama of kiba minzoku by rendering the impression that Koreans with horses rather than north Asian horseriding people came to Japan. In this regard, Okuno's observations notwithstanding, it is noteworthy that the paradigm didn't even encompass the contents of the coverage at the time. On the contrary, with the exception of the Egami article plus the supplement, the focus of the media's response was within the context of Japan historical Korea. Too great a cultural perspective had switched the media conceptually to a track quite different from the mythical line, to one which was concerned with the extent of impact of Korean culture on ancient Japan, or vice versa, or in its most political form, with exploring the existence of the 4th to 6th century Japanese colony of Mimana in southern Korea. Specifically, the media's focus was Mimana-oriented. Although Egami heralded Taesung in his article as providing the missing link in the horserider theory[5] and thereby incontrovertibly proving that horseriders came to Japan, the media failed to pursue his lead and hitch the mythical paradigm to a Korean-made chariot. The fact that *Gekkan Asahi* allowed its pages to be used as a platform by Egami for his theorizing reflected Egami's high status within Japanese society as well as his association with an origins' image which society valued. But it was revealing that *Gekkan Asahi* didn't offer any non-Egami-produced follow-ups on the meaning of the recent excavations. There was no indication of any intent on the part of the editors to turn the myth of Japanese origins on the head of an expanding Korean needle.

The only article which followed didn't appear until eight months later and it was not an independent production, but a presentation of a conversation between Egami and the archaeologist Koichi Mori of Doshisha University. The exchange did not center on Taesung per se, but on "Coming to See that Kiba Minzoku Came by Boat," with Egami transforming his land nomads into horseriders adept at exploiting water resources and transport even while in Manchuria and attributing to them the premeditated intent of coming to Korea to invade Japan.[6] The context and course of the conversation evinced, however, the marketability of the Egami profile. For instance, Mori opened the discussion with great praise for the accomplishments of the 85-year-old former University of Tokyo professor and current curator of the Ancient Orient Museum in Tokyo. Scholars as far back as Taisho (1912-1926), according to Mori, knew about kiba culture, but before Egami came along some 40 years ago, nobody attempted to build up a theory, leaving the Japanese government free to guide the world of scholarship into legendary accounts and imperial aggrandizement. One should keep in mind that whereas Egami is more apt to be viewed among scholars as dealing with the origins of the imperial family, mass culture doesn't necessarily make such a distinction in its horserider imagery. Mori continued, noting that the Japanese government had now presented Egami with a national culture decoration (bunka kunshō) and although this didn't necessarily mean government recognition of kiba culture, it did represent an admission of Egami's scholarly achievements in this regard. He therefore offered his congratulations to Egami on the award. As for Egami's critics,

Mori was quite emphatic, explaining that these people grasp on to only minor parts of the theory and, as for the structure of Japanese history, they offer no alternative to Egami's matrix.[7]

In the same issue of the *Ancient Culture of East Asia* in which Okuno's article appeared, Toshiyaki Tanaka, an authority on ancient Korea, in reflecting on the Taesung finds, offered his views on the mass media's reaction in Japan as well as Korea. Whereas Okuno had found the response rather thin, Tanaka was surprised about how much interest the Japanese mass media showed in the excavation. It was much more than he had expected, even though he understood how fond Japanese were with delving into the Mimana question. In this regard, he noted that what was at the bottom of the media's behavior was the possibility of Taesung offering up a solution to the Mimana issue. In contrast, the robust manner in which the Korean mass media dealt with the story didn't surprise Tanaka at all. He explained that everytime the Korean media covered a new archaeological dig, they always peppered it with the title, "Japanese Scholars Overturned." Indignantly, he wrote that Japanese scholars weren't always in agreement and that most of the time, the matter overturned was an idea which did not enjoy wide support. However, he tempered his response by considering the motivation of the media and rather than giving into his anger over the ignorance of the medium, he came to think of its focus as being quite reasonable since its executives were taking advantage of a good thing in order to sell a product.[8] Perhaps, herein, the observations of Wontack Hong, a professor of international economics at Seoul University and the author of a book which weaves Biten-Yasumoto-like through the ancient Japanese chronicles to arrive at a Korean origins for the Yamato State, may provide some background for Tanaka's thoughts on good salesmanship. In Hong's words...

> The Japanese, almost without exception, claim that Japan had maintained a colony named Mimana in the southern part of Korea for more than two centuries beginning in the late fourth century. Mimana is the traditional kana rendering for "Imna." The Japanese claim is inspired by the fairly confusing records on Imna that cannot be found in chronicles of East Asia outside of Nihongi.

The imperialistic expansion of the Japanese military power to Korea in the early twentieth century was typically justified with an arbitrarily fabricated Mimana story such as [Yoshi] Kuno's: 'The power of Japan to rule in Korea began with the creation of the State of Mimana as her protectorate so that Shinra [Silla] could not invade it. Japan's power in Korea began to decline with the destruction of her government-general in Mimana by Shinra and finally, when the allied armies of China and Shinra, in 663, annihilated her military force in Korea, Japan was forced to abandon all her claims there. She did not regain authority in Korea until after the Russo-Japanese War. The date of the founding of Mimana is therefore essential to a determination of the period of suzerainty that Japan exercised over Korea prior to 1905.'[9]

Another authoritative voice reflecting the intensity of present-day Korean opinion on Japan and ancient cultural matters is the veteran archaeologist and professor emeritus of Seoul University, Wonyong Kim. In explaining Japan's archaeological intentions in Korea during the colonial years, Kim related in a *Korea Newsreview* interview that the undertaking was very political and "generally speaking, the Japanese colonists worked hard to prove through archaeological and historical research that ancient Korean culture was a minor, peripheral phenomenon."[10] Also, in this news magazine, one can find further confirmation of strong popular feelings on what is described as "misrepresentation of history" of ancient Korea and Japan. One op-ed writer put it this way:

But what does matter is that history should never be intentionally twisted or misrepresented for whatever reason. Japan's record of hiding or glossing over certain historical events when they do not suit their convenience is well known in this part of the world.[11]

The pride of national resurgence evident in Hong's work and the above comments are supportive of Tanaka's good-sales association. In addition, one could speculate that the popular enthusiasm in Korea surrounding the demise of the Mimana theory reinforces the popularity of the Mimana Japanese Government subject in Japan in view of the close ties between Japan and South Korea today. Nevertheless, Tanaka did not follow this line of reasoning. Instead, he saw a parallel in Korean and Japanese media's intentions. He found the attitude of the Japanese also to be rooted in good salesmanship of a sort. In this regard, he related that Japanese history fans' knowledge was not so deep and that the intentions of publishing companies were mislaid in that they continued to harp upon proven formulas rather than break new ground to appeal to this target audience. From his perspective, the views of academics and editors dedicated to good scholarship were prone to be neglected by the media.[12]

Tanaka was particularly critical of the Japanese television broadcasts about the Taesung remains. For him, it was not the answer to the question which these broadcasts presented to their audience which was incorrect but the question itself. The query to which he objected pertained to whether Mimana existed or not. He maintained that the question should be what Taesung could tell us about the political history of the Kaya Kingdom, the Korean state which had repeatedly been associated in part or in its entirety with Mimana on the basis, in his understanding, of the highly ideological and untrustworthy *Nihon Shoki*. Tanaka's position on Taesung reminds one of Sahara's stance on the value of the Yoshinogari tradition.[13]

Nevertheless, the Japanese media was not Mimana-biased in its approach to Korean-Japanese cultural relations. Its bias or, more appropriately, its conceptualization rested elsewhere. A blindness to tribal events in nomad country would perhaps best define this tendency. For instance, in May of 1986, when NHK-G's cameras journeyed to North Korea to broadcast for the first time the wall paintings within the stone chambers of the Koguryo tombs, the presentation allowed for no degree of deviation from the pattern within Japanese Historical Korea.

The 4th century in Korea witnessed the development of the Three Kingdoms: Koguryo, Paekche and Silla. The power of the aristocratic monarchy of Koguryo, with a strong warrior-horseriding heritage, extended from lands bordering the nomadic steppes to a much more sedentary world south of modern-day Seoul. In the southern extremity, sandwiched between the growing power of the Paekche monarchy and the relatively weak Kingdom of Silla was the Kaya Kingdom, which consisted of a grouping of states. Koguryo's warlike prowess had been tested in repeated conflicts with

China and in 313 Koguryo seized the last remaining Chinese commandery in the Korean peninsula, which had exercised a strong political and cultural influence over the area since the outset of the 1st century B.C., and occupied the Taedong River region (Pyongyang and environs).[14]

The primary objective of the NHK-G special on "The Beauty and Power of Koguryo" was to compare the style and content of the Koguryo paintings with those in 7th century Takamatsuzuka tomb in Japan. The concept, therefore, centered on the constitution of a Korea-Japan cultural movement dating back to the 4th century, leaving little room for nomadic genes to enter the picture. The murals of the Koguryo tombs were scanned and Chinese and nomadic influences revealed. The program vividly assessed the process of cultural admixture. One of the oldest Koguryo tombs, of the second half of the 4th century, contained a huge mural showing a high-ranking person. In proximity, there was a painting of his wife and her female attendants. The inscription on the wall of the tomb referred to Toju, a Chinese military commander known to have sought political asylum in Koguryo, and the issue in ancient Korean history (Chinese vs. Korean scholars) of whether this was the tomb of a Chinese general or a Korean king was raised. A North Korean scholar appeared during the filming of these murals and presented his view that the reason why Toju's name appeared in a royal tomb was because it was so unusual to have a Chinese military commander running away to Korea and entering into the service of a Korean king. However, the announcer pointed out that the hairstyles of the ladies were definitely Chinese.

In considering this very early Koguryo tomb and other tombs, the broadcast made continuous references to images associated with Japanese stone-chamber tombs or Japanese design motifs. There were wall paintings of horses wearing horse masks (a horse helmet having been found in a tomb in Japan) and of a kiba-minzoku-type warrior caught in the act of shooting an arrow. On one wall was found the "tanebata" story, a well-known children's tale in Japan, of two heavenly lovers separated among the stars. Also, the murals provided a cameo of sumo-style wrestlers and a painting of a "kirin," the stylized giraffe which is the hallmark of a famous Japanese beer. In addition, the camera scanned a metal ornament with the three-legged black crow which served as Jimmu's guide.

The production even journeyed beyond the tombs to make its point. For instance, the "yamajiro" (mountain castle-) above-a-palace configuration style of Koguryo was compared with the layout of the Dazaifu military command in Kyushu built in 660 with the assistance of a military person from Paekche. The announcer indicated that there were many yamajiro in Japan.

The Takamatsuzuka murals were featured at the end of the broadcast and consideration was given to the dress of the female figures, a two piece suit with a pleated skirt. It was noted that although this fashion was in the Koguryo tradition, the structure of the drawing was Chinese. The Takamatsuzuka pièce de résistance, consisting of paintings of the Chinese-derived protective spirits of the four directions, including the azure dragon of the East, the white tiger of the West, the phoenix of the South and the tortoise-snake combo of the North, was shown and compared with that in a 7th century Koguryo tomb. The observation was related that the dragon bore the same three-colored necklace.

What was evinced in the program pertained to the powerful emission of cultural elements emanating from Koguryo and passing to Japan via Paekche from the 4th century until Koguryo ceased to exist in 668 when this kingdom was destroyed by the combined forces of an emerging Silla and its ally, Tang China. Silla had dispatched Mimana much earlier in 562. Paekche succumbed to a Silla-Tang offensive in 660.[15] Instead of an invader's arrow passing through a map of Korea, the viewer witnessed the formation of a gigantic red clot (delineating the Koguryo Kingdom) dominating the Eurasian route to Japan, one which covered the area from the Sungari River in Manchuria to the Han River of southern Korea.

In a similar vein, neither of the two Taesung NHK programs broadcast on February 5, 1991 at 8 to 8:45 PM and March 4, 1991 at 10 to 10:45 PM were interested in turning up nomadic invaders in perusing

Japanese-Korean intercourse. The titles of the "Modern Journal" program of February 5 underlined the Korea-centered focus of analysis. The program was called "Ancient Japan After Himiko," with a subtitle reading "An approach from the Korean peninsula."

The opening of this "Modern Journal" surveyed recent Kaya archaeological undertakings. An excavation overlooking the port area was shown and the narration unfolded a story of Japanese-related finds which the diggings had uncovered over the past ten years from this Pusan Kaya tomb group. References were made to big stone lids for coffins, a vertical-pit-style stone room to house the coffin, iron grave-goods dating from the beginning of the 5th century and iron bars or "tetsutei." The narrator noted that in the Tomb period, Japan imported these tetsutei to use as money. It was also pointed out that for the first time, an iron horse helmet had been excavated in Korea, one similar to that found in Otani tomb, of the mid-5th century, in Wakayama Prefecture, although 40 to 50 years older. The statement that iron ore had been found with which to make these products implied a strong commercial reason other than the trade in crafted goods for close relations between Kaya and Japan. The narrator then related the significance of Taesung situated in Kimhae County, west of the Naktong River. He explained that an excavation begun in the spring of 1990 had already yielded what seemed to be a grave of a king and a wealth in iron horse-trappings and iron armor. An unexpected discovery, according to the broadcast, pertained to the bronze artifacts unearthed, objects which people had thought only existed in Japan.

The 4th and 5th centuries in Japanese history are known as the mysterious centuries ("nazo no seiki") because there is no record in China of contact with Japan from the time of the last mission of Yamatai to the Wei court in the 260s to a revival of Japanese-Chinese relations in 413. Within this interval, when the Japanese government in Mimana was supposedly established and flourished, all was "kūhaku" or blank, notwithstanding the documentation in the *Nihon Shoki*. With this observation, the broadcast proceeded to fill in this blank page in history within the framework of a panel discussion.

Among the archaeologist-historian panelists gathered to consider the significance of the finds were Wonyong Kim and Kyotari Tsuboi. They were joined by the Korean Chinhee Lee, of Japan's Meiji University, and the Japanese scholar Kenji Kadowaki, of Kyoto Furitsu University. Regarding their overall impressions, Kim was the first to offer a response. It is interesting to note the effort on the part of NHK to give equal weight to the opinions of Korean scholars on ancient Japanese-Korean relations, leaving one once again to speculate on how the intensive presence of Korean perspectives contain the media's focus within a cultural frame. Kim's point of view, for instance, would definitely be grounded in a Kaya mold since he had devoted his career, in his own words, to defining the role of Korea in East Asian culture, his opinion being that "Koreans enriched the China-oriented culture and civilization, and transmitted it to Japan."[16] As for his comments, Kim explained about the national pride involved in the undertaking at Taesung, relating that young Korean archaeologists were excavating the place as if it was their own ancestors' graveyards. Nevertheless, he held that the excavation had yielded two strong impressions: (1) Kaya was much stronger than anyone thought militarily and economically and therefore wouldn't have been easily conquered by Japan. (2) In view of the first-time findings of "tsutsugatadoki" – a handle-like cylindrical object – and "tomoegatadōki" – a rotary-blade-style shield ornament – there existed a need to develop a new theory to explain the roots of bronze vessels.

Kadowaki, whose perspective was sympathetic to Kim's assessment, followed mentioning that the *Nihon Shoki* was untrustworthy. He realized that the aristocratic society of the past wanted to believe their ancestors were great men, but he pointed out that the dating of the *Nihon Shoki* for Mimana – even if accepted as an existing entity – had to be adjusted back 180 years. Kadowaki said that when he went to lecture in Pusan, Kim had told him to tell those attending what Japanese scholars thought about Mimana since their response might prove quite revealing, perhaps providing him with some new ideas to consider. The aura of Korean culturalism hovered heavily over the broadcast.

Tsuboi's initial comments kept the discussion moving in the Kaya-Mimana cultural court but from a different angle. He felt that if culture could move to Japan from Korea, then, it could certainly travel in the opposite direction. He observed that at Yoshinogari, a mold had been found for making of tomoegatadōki, but nothing like that had been discovered in Korea. Tsuboi's response revealed how the Kaya-Mimana issue could develop into a debate of Korean vs. Japanese culturalism, but still with the emphasis on Korean-Japanese intercourse and Korean cultural developments, no third parties from the steppe being required to resolve the dispute.

Lee, in his introductory remarks, steered the program back to its original coordinates. He referred to the need to reconsider the Mimana issue in the light of what he perceived as so many common things being excavated. While Lee spoke, the telecast examined visuals of the Korean tsutsugatadoki of the 4th and 5th centuries and Lee and Tsuboi discussed the possible uses of the instrument, such as a spear grip (but, perhaps too fragile) or a cane handle (but, the wooden part would extend outside of the grave). Lee thought that it might be a ceremonial musical instrument since a sound-producing element had been found inside a tsutsugatadoki. Lee's general conclusion was that Korean archaeology which had been backward in the past had taken a giant leap forward with economic development and new buildings. He claimed that maybe the grave system of Kaya differed from that of Japan, but inside the burials many common things had been found. Kim and Tsuboi agreed with Lee's exposition of commonness. Tsuboi noted that although it had not been shown, a type of stone spearhead had been found like the ones he had come across in Gifu Prefecture.

In *Gekkan Asahi*, Egami had mentioned that one of the telltale signs of a nomadic kingdom in Kaya-Mimana was "mokkakubo" or a grave site with a wooden structure protecting the coffin. According to Egami, these types of tombs revealed that the Kaya rulers were from Siberia or other wooded steppe areas where wood was fully available and they moved to Korea with their mokkakubo culture around the 3rd to 4th centuries.[17] However, when Tsuboi raised the question during the following discussions regarding the development of the Kaya burial structure, the focus remained Mimana Japanese Government and not nomadic Mimana kingdom. Kim responded that previously, there was no information on 4th century graves, but now there was evidence from even the 3rd century. He explained that initially, graves held wooden coffins and a wooden structure and such burials became bigger in the 4th century. Afterwards, he noted that stone structures developed. He continued that since a lot of Japanese-type items were found at Taesung, scholars might conclude that Mimana existed. As for himself, he felt that the cultural evidence offered quite a different resolution than a Mimana Japanese Government. In his estimation, the bronze vessels might originally be Korean products and even Kofun ("hajiki") pottery might not have originated in Japan.

Neither the NHK moderator nor anybody on the panel even referred to the practice of "junsō," or human immolation at the Taesung burials, some trace of which had been observed by Egami. According to Egami, such a custom was characteristic of ancient kiba minzoku and was carried out to show great sorrow and calm the soul of the deceased. Also, no reference was made to Egami's ordos kettle from the grasslands used for cooking and sacred festivals or the special nomadic-style belt hooks. The discussion merely continued to become more heated on the old Mimana theory, with even less attention being given to what was found at Taesung and more on the past foundations for this theory. Lee related that the archaeological underpinnings for Mimana's existence rested on a 4th century Koguryo stele, a sword inscription and armor without leather straps. He didn't detail his opinion on the first two, perhaps indicating by omission his understanding on the ambiguity of their meaning or relevance. He related that previously people didn't think the iron armor found in Kaya burials was made there because of the absence of leather straps to tie the parts together, but now many examples had been discovered. He mentioned that there was even evidence of pre-armor dating to the 4th century and an iron horsemask had been found as well. Lee could have substituted kiba minzoku for Japanese in considering the history of Kaya weaponry, which would have taken him down the Egami path. Instead, he stated emphatically that Koguryo influenced Kaya military styles.

Kadowaki considered Lee's points appropriate, but he thought Mimana and Mimana Japanese Government had to be separated, holding that Mimana existed as a place in view of the evidence of the 4th century Koguryo stele, the references in the *Nihon Shoki* and an inscription found on a small monument in Japan. In addition, he put forward the documentation provided in the 6th century Chinese dynastic record of the *Sung Shu* which offered an account of four successive Japanese rulers who sought confirmation of their titles from the Chinese court. One of these titles dating back to 425 A.D. was "Generalissimo Who Maintains Peace in the East Commanding with Battle-Ax All Military Affairs in the Six Countries of Wa, Paekche, Silla, Imna [Japanese read as Mimana], Chin-han and Mok-han."[18] In his estimation, this was just a title and did not reflect the political situation. In this respect, he noted that confirmation of the existence of Chin-han and Mok-han at that time had never been found. Lee intervened to remark that the title was kind of inflated. However, Tsuboi countered that because of turmoil and shifts in power in Korea, opinion continually changed, just like at the time of the Gulf War.

The second NHK program just about continued along in the same manner as the "Modern Journal"'s panel discussion in its final segment, being more caught up in the Mimana Japanese Government issue than the Taesung discoveries. Consequently, from the outset of this broadcast which was aired as part of NHK-G's prime-time historical variety series, there was no reason to expect an interpolation of nomadic adventure. Entitled "The Riddle of the Mimana Japanese Government: Ancient Japan and the Korean Peninsula," the production's storybook was very tightly drawn within a polemical context, with the solution to the riddle being slanted in favor of the nonexistence of the Mimana colony. In the initial segment, two NHK reporters gathered around a table on which lay three high school history textbooks, two Japanese, one Korean. The Korean textbook included a map showing Kaya and contained no reference to Mimana or Mimana Japanese Government. The old Japanese source, which the middle-aged commentators indicated was similar to their schoolbooks, had Mimana rather than Kaya on the map and had it occupying much more territory than indicated in the Korean text. There was also a parenthetical caption explaining that Mimana Japanese Government governed Mimana. However, the recent Japanese schoolbook designated the area on the map as Kaya, with Mimana in parenthesis, and included an explanation to the effect that Yamato advanced on Kaya and established a strong base there. Through such a presentation, NHK made evident the increasing fragility of the case for Japanese rule in ancient Korea.

The broadcast then proceeded to show how the "Mimana focus" had been torpedoed into Japanese history as much by propaganda as by historical analysis. It was related that the Meiji government at the turn of the century in order to dramatize their legitimate right to rule Korea as part of Japan promoted the Mimana precedent to the extent that a large number of top scholars were dispatched on an unsuccessful undertaking to southern Korea to excavate incontrovertible archaeological substantiation of the existence of Japanese dominance. One could almost sense the force of Korean nationalism or a feeling of Japanese regret for the many injustices done to Korean people from the beginning of Japanese colonial rule in Meiji until the end of World War II in the production's shading of the issue. Between 1990 and 1992, there was a flood of stories concerning discriminatory practices regarding third-generation Koreans living in Japan and revelations about past brutalities, such as the fate of Korean men forced into labor camps or conscripted into the army and Korean women, even primary school children, enlisted by the Japanese military as "comfort girls" for front-line Japanese troops. TV broadcasting, including NHK, responded quite sympathetically to Korean demands for the Japanese government to make adequate amends. For example, NHK's treatment (in "Asia-Pacific War" program of August 14, 1991) of the lack of compensation for Koreans who served in the Japanese military and were even tried after the war as Japanese war criminals was highly favorable to the Korean position. In general, one can conceive of the media's emphasis on a Korean cultural perspective on ancient Japanese history as being bolstered by the prevailing political atmosphere and thereby as reflecting a social attitude of goodwill directed toward softening the wrongs of the past.

In sifting through the early archaeological evidence which had in the past been interpreted as supporting the existence of the Japanese colony of Mimana, the NHK-G production found the materials lacking in convincibility. One of these, the stele of King Kwanggaet'o of Koguryo (391-413 A.D.) mentioned by Lee and Kadowaki in the NHK-E program was found in 1882 in an area north of the Yalu River. Among the inscriptions on the stele was a line from the year of Sinmyo, 391 A.D. According to Hong, in his book, "The Japanese interpreted the line of inscription in the following fashion: 'Paekche and Silla had been the subject of Koguryo and paid tribute to Koguryo. Since the year of Sinmyo (or in the year of Sinmyo), however, the Wa came (and) crossed over the sea, (and) conquered Paekche...Silla, (and) thereby made (them Wa's) subject.'"[19] As related in the NHK-G broadcast, Japanese scholars had believed that the Wa must have had a strong base in southern Korea to launch their successful assaults against two of the three Korean kingdoms and defend against a third. However, the explanation was offered that the Sinmyo line cut two ways and could be read in this way: The Wa came and therefore the King of Koguryo crossed the Yellow Sea to defeat Paekche and Silla and make them his subjects. Another source of equivocal evidence noted by Lee was the seven-branched sword. The program presented the vagaries in the reading of the sword's inscription. It was indicated that one interpretation had Paekche presenting the sword in homage to Wa, thereby, together with the stele, offering implicit confirmation of the existence of a Japanese Mimana Government, while a second had the King of Paekche bestowing the sword on Wa, its vassal state. The commentator concluded that it was impossible to say whether Mimana

Japanese Government existed on the basis of these two sources. Aside from the quandaries of interpretation, he referred to the virtual indecipherability of some of the characters of these time-worn inscriptions.

Having disposed of previous archaeological discoveries, especially those left unchallenged in the NHK-E program, the "Riddle" finally turned to what could be resolved from the Taesung finds. And it was as if Wonyong Kim who had stressed Kaya power in the earlier broadcast had ghost written the resolution. The viewer learned that it would have been difficult for a Mimana Japanese Government to have thrived within the womb of Kaya since Taesung had resurrected what appeared to be the burial remains of a Kaya royal family who enjoyed the prerogatives of power, such as material luxuries, and had a well-armed military force at its disposal. Aside from this evidence of a great power in place, Taesung, according to the narrative, revealed the existence of a distinctive cultural entity rather than a Japanese import. The viewer was informed about mokkakubo-style graves within the context of such structures being found in Korea a lot but not in Japan. No suggestion was given to cause any entertainment of Egami-style speculations on nomads from the steppe. In addition, instead of making a great ado about an ordos kettle, reference was made to pottery of a type never fired in Japan. At one point in the program, the laboratory of a Japanese steelmaker was visited and iron bars from Taesung of the 3rd century and iron products from 5th and 6th century Kyushu were analyzed. The laboratory found that the composition of the samples was similar and that the Japanese products, e.g., farm tools and weapons, were made from Kaya materials. Consequentially, the program set forth the observation that instead of having a colony in Korea, Japan received materials, products and many kinds of techniques from Kaya. It was noted that even tsutsugatadoki was imported, the logic on export-import in this case being based on the concentration of the find at Taesung, i.e., 16 items, whereas in Japan only 2 or 3 examples had ever been found at one site. A popular writer, Jugo Koroiwa, who appeared on the program spoke about the Kaya-Kyushu area as if it was what would be considered today to be a borderless society. He explained that the area in question was a garden with people moving freely back and forth and therefore, there was no need for a Wa base, such as Mimana Japanese Government. The archaeologist Tadashi Nishitani, of Kyushu University, who also was interviewed, remarked that academic thinking tended to place the unification of the Japanese state in the 4th century, but, in view of the lack of substantiation of a colonial landmark, maybe unification didn't take place until the 6th century.

With this March 1991 historical variety program, media focus on Taesung per se dimmed, but only momentarily. Toward the end of 1991, evidence of the undiminished strength of Japanese Historical Korea in the media's approach to Kaya was once again forthcoming. In addition, confirmation could also be found at the time that the media was disposed to integrate perhaps not the substance of the Kaya finds, but certain images associated with them to bolster Japanese Mythical Korea. The structure of the mythical paradigm made it quite easy for the media to make the addition or association since extensive explanations were not required, symbolic forms from the excavations rather than historical context being sufficient for the presentation. The popularity and prestige of a nomadic origins permitting the media to edit out ethnic Kaya and transform history.

However, when Kaya was "the lead" in the media in the winter/spring of 1991-1992, there was no origins' linkage and treatment remained cultural, not racial. On December 8, *Asahi Shimbun* reported on the excavation of the biggest Kaya tomb group ever excavated.[20] According to the article, two-hundred and six graves had been unearthed, including a king's class grave, from a tomb group located in Yangdong village in Kimhae County and the expectation was that the number would rise. The report noted that the archaeological team which had begun its investigation in November of 1990 had uncovered six different grave systems depending on the period of construction and more than a thousand artifacts – ironware, bronzeware, necklaces, beads and earthenware – dating from the 1st to the 4th century. The article was emphatic in its observations which revealed a close linkage between Kaya and Wa culture. It was related that nine Chinese-type bronze mirrors – the first time that so many had been excavated together in Korea – had been found in the king's class grave. This find consisted of two Hankyong and seven Pangjekyong. The Hankyong are mirrors made in Han China; the Pangjekyong are modeled after the Hankyong. This grave measured five meters and was late 2nd century. Also, in view of the discovery of a sword and beads, *Asahi Shimbun* reported that the three symbols of power ("sanshu no jingi" within the Japanese emperor system) were present and therefore the assumption was high among the excavators that royalty was buried there. The article even appeared with a picture of these three *Nihon Shoki* symbols. Among the finds from the other graves, according to the newspaper, were an 80-cm bronze spearhead and an iron sword with a handle with bells, artifacts familiar to Japanese archaeology. Byonsam Han, head of Korea's National Central Museum, was cited as saying that this cultural treasure store would strongly support the position that Kaya was a powerful state, which had iron and a stratified society and whose existence coincided with the Japanese Yayoi-Kofun periods.

Of the finds, the bronze mirrors received special attention, Han providing this observation: "Careful study has to be undertaken in the future in order to arrive at a result on whether the source of the Japanese bronze mirror was Kaya." This response was echoed by the Japanese archaeologist Koichi Kondo, of Yamaguchi University, in the article. He was quoted as saying that although bronze mirrors had been excavated before in Korea, he was surprised that so many (ten in all) had been found at one time and that among them were Hankyong mirrors, a point in common with northern Kyushu in the Yayoi period. He continued: "Because of this excavation, it will be revealed whether the root of the bronze mirror is Korea or Japan. But further study is required."[21]

On January 5, Kaya made front page news in the *Asahi Shimbun*, but not in terms of the uncovering of a new treasure trove of artifacts. A related article also appeared inside the paper. An exhibition on Kaya at the Japanese National Museum in Tokyo scheduled for June 30 to August 9 was heralded by the editors as one of the two main cultural events of 1992 in

Japan in a survey of the top attractions. It was noted that the exhibition would also travel to Kyoto and Fukuoka. The *Asahi Shimbun* underlined the significance of the exhibition by explaining that recent excavations had brought to light objects never thought to exist before in southeastern Korea as well as products similar to wares of northern Kyushu and Yamato, proving that Japan had an active commercial relationship with Kaya in the Yayoi-Kofun period. The Kaya event was headlined "Kaya Culture Exhibition: Root of Japanese Ironware."[22]

With this announcement, Kaya excavations debuted as a feature story within the *Asahi Shimbun* and the newspaper set out to develop Kaya Kingdom as a new source of cultural information for resolving the mystery of Japan's 4th and 5th centuries.[23] Two events in March sponsored by *Asahi Shimbun* were widely covered within the pages of the newspaper. One was heralded as the first time that information had been gathered in Korea by a foreign-press helicopter and referred to an aerial survey of the Kaya ruins. Headlined as tracing ancient intercourse between Japan and Korea from the air, this feature story received front page, color photo (of Taesung) coverage in the March 5th morning edition. On board for this historical flight was a group of Korean and Japanese archaeologists. A follow-up story on the next day proclaimed that the mystery of Kaya was in the process of being resolved. Tadashi Nishitani, who had been aboard the helicopter, explained that "Phantom Kaya" had been spotted. The article went on and indicated that this area which is closest to Japan is undergoing a development rush and consequently an archaeological excavation boom is taking place. With a continuous flood of new finds, the article foresaw the rewriting of the closeness of the relationship between ancient Japan and Korea. The evening edition of March 19 presented a 3/4 page, color photo spread from the air of the Kaya ruins and of the infrastructure development taking place in the vicinity of the excavations. The text underlined the potential for even greater archaeological news in the near future.[24] The aerial expedition was followed by a conference on Kaya and the proceedings were encapsuled in a two-page spread in the evening paper of March 16.[25] The conference of Korean and

Japanese scholars included the leaders of the major archaeological expeditions, Kyungcheol Shin (Taesung), Yongche Cho (Okchon) and Hyotaek Lim (Yangdong) as well as Byonsam Han. According to the newspaper's summary and accompanying headlines, the initial focus of discussion was on how to interpret the significance of the rise of mokkakubo culture in the 4th to 5th centuries in the Kaya area. Cho, in his comments, explained that the Okchon area located to the north and west of Yangdong and Taesung harbored a powerful military state of the Kaya confederation, Tara, whose economic strength rested on trade and iron production. He asserted that Tara enjoyed a special relationship with Koguryo and the development of mokkakubo culture with its cache of crowns, armor, ring-pommeled swords, helmets, horse masks (six in all) and horse-trappings was indicative of the depth of this association. According to Han, in his interjected observation, the only conclusion possible on the basis of the excavated evidence was that horseriding customs, not horseriding warriors, came to Tara. But, as he himself noted, Okchon contained many important ruins from the late 4th to 5th century.

Shin took a very different point of view on the basis of Taesung dates: Large mokkakubo were present in the late 3rd century and horseriding-related artifacts could be traced back to as early as the beginning of the 4th century. He did not disagree with Cho on the power of Tara, although he did add his idea that the basic economy of Kaya was agricultural, not maritime, based upon the relative lack of fishing equipment excavated. Definitely, *Gekkan Asahi* could not have supported Egami's second article with a Shin footnote. However, his period of perspective led him to the conclusion that the appearance of mokkakubo culture in its most fundamental form in the late 3rd century marked the establishment of Kaya Kingdom and the vanquishment of all rival powers in the area. He assumed that the flow of north Asian type culture to southeastern Korea emanated from Manchuria and passed down the east coast of the peninsula. The nature of the flow was not mentioned at this time, although Shin would intimate at a subsequent meeting in Tokyo that such a flow might have involved the arrival of a new group of people in the area.

Han took exception to Shin's position, holding that fundamental elements of mokkakubo culture were generated as a result of the influence of the Chinese military commandery of Lolang. Shin countered, however, that although he could concede the ordos-style kettle as a possible Lolang cultural import, he was emphatic on the point that Lolang didn't have the custom of junsō or armor for horseriding. For Shin, Lolang was the impossible route. For Han, mokkakubo culture scholars were either Lolang or Koguryo oriented, a north Asian source being quite a hypothetical jump. Han thought Shin's position strange, maintaining that the roots of Kaya lay more in the earlier sociopolitical state of southeastern Korea. He admonished Shin, stating that it was impossible to punctuate the period and that he had better stop doing just that. The impact of Han's position was strengthened within the context of the *Asahi Shimbun* article since the editor introduced the possibility of a "Lolang route" with a bold, large-print, lead-in heading.

The next focus of discussion concerned what could be learned about ancient Japan from the new discoveries. At this point, Shin parted whatever company one might have thought he was keeping with Japanese horserider theory enthusiasts, especially in light of his *Gekkan Asahi* piece. As indicated earlier, it would be very difficult to pursue a Japanese racially oriented paradigm within the media in view of the strong cultural concerns coming out of Korea. He explained that the royal family which established Taesung entered into relations with Kinki from late 3rd to 4th century. As for the evidence of such a relationship, he referred to the finds of tsutsugatadoki, tomoegatadōki and jasper arrows. He also held that stone cylinders ("hekigyokujō") for the top of a ritual wooden wand had been found mainly in Kinki. In all, he favored the idea that the Kaya area switched its intercourse with ancient Japan from northern Kyushu to Kinki in this period. At this point, the moderator tried to move Shin to make some comment on the formation of Yamataikoku. His response was quite emotional: "Yamataikoku is a Japanese problem. We have nothing to do with that!"

Specifically, Egami's theory was mentioned at the conference within the context of the Mimana question, but it was brushed aside quite quickly. Han dismissed the notion as without merit and Nishitani agreed that only horseriding customs came to Japan. The last major topic of discussion featured in the article concerned the Mimana issue. As expected, the Korean scholars were very emphatic on the point that there was no basis for Mimana Japanese Government in the Korean archaeological record. Shin put it this way: He referred to the difference in the grave systems, mokkakubo vs. key-shaped tombs. The fact that similar things were found in these grave systems, in his opinion, didn't prove Mimana Japanese Government was in place since Kaya was rich in iron and an international kingdom with multilateral relations. He reiterated that the most important cultural influence was not Japanese, but north Asian.

The second main event of March was an Asahi Shimbun sponsored symposium in Tokyo on Kaya which was co-sponsored by All Nippon Airways with the cooperation of NHK and the Cultural Affairs Agency. The two-day conference of March 14 and 15 was presented as a 3/4-page article on March 31. Although Shin was the only Korean scholar on the panel, the topics of discussion were the same as in the Korean meeting and the issues, which received attention, also overlapped. The article itself was entitled "Gigantic Tombs and Kaya Culture: Seeking to Fill in the Blank 4th and 5th Centuries."[26]

Indubitably, one could see that horserider theory enthusiasts, such as Okuno, would not have been pleased with the manner in which Kaya rose to distinction within the pages of the *Asahi Shimbun*. Moreover, the scheduled exhibition in June at the National Museum in Tokyo did not hold out much hope for any change in media treatment since the display was based on a Korean National Central Museum event held in the summer of 1991 in Seoul.[27] One could hardly see an exhibition based on a purely cultural concept at Egami's Ancient Orient Museum. Interestingly enough, in 1991, the Ancient Orient hosted an exhibition of "The Treasures of Nomadic Tribes in South Russia," focusing on the nomadic civilizations of the steppe region extending north of the Caucasus Mountains to the Black Sea from the 8th century B.C. to the 13th century A.D., including the ancient kingdom of Scythia and its successor, the Sarmatian realm. In a large advertisement in the English-language *Asahi Evening News* for the exhibition, Egami's photo appeared beside a quote reminiscent of earlier pronouncements intended to define Japanese character on the basis of a kiba minzoku cutout: "Japanese culture contains two elements – the culture of the mounted nomadic tribes and the culture of the farming tribes. The capacity to comprehend foreign cultures and harmony with nature – the role that these special characteristics can play in the international society is big."[28] Egami apparently encountered no difficulty in making the horserider theory a part of Japan's global society to appeal to the international readership of this English-language daily. But then again, the Huns and the Mongols were anything but passive in their capacity to comprehend or should we say apprehend foreign people and cultures.

Nevertheless, the winter/spring of 1991-1992 did find the media venturing into Egami country, if not in a highly theoretical way, at least in a manner which fit into the earlier indicated Japanese Mythical Korea approach. Horseriding invaders of Japan were not to be so easily vanquished from their Korean stepping stone. Although these media events, which were broadcast at the end of November on NTV, were the only pertinent instance of a Second Korea operative within the Kaya zone since the unveiling of Taesung, there is every reason to believe that more will follow. Although the cultural aspect of Japanese-Kaya relations during the Yayoi-Kofun period will continue to be portrayed by the media in increasing detail, the other Kaya will appear from time to time as part of the creative letting go of the arrow of Japanese origins. To understand the "why" behind such an expectation, it is necessary to realize that the steppe nomads of ancient times not only are the prime motor of the modernized mythical engine of origins but also are the phantoms of history. Nomadic tribes appear suddenly in the pages of history as political entities with distinct ethnic identities and disappear almost as mysteriously in case after case, e.g., Scythians,

Sarmatians, Huns and Hsiung-nu, after being vanquished by a superior enemy. A cloud of anonymity also lingers over their days in power. The archaeologist Roger Cribb in his book, *Nomads in Archeology*, points out that it's difficult for the archaeologist to pin nomadic people down historically since they are highly mobile, have no fixed assets and are always seeking military advantage.[29]

The ancient nomads were the people of the old grassland roads of some 6,000 miles. They occupied a steppe belt, encompassing a broad land route of gentle relief with intermontane corridors stretching from north of the Black Sea to the plains of Manchuria. The steppe was the preeminent means of long-distance communication for people, cultural innovations and goods across this landlocked region of Eurasia.[30] The nomads moved along the steppe with their herds – horned cattle, camels, sheep, goats or horses. Their economies were self-sufficient, their livestock providing them with their basic necessities, but movement was imperative to prevent overgrazing. They were people, according to the Chinese stereotype, who followed the grass and the water. But they also possessed the potential to develop a powerful political unit centering on the era's most formidable weapon, which was also a very valuable item of trade, i.e., the horse.[31] In comparing the steppe-belt people with the fishermen, hunters and reindeer breeders of the adjacent taiga and tundra zones, the Altaic studies scholar, Denis Sinor, writes:

> But, unlike the inhabitants of the tundra or the taiga, the nomads could congregate with great speed and important masses of men and beasts could stay together for relatively long periods of time. In other words, the population-carrying capacity of the steppe, within a fixed area, is superior to that of either the tundra or the forest. The environment could and did allow the creation of strongly centralized states and was able to maintain such a political superstructure for as long as the community could complement its basic production with commodities obtained from other, mostly agricultural regions.[32]

It was the sheer number of horses possessed by the nomadic state's cavalry force which gave it such a hold over the bordering agricultural economies and allowed it to overpower the defenses of civilization and carry away booty to keep the state whole and intact under the leadership of an elite grouping. In many instances, the threat of force was all that was necessary to exact the booty, among which were the highly evaluated goods of textiles, craft products, tea and grain as tribute. The horse was also a negotiable commodity of great importance in those days given the agricultural communities' need to defend against nomadic incursions and therefore the nomadic power could often obtain what it wanted through trade.[33] One of the major military innovations of ancient times, one which would determine the nature of warfare for centuries to come, was the saddle and its accouterments. These trappings made the horse a supercharged vehicle of swordsmanship and archery.[34] The putting of saddle equipment on the horse was the value-added factor which increased the worth and saleability of this livestock.

Nomadic mobility made national borders superfluous and the cultural tracks of a powerful phantom were widely dispersed. Consequently, the archaeologist and historian are confronted not only with dilemmas of appearance and disappearance, but also of presence. In truth, the dilemma of presence when it touches upon the other two dilemmas loses its distinctiveness and issues driven by mobility become omnipresent. The archaeologist is left to determine whether antiquity's clues of trespass represent evidence of the phantom in place, or cultural assimilation, or imitation by a different ethnic people, pastoral or sedentary. The Russian scholar of Inner Asia, A. I. Melyukova, in writing about the Scythians who inhabited the Central-Eurasian steppes, the north Black Sea area, from the end of the 7th century B.C. to the 4th century B.C., pays particular attention to all three dilemmas. Firstly, on the appearance of the Scythians, Melyukova indicates that the most important work, Herodotus' *The Histories* of the 5th century B.C., stresses the unity of the whole Scythian world bordering the Black Sea and extending from the Don to the Danube Rivers. However, she relates that the literature of antiquity, which has another story to tell, puts the Scythians in the beginning in Eastern Europe and Asia as

well as in their usual place.[35]   But then again, there is the historical
information which places two tribes in the Black Sea zone in the 9th-8th
centuries B.C., the Scythians and the Cimmerians, On this matter, she
maintains: "The most probable explanation for this is that the Cimmerians
and Scythians were kindred people, indistinguishable in origins and culture.
Many archaeologists, also leading authorities on the Iranian languages,
nowadays adhere to this point of view."[36] Secondly, on the exact extent of
Scythian power, this Russian specialist finds Herodotus' geographical data
lacking and the written record and archaeological data difficult to reconcile.
She makes mention of the problem of identifying bordering agricultural
tribes as Scythians or Slavs.[37] Thirdly, on the subject of where did they go,
Melyukova is also skeptical about how much could be said for a Slavic cloak
made from Scythian material. She offers the following in this respect:

> All contemporary historians, archaeologists and linguists are
> agreed that since the Scythian and Sarmatian tribes were of the
> Iranian linguistic group neither could have played a direct role
> in the ethnogenesis of the Slavic tribes that, in the second half
> of the first millennium A.D., settled in the lands of Eastern
> Europe, which include the north Black Sea area. At the same
> time, in the culture and especially in the art of the Slavic
> people, right up to the Middle Ages, the preservation of some
> traditions of Scythian and Sarmatian culture can be observed.
> Reminders of the art of the Scythian animal style and of
> Sarmatian zoomorphic art survive, especially in the art of
> ancient Rus.[38]

Whereas nomadic movements create dilemmas of analytical interest
for scholars, they also provide fuel for popular interest of the sort of whether
a group came this far or passed this way. A kind of unidentified riding object
mystery unfolds. There is no need for the image maker to enter into an
analysis of cultural developments and relationships if motion dominates the
scene. All that is necessary is to fasten onto one or more signs or symbols to
catch a glimpse of the phantom riding by. The Second Korea derives its
integrity within the modernized mythical paradigm of the Japanese origins
because of the barbaric essence of the paradigm. Sinor divides the Eurasian
expanse into civilized and barbaric cultures, the nomadic being the

progenitors of the latter. He writes that the barbarian was as free as the wind from rules based on abstract standards and since he was always being pushed forward by an insatiable greed, he possessed no proper place in the universe.[39] With this distinction in mind, the ethnogenesis of the Second Korea within the mythical paradigm is in keeping with the essential character of the paradigm, being unburdened with the details associated with civilized societies. It really doesn't even need the continuing support of an intellectualizing Egami.

More to the point is an NHK-G program broadcast in November just prior to the first Second-Korea-related show. This special appeared in the 9 to 10 PM slot on Japan's national holiday, Culture Day, and was entitled "The Riddle of Kiba Minzoku," with the subtitle "The Excavation of a Scythian Tomb." The production chronicled a Russian-led international expedition on an excavation of a king's class Scythian tomb on the grasslands within the Altai Mountains. The Russian archaeologist leading the expedition commented that the reason for excavating here was the possibility of finding in such an inaccessible place a mokkakubo grave which had not been stripped by grave robbers. However, the artifacts to be discovered were only one part of the drama, the other part being centered on the mobility of the phantom and on the possibility of nomadic people, not unlike the Scythians, trekking to Japan.

At the beginning of the program, the viewer learned that the area bounding Mongolia and China was 4,000 kilometers away from the Black Sea where the kingdom of Scythia was located. Later on, a map depicting a Scythian dominated grassland trade road extending from the Black Sea across to Manchuria, with Scythian commanderies, such as the one in the Altai, occupying strategic locations along the route was explained. The drama of the expedition was heightened by the possibility of uncovering another frozen tomb in the area. The first frozen mokkakubo, which was excavated in the late 1940s and dated 5th to 4th century B.C., revealed an amazingly preserved human specimen and a horse. Even clothing was recovered. The museum housing these finds was visited during the program and the narrator related that the body because of its high nose was judged to be Indo-European and the castrated horse because of its size was considered to be a West Asian breed. Since the head of the dead horserider rested in the East and he was buried with his horse, which in the Bronze Age was believed to be the incarnation of the sun, it was indicated that the interment accorded with the Scythian sun cult. As for the revelation of a trading connection, silk work from China and Persian tapestry were televised.

However, the excavation did not meet the expectations of either the archaeological or NHK production team. The tomb had not been bitten by the frost and therefore the natural world could not be brought to light once again. But even more disappointing was the discovery that grave robbers had already discovered the place and even the usual cache of precious Scythian gold objects would not be retrieved. Yet, the archaeologists could take comfort in the finding of an artifact which confirmed at least the tomb to be a Scythian one and NHK was heartened to be left with a symbol with which to develop a climactic conclusion.

The artifact/symbol in this case was a gold griffin. The program unraveled case after case in which this imaginary, winged creature which, according to Herodotus, was a Scythian sacred animal thought to protect gold from theft, became a common motif among Mesopotamians, Persians, Afghans, Turks and Greeks. The gold griffin became evidence of the wide-ranging exploits of the Scythian cavalry. It was maintained that even China's fantastic horse with feathered wings was a modified griffin. Where were all these griffins leading? Of course, Japan! Egami, who had appeared earlier in the broadcast, at the site of the excavation, to proclaim that since he proposed his horserider theory, it had been proven time and time again, reappeared to offer his agreement with the production's idea that the origin of the Japanese kirin was the Scythian griffin. Once again, the sign of the phantom had revealed itself. One could ruminate at the time on whether kirin and griffin were really artistic cousins or whether the Japanese couldn't have derived the kirin motif from China via Koguryo where such a motif was known. One might even consider the pertinence of Melyukova's analysis of

Slavic origins, if one had access at the time of the broadcast to the book in which it appeared. Yet, all this is very intellectual. For most of the audience, the griffin-kirin similarity would conjure up the coming of the phantom as hoped for by the production. The program offered the viewer no reason to challenge this image since, from the producer's perspective, this idea was popularly appealing and quite dramatic.

It is also not startling to find Japanese television portraying the Mongols of Chinggis Khan's time (ca. 1167-1227) in the same manner as the Scythians, as the phantoms of history, despite their rather recent exploits. Of course, Chinggis Khan's Mongols went on to establish a great Eurasian empire which included a Chinese dynasty and therefore, the Mongol horde is quite a well documented phenomenon in world history. Also, there is the present state of Mongolia or for that matter, the Buryat Mongols. The ethnic Mongols didn't exactly disappear. But the nomadic tradition of Chinggis Khan's Mongols provides sufficient occasion for an envisioning of the phantomlike character of a people. A two-hour special on NTV on November 28, 1991, which aired in the 9 to 11 PM slot, took the viewer on a journey to modern Mongolia with the latest in high-tech exploration equipment to search for the tomb of Chinggis Khan himself. Perhaps, the Mongols are still with us today, but the monument to this great leader has yet to be found, perhaps hidden forever by a people who sought security for the dead and their treasures. It was within the portrayal of this undertaking that the Kaya excavations appeared for the third time on television in 1991 and for the first time in the guise of the Second Korea model. The program's title should have been at least for the benefit of this chapter not "The Search for the Tomb of Chinggis Khan" but "The Search for the Nomad in Asia." In any event, this story of detection concerning Chinggis Khan was complemented by a secondary theme concerning Egami's effort of some 50 years to secure proof for his horserider theory. As a matter of fact, the titular leader of the NTV search party was none other than Egami himself.

At the beginning of this archaeological journey to the Mongolian grasslands, the production detoured for a while to follow Egami and an actor-companion through the streets of Beijing. The narrator explained that Beijing was Egami's youth, the place where he had studied ancient Asian history and archaeology. The viewer was told that this sprightly 85-year-old walked around in a place just like the one seen here today and during his early wanderings, his thoughts coalesced and kiba minzoku theory was born. At this point, the scene suddenly shifted from Egami and Beijing to a horse racing across snow-covered grasslands and then a magazine titled *Minzokugaku no Kenkyu* (Studies in Ethnology) filled the screen. According to the voiceover, 43 years ago this issue of the magazine created a big sensation because within its pages – the pages of the magazine being turned before the camera to the correct place – Egami, at the age of 42, first introduced his horserider theory. Proclaimed as being a really original and creative theory, Egami's approach was also heralded by the broadcast as breaking the taboo which pre-1945 history could not break. The magazine visual was followed by a map with the usual Northeast Asian red arrow pointing in the direction of Japan from Korea, the narrator relating that a group of kiba minzoku in the years before Christ began to move slowly toward Japan.

The next stop for the camera's eye was Pusan port and the Pusan tomb group, the production using a more scenic setting than offered by the Taesung ruins which Egami had found so supportive of his theory. The pronouncement was that this excavation, which had been proceeding for a few years, had finally – actually some time ago – delivered the evidence proving kiba minzoku theory. The evidence in question flashed across the screen for only a few seconds and consisted of a comparison of stills of the Pusan and Wakayama horse helmets. The only explanation deemed necessary to substantiate the authoritativeness of Egami's "gigantic hypothesis" was that the two helmets were very similar. A map and a horse helmet? A map and a griffin would have sufficed just as well, if such a gold ornament had been found. In fact, a map and any aspect of steppe horseriding culture would appear to be all that is required to interpolate the mythical paradigm into a media presentation focusing on nomadic movements and ancient Japan. A lengthy exposé which would entail historical relationships would appear to be unnecessary for imaging a Second Korea within such a scenario since this entity is supportive rather than substantive and exists within a split second of many minutes devoted to steppe history and culture.

A disposition on the part of the media to de-chronologize Korea and transport it into timelessness together with the Phantom might very well derive from Egami's rendition of his horserider theory. In his writings and commentaries, Egami tends to provide much more information on the nomadic system of the steppe than on the ethnicity of his horseriders. In discussing Egami's 1967 book, Ledyard remarked that "fully half of *Kiba minzoku kokka* is devoted to a description of the historical nomadic confederations that have periodically arisen in central Asia to batter and sometimes engulf the classical centers of civilization."[40] In reading or listening to Egami, one is left with the impression that the Phantom is a conglomerate of periods and tribes, Scythians, Sarmatians, Mongols, etc., rather than a specific Northeast Asian people although he does vaguely identify such a group (a group related to the Puyo people who emerged in the Manchurian steppe around 400 B.C.).[41] In a NTV "World Special" entitled "Birth of Japan" for National Foundation Day on February 11, 1992, which was aired from 4:30 to 6:00 and targeted children rather than adults, the media and Egami performed in unison on a presentation of his theory. Interspersed with Egami's comments from the Ancient Orient Museum was a cartoon which traced the trials and tribulations of a stylized "kappa" (an imp-like character in old Japanese folk tales) family from Yayoi to horseriding days. Egami referred in one sentence to the ethnicity of the horseriders who came to Japan and then proceeded to talk at length about the history and traditions of the steppe. The audience learned little more than the name of the invaders, but, as for the nomadic system, Egami waxed eloquently on and on, explaining how adept the nomadic system is in integrating people with diverse cultures, languages and religions into a centralized unit. He spoke about the steppe nomads as being liberal and international. In the 1990s, apparently, Egami discovered the popular Japanese 1980s' catchword of international rather than the more up-to-date catchword of global. Instead of emphasizing the genetic-culture attributes of kiba minzoku which made Japanese good businessmen and politicians as he had in the past, Egami offered a new edition of Japanese kiba minzoku identity, the international person. Once again, however, Egami proclaimed that kiba-minzoku-type people are good at adapting to a variety of situations and taming other people. Also, in this program, an aerial view of the 5th century Ikeno-ue tomb group in Fukuoka Prefecture, a map pinpointing Kaya, and pottery with pedestals from Ikeno-ue and Kaya were shown in split-second succession. The point was made that kiba minzoku came to Fukuoka from Kaya. Kiba-minzoku-style weapons, horse-trappings and gold earrings from Ikeno-ue were also presented to support this line of invasion. None of the recent Kaya excavations were shown nor was the "missing link" in Egami's theory discussed, although the program had been subtitled as the "new" horserider theory. The point had been made. In this broadcast, at least, Taesung, etc., was irrelevant. In any event, Kaya received only passing notice. The Phantom dominated the story and Kaya appeared within the Second Korea construct, peaking through a mass of detail about the nomadic system. A buried lead; a buried history!

Although portrayals of both Japan historical Korea and Japan mythical Korea exist in Japanese media presentations of the 4th and 5th centuries, the former dominates the media's story of the development of events while the latter exists within the womb of nomadism. Second Korea's association with the phantom of history allows the media to remove Kaya artifacts from their historical context and relate them symbolically to the powerful image of an invasion from northeast Asia in spite of the strong presence of historical Korea. Moreover, although Second Korea exists in the 4th and 5th centuries, it is not of these centuries particularly. Symbols of culture rather than culture itself prevail within Japan mythical Korea. Second Korea is as timeless as the phantom. The media's imaging of Scythian nomads, a gold griffin and Egami's horseriding invaders had as little to do with chronological time as horseriding invaders and Yoshinogari. Horseriders' ride persistently through Japan-time according to the tenets of the modernizing myth and the needs of the consumer.

CONCLUSION

The Media's Message

The myth of Japanese origins occupies a space in time which covers a period of some eight centuries, extending from the 3rd century B.C. to the 5th century A.D. Within these contours, information undergoes transformation and symbolization according to the parameters of the mythical paradigm. The modernizing instrument of the traditional myth is the mass media, which updates mythical images to attract a mass market for its publications or programs. The continual chronological and contextual distortions in media presentations to construct a set of origins' images for mass consumption reveals the extent and intensity with which the masses identify with the elevated consciousness of being inherent in the message. In this sense, the media is a captive of the myth and of mass culture which highly evaluates the mythical format. For the average individual, the vision of racial uniqueness which blends socio-political and biological evaluations is a highly meaningful and rational one, enabling the transcendence of the realities and limitations of personal history and the recovery of a highly satisfying and socially rewarding sacred time.

The mythical paradigm's format consists of three layers: the ancient Japanese chronicles, the Chinese record and the media-linked modernizing message. The foundation layer of the *Kojiki* and *Nihon Shoki* offers a miraculous period of ancestral gods who overcome a myriad of obstacles, challenge natural and superhuman forces and restore order and stability to the universe of the god-children. Complementing the foundation layer is the *Wei Chronicle*, a 3rd century A.D. Chinese dynastic record which provides an historical instrument for viewing and reviewing the places and events within the basic paradigm. Through textual analysis of the meanings inherent in these writings, the myth of the unique origins of the Japanese people is enlivened and reenacted for popular consumption. Nevertheless, in a world filled with scientific and social scientific values, ancient traditions of descent have to be reformed with archaeological, anthropological and biological images to sustain credibility and interest within a modern-day educated population. The creative instrumentality of the media is essential for neutralizing the disparities within traditional and modern contexts, for promoting innovative formulas of myth to meet social demand within a world of affluence and fashion. Through media renovation, the legend of racial uniqueness is imaginatively retold, redistributed and relived for "everyman."

Reform necessitates the insulation of the mythical format to prevent dissonant patterns from disturbing the tranquility resonant within the house of myth or the mythical paradigm. This is reflected in the media's disposition to separate Western from Japanese concerns on the evolutionary tides of humankind. The media creates time zones for the categorical treatment of issues and events which are calibrated according to two clocks. Certain developments which fall within the boundaries of public curiosity are presented by the media within a Western-time standard. Others pass into the Japan-time realm of high-profile, national identity idolizations. Educational circles in Japan generate origins' structures which seek to integrate the two time zones to the detriment of the credibility and authoritativeness of the mythical paradigm. Media coverage of their performances, however, reveals the impermeability and durability of the paradigm within mass culture in that spawned concepts of integration are locked out. The outcome would appear to be the same whether the dissonant, Western-oriented pattern tries to enter the house of myth through the door of multi-regional evolution or the window of out-of-Africa theory. The media's view from within the house of myth remains from the inside looking out. There is no need for the media to rearrange the interior of the house. In this respect, there is the case of *Newton* magazine which utilized the same interiors for both its mainstream anthropological and revolutionary mitochondrial DNA stories on the search for modern man.

Within the framework of this distortional insulation, information undergoes transformation and symbolization. In 1989, Yoshinogari, a 3rd century excavated ruins, became a top performer within the mass media. The features of this kangō shūraku were compared to the description of the queendom of Yamatai recorded in the *Wei Chronicle*. The entrance of Yoshinogari into the media's retelling of mythohistory uprooted the excavated evidence from its place in history, setting it down whenever, wherever and in whatever form mythical dictates warranted to fulfill a modernized rendition of Japanese origins. The patterns of conformity rested within the following continuum: (1) an invasion of a new population from the continent to Japan in the Yayoi period and ensuing conflict; (2) the dominance of this population and the establishment of a consolidated and unified kingdom. The evidence of Yoshinogari was transformed by the media to integrate this popular archaeological find into either end of the continuum. Yoshinogari was portrayed as representing invasion-conflict or consolidation-unification and the excavated findings were deposited for discovery in both the 2nd and 3rd centuries depending on the needs of the dramatization. A touch of timelessness was added to the transformation as the media introduced images associated with periods existing outside of the Wei record to focus on the nature of the invasion and the constitution of the invaders. In fact, vital signs of the rise of Yamatai at Yoshinogari, such as a gigantic tomb fit for a queen, were much earlier than the period chronicled in the Wei record. From the watchtowers of Yoshinogari, the media looked out upon the conquest of a new race which would destroy or absorb the local population and give birth to the Japanese people. This new race was associated not only with homogeneity but also with values of importance for national identity, e.g., dominance, aggressiveness, flexibility and ingenuity, and with a vision of an heroic ancestry. The house of myth in which the media and Yoshinogari found themselves consisted of two separate but connected rooms and all the new props had to match the decor of one or the other. Aside from the distortion of time and the nature of events, discontinuity in historical development was an inherent bias in media productions. By 1990, the media had processed Yoshinogari so thoroughly through the mythical paradigm that Yoshinogari itself had become firmly associated with mythohistory. As a result, the media could employ the view from the watchtowers as a symbolic liaison to appropriate other archaeological excavations for mythohistorical accounts, Yoshinogari thereby becoming an image to be evoked by the media to enhance credibility of a story.

But it was not just archaeology which was being coopted by the media to modernize the mythical paradigm. "Yoshinogari as evidence" had been blended with physical anthropology to dramatize the break between Jomon and Yayoi periods. Skeletal remains and computer simulations of population movements were presented to confirm a racial change in the population. "Yoshinogari as symbol" surfaced with climate studies, ecology and animal behavioral psychology. From this perspective, it is not surprising that the social/natural sciences could serve up its own idol for the media, a substantive as well as a symbolic performer. Perhaps, the thought of genetic markers of human immunoglobulin becoming the darling of TV origins' productions would appear somewhat unlikely. However, such was the case in the mid-1980s when Hideo Matsumoto, a doctor of legal medicine, associated the Buryat people of Lake Baikal with the Japanese race with his findings on Gm haplotype frequencies. The media enhanced the audience appeal of Gm by metamorphosing the dynamics of Matsumoto's theory into the simple expressiveness of a human face. Central to the modernizing mythical paradigm was the dispersal of nomadic, horseriding people who were courageous, energetic, adaptable to circumstances and invaders par excellence, people who were rooted in neither time nor place. The faces of the modern-day Buryat people were visions which, from the media's vantage point, added personality and depth to a characterization outlined in rather sterile scientific terms. The facial context coated the dating of Gm theory of 10,000 or 13,000 years ago and allowed it to be swallowed by the "Great Flexed Time" of Yayoi to Kofun without any dissonance whatsoever. Almost immediately, Gm became a symbol of the mythical play. Buryat people were creatively incorporated into a southern Mongoloid-northern Mongoloid pattern of confrontation. Nonhorseriding, nonphysical anthropological aligned concepts of Matsumoto were selectively disregarded or overwhelmed with disassociation imagery or reasoning through editing, arrangement and direction. Through the workings of television, Matsumoto's bearing on Japanese racial origins interfaced with that of Kazuro Hanihara who postulated an hypothesis on the human body and cold climate adaptation which effectively incised into a Yayoi calendar a new racial age compatible with the formatted telling of sacred events.

The media's performance in integrating Gm into a horserider parable parallels a broader preoccupation of infusing nomadic content and descriptions into appraisals of the conflict-invasion phase of the paradigm. Within nomadism lies the phantom of history – with mysterious appearances and disappearances or a masked vision which can move almost undetected through time. Nomadism allows the media to make room for a skeletal treatment of Korean reality of the 4th and 5th centuries in spite of a media agenda calling for an in-depth examination of Japan-Korea cultural relations in this period. This Second Korea, which is as phantomlike as the intruder who passes within its boundaries, co-exists with the more detailed depiction of Japan historical Korea. Moreover, "phantomization" of the invasion sequence permits the media to swoop down on Korean and Japanese archaeology and carry remains in symbolic form to a prior period to create a story of the coming of the horde more in conformity with the other patterns of the modernized mythical paradigm.

Images of exclusiveness within Japanese society are not purely cultural. The continual twisting of the pen and the gyration of the camera to highlight culturally compatible values of racial import reveals a bias within mass culture with much broader and less intellectual ramifications than those founded solely in nihonjinron philosophies. Since values of racial and cultural exclusiveness are so very much alike, it's difficult to differentiate the two and very easy to choose one over the other. As such, cultural exclusiveness would appear to be less instantaneously equated with bigotry than its racial cousin and therefore much more likely to appear in critical but gentleman-scholar-type evaluations of Japanese behavior. However, the pull of a made-for-myth past on the media and the masses reflects the perpetual need of Japanese society for a racial mirror of national identity. Japan remains in the post-war era a society of many persuasions, one of which is distinctly racial.

INTRODUCTION ENDNOTES

1.   Ross Mouer and Yoshio Sugimoto, *Images of Japanese Society* (London: Kegan Paul International, 1986), 21-22, 56.

2.   Yoshio Sugimoto and Ross Mouer, eds., *Constructs for Understanding Japan* (London: Kegan Paul International, 1989), 4-8.

3.   *Ibid.*, 21.

4.   *Asahi Evening News*, Oct. 24, 1986, Apr. 11, 1990. John Dower, *War Without Mercy* (Pantheon: New York, 1986), 315.

5.   *Asahi Evening News*, Apr. 11, 1990, Sept. 22, 1990.

6.   *Japan 1991 Marketing and Advertising Yearbook* (Tokyo: Dentsu, 1990), 327, 341-342.

7.   K. Goto, H. Hirahara, K. Oyama and M. Sata, *A History of Japanese Television Drama* (Tokyo: Japan Association of Television Broadcasting Art, 1991), 6, 9-10.

8.   Public Opinion Poll on Leisure and Travel, Prime Minister's Office, 1986, Foreign Press Center.

9.   Sugimoto and Mouer, eds., *Constructs for Understanding Japan*, 21-22.

10.   *Ibid.*, 22.

11.   *Ibid.*

12.   Stephen Molnar, *Human Variation: Races, Types and Ethnic Groups* (Englewood Cliffs, N.J.: Prentice-Hall, 1983), 16-17.

13.   Kazuro Hanihara, "The Origin of the Japanese in Relation to Other Ethnic Groups in East Asia," in *Windows on the Japanese Past: Studies in Archaeology and Prehistory*, ed. by Richard Pearson (Ann Arbor: Center for Japanese Studies, University of Michigan, 1986), 76.

14.   Molnar, *op. cit.*, 131.

15.   Rebecca L. Cann, "DNA and Human Origins," *Annual Review of Anthropology*, XVII (1988), 137.

16.   *Ibid.*, 138.

17. Molnar, *op. cit.*, xvii, 21, 131.

18. *Ibid.*, 128-129.

19. Hanihara, *op. cit.*, 75.

20. "Jinshu to minzoku wo kangaeru," [Thinking about Race and Nation], *Mongoroido* [Mongoloid], No. 5 (summer 1990), 5.

21. *Ibid.*, 6.

CHAPTER I ENDNOTES

1.   Niles Eldredge and Ian Tattersall, *The Myths of Human Evolution* (New York: Columbia University Press, 1982), 1-3, 29-32. Roger Lewin, *Bones of Contention* (New York: Simon and Schuster, 1987), 302-303, 313.

2.   Eldredge and Tattersall, *op. cit.*, 2.

3.   *Ibid.*, 3. See how Gould answers the question of "Do species change by random molecular shifts or natural selection?" in Stephen Jay Gould, "Through a Lens Darkly," *Natural History* (Sept. 1989), 16-24.

4.   Christopher Wills, *The Wisdom of the Genes* (New York: Basic Books, 1989), 52, 74-96.

5.   Stephen Jay Gould, *The Mismeasure of Man* (New York: W. W. Norton, 1981), 24.

6.   *Ibid.*, 21-22.

7.   Michael H. Brown, *The Search for Eve* (New York: Harper and Row, 1990), 223.

8.   Gould, *The Mismeasure of Man*, 73-112.

9.   *New York Times*, Dec. 23, 1990.

10.   "The Search for Adam and Eve," *Newsweek* (Jan. 11, 1988), 47.

11.   *Ibid.*

12.   Brown, *op. cit.*, 215.

13.   Leszek Kolakowski, *The Presence of Myth* (Chicago: University of Chicago Press, 1989), 2.

14.   *Ibid.*, 1-8.

15.   Thomas Kuhn, *The Structure of Scientific Revolutions* (Chicago: University of Chicago Press, 1962), 24.

16.   Kolakowski, *op. cit.*, 3.

17.   Donald Johanson and James Shreeve, *Lucy's Child* (New York: William Morrow, 1989), 32.

18.   Wendell C. Beane and William G. Dotty, eds., *Myths, Rites, Symbols: A Mircea Eliade Reader*, I (New York: Harper and Row, 1976), 2. Ivan Strenski, *Four Theories of Myth in Twentieth-Century History* (London: MacMillan Press, 1987), 72.

19.   Mircea Elaide, *Myths, Dreams and Mysteries* (New York: Harper and Row, 1960), 16.

20.   Beane and Dotty, eds., *op. cit.*, 9.

21.   Eliade, *op. cit.*, 33.

22.   Beane and Dotty, eds., *op. cit.*, 10.

23.   *Ibid.*, 6.

24.   Biten Yasumoto, *Yamataikoku e no michi* [The Road to Yamatai Country], (Tokyo: Tokuma Bunko, 1990), 66. This book was originally published by PHP in 1983 under the title *Himiko to Yamataikoku* [Himiko and Yamatai Country]. Between 1989 and 1991, there were over fifteen published titles by Yasumoto on ancient Japan. There were titles such as "Did Himiko (Yamatai's queen) Speak Japanese?" Between 1976 and 1991, Yasumoto authored over 35 works in this field. He also found time to write books on psychology and persuasive writing skills.

25.   Masao Okuno, *Yamataikoku wa koko da* [Yamatai Country Was Here], (Tokyo: Tokuma Bunko, 1990), 5-6. This book was originally published by Mainichi Shimbun in 1981. From 1985 to 1991, seven books by Okuno on Yamatai, Yoshinogari or the coming of horseriding people were published.

26.   The above Okuno and Yasumoto citations are mini-books which were published at the same time. Also issued on Mar. 15, 1990 in mini-form was: Biten Yasumoto, ed., *Yoshinogari wa Yamataikoku nanoka* [Wondering if Yoshinogari Is Yamatai Country], (Tokyo: Tokuma Bunko, 1990). Yasumoto wrote the introduction, pp. 17-34, and a section, pp. 153-195, on the historical relationship between this ancient Kyushu ruins and Himiko's Yamatai country. Okuno contributed "Yoshinogari koso Yamataikoku da," [Yoshinogari is Indeed Yamatai Country], pp. 127-152. In 1990, both authors published booklets on ancient Japan as well.

27.   Masao Okuno, *Yamataikoku wa kodai Yamato o seifuku shita* [Yamatai Country Conquered Ancient Yamato], (Tokyo: JICC, 1990), 3, 62-63.

28.   See a discussion between the popular writer Jugo Kuroiwa and the academic Atsumu Wada, of Kyoto Educational University, "Kojiki wa gishō setsu no shinsō ni semaru," [Approaching the Truth Regarding the Theory

that the *Kojiki* Is a Falsified Document], *Gekkan Asahi* [Monthly Asahi], Vol. 3, No. 3 (Mar. 1991), 126.

29.   *Ibid.*,   120-123.   Also,   Himiko   can   be   tied   to Yamatototohimomosohime. See Okuno, *Yamataikoku wa koko da*, 6.

30.   W. G. Aston, trans., *Nihongi* (Tokyo: Charles E. Tuttle, 1972), 10-30.

31.   *Ibid.*, 64.

32.   *Ibid.*, 64-73, 92-108.

33.   *Ibid.*, 109-110.

34.   *Ibid.*, 110-111.

35.   *Ibid.*, 112-132.

36.   As for an overview of the modern scholastic controversy on the historical value of the *Nihon Shoki*, refer to the translator's introduction in Taro Sakamoto, *The Six National Histories of Japan*, trans. by John S. Brownlee (Tokyo: University of Tokyo Press, 1991), xxiii-xxviii. Sokichi Tsuda, of Waseda University, who was persecuted during World War II for his views on the *Nihon Shoki*, theorized that the tales of origins weren't historically true, being created merely to justify the imperial house. Many scholars came around to Tsuda's point of view after the war. One who didn't was Taro Sakamoto, of Tokyo University, who professed great respect for the imperial household. However, even the conservative Sakamoto who believed that the origins' myths were not concocted in the late 7th and early 8th centuries but were the product of a long history was not oblivious to the ancient propaganda value of the *Nihon Shoki*. On p. 55 of the text, Sakamoto admits: "No one would deny that the materials were manipulated" to achieve imperial ends. Okuno, also, relates that there remains a strong scholarly opinion, which he doesn't agree with, of course, which considers efforts to discover historical facts in the ancient legend as unscientific and dangerous. See Okuno, *Yamataikoku wa koko da*, 5-9.

37.   Sakamoto, *op. cit.*, 49-51, 57.   G. W. Robinson, "Early Japanese Chronicles: The Six National Histories," in *Historians of China and Japan*, ed. by W. G. Beasley and E. G. Pulleyblank (London: Oxford University Press, 1961), 221-224.

38.   Yasumoto, *Yamataikoku e no michi*, 80-81.

39.   *Ibid.*, 82-83, Note: Kinai and Kinki refer to central Japan.

40.   *Ibid.*, 97-98.

41.　*Ibid.*, 84-87, 95-97.

42.　*Ibid.*, 80-81.

43.　"Gishi Wajin-den," *The East*, Vol. 25, No. 5 (Jan.-Feb. 1990), 9-10. For an older English translation, see Ryusaku Tsunoda and L. Carrington Goodrich, *Japan in the Chinese Dynastic Histories* (S. Pasadena:　P.D. and Ione Perkins, 1951), 13-16.

44.　To understand just how brief the Wa description is in the *Wei Chronicle*, see the "Eastern Barbarian" section of the *San-kuo chih* [Account of the Three Kingdoms].

45.　Regarding the age of the information in the *Wei Chronicle*, the scholar in question is Namio Egami and his observation as to a Han period derivation (prior to 220 A.D.) is cited positively in Makoto Sahara, "Yoshinogari to Wajinden," [Yoshinogari and Wajinden], No. 6, *Yomiuri Shimbun* (July 3, 1989), 11. Also, as for the possibility of dates outside of the Wei period, there is an hypothesis among Japanese scholars that cultural attributes such as diving for fish, tatooing and fashion are similar to the customs of ancient Wu and Yueh (6th to 4th century B.C.) in China. The opinion is that these elements entered Japan with the fall of these states. See Taryo Obayashi, "The Ethnological Study of Japan's Ethnic Culture," *Acta Asiatica*, No. 61 (1991), 8-9.

46.　"Gishi Wajin-den," 9.

47.　Seicho Matsumoto, "Reiryoku wo ushinatta Himiko wa jinmin ni korosareta ka?" [Himiko Who Lost the Shaman Power Was Killed by the People], *AERA* (June 13, 1989), 26-27. See map and explanation in Okuno, *Yamataikoku wa koko da*, 157-158, 162.

48.　Yasumoto, *Yamataikoku e no michi*, 80-81, 187 (for Yamatai equals Yamato).

49.　*Ibid.*, 189.

50.　Okuno, *Yamataikoku wa kodai Yamato o seifuku shita*, 4-8, 56-57.

51.　Masao Okuno, *Himiko: Yamataikoku eiyūden* [Himiko:　The Heroic Story of Yamatai Country], (Tokyo:　President, 1991), *passim*.

52.　Sahara, *op. cit.*, 11.

53.　Jacques Ellul, *Propaganda* (New York:　Alfred A. Knopf, 1968), 75.

54.　*Ibid.*

180

55.   *Ibid.*, vii.

56.   *Ibid.*, 36.

57.   Dower, *op. cit.*, 215-227.

58.   *Ibid.*, 204-205.

59.   Edward S. Herman and Noam Chomsky, *Manufacturing Consent: The Political Economy of the Mass Culture* (New York: Pantheon, 1988), xi-xv.

CHAPTER II ENDNOTES

1.   See Takeru Akazawa, et. al., "Introduction," *Abstracts: The Evolution and Dispersal of Modern Humans in Asia, November 14-17, 1990* (Tokyo: Tokyo University Museum, 1990), vi-vii.   Also, Takeru Akazawa, "Introduction," *Prehistoric Mongoloid Dispersals*, No. 7 (special issue, 1990), v-vi. Note: The completed and revised papers were published two years later at the time of the second international conference by Hokusen-sha and entitled *The Evolution and Dispersals of Modern Humans in Asia.*

2.   Akazawa, et. al., *op. cit.*, vi.

3.   Symposium invitation letter from Takeru Akazawa, et. al., Feb. 21, 1990. According to Rebecca Cann, on being invited to the 1992 symposium, Akazawa said that she could speak on any topic. However, when she replied "Polynesia," Akazawa wrote back: "No, Please Eve."

4.   Eldredge and Tattersall, *op. cit.*, 78-83, 86-93. Kenneth F. Weaver, "The Search for Our Ancestors," *National Geographic*, Vol. 168, No. 5 (Nov. 1985), 578-579.

5.   Brown, *op. cit.*, 141-142. Weaver, *op. cit.*, 585-593.

6.   Brown, *op. cit.*, 143-150. Weaver, *op. cit.*, 590-592. Johanson and Shreeve, *op. cit.*, 109-115, 207-209, 269.

7.   Johanson and Shreeve, *op. cit.*, 121.

8.   Stephen Jay Gould, *Wonderful Life* (London: Penguin, 1991), 28-35. Brown, *op. cit.*, 16-17.

9.   Weaver, *op. cit.*, 574-577.

10.   Brown, *op. cit.*, 47-53.

11.   *Ibid.*, 23-24. Rebecca L. Cann, Mark Stoneking and Allan C. Wilson, "Mitochondrial DNA and Human Evolution," *Nature*, CCCXXV (Jan. 1987), 33-34.

12.   Motoo Kimura, "The Neutral Theory of Molecular Evolution," *Scientific American*, Vol. 241, No. 5 (Nov. 1979), 98-99.

13.   Gould, "Through a Lens Darkly," 16.

14.   Cann, "DNA and Human Origins," 127, 130-138. Roger Lewin, *Evolution* (Boston: Blackwell Scientific Publications, 1989), 109-111.

182

15.   Mark Stoneking and Rebecca L. Cann, "African Origin of Human Mitochondrial DNA," in the *Human Evolution*, ed. by Paul Mellars and Chris Stringer (Princeton: Princeton University Press, 1989), 19-23. Brown, *op. cit.*, 26

16.   Milford H. Wolpoff, "Multiregional Evolution: The Fossil Alternative to Eden," in *The Human Evolution*, 63-67.

17.   Rebecca L. Cann, "In Search of Eve," *The Sciences*, Vol. 27 (Sept.-Oct. 1987), 30.

18.   Cann, "DNA and Human Origins," 127.

19.   Lewin, *Evolution*, 112.

20.   *Ibid.*, 111. Brown, *op. cit.*, 220, 270. Wolpoff, *op. cit.*, 69.

21.   "The Search for Adam and Eve," 47.

22.   Wolpoff questions the assumption of branching analysis that population differences can be mapped from a common ancestor, with consideration being given to population splitting and isolation factors. In his opinion, "just as a correlation analysis will provide a 'number' even when comparing apples to oranges, a branching analysis will provide branches to the form of the structure assumed to underlie population relationships whether or not these actually characterized population histories." For Wolpoff, the following historical agenda is much more pertinent: "there have been numerous invasions, and a marked rate of gene flow between human populations since the end of the Pleistocene. These have affected every human population on the planet. All populations, therefore, should appear genetically and morphologically to be more closely related than they might actually be, if the analysis of population relationships assumes a splitting model of populational divergences. Another Holocene phenomenon that affects modern genetic variability in unknown ways is the demographic instability of the past two millennia, with numerous population replacements, ubiquitous admixture, and dramatic population expansions." See Wolpoff, *op. cit.*, 67-68.

23.   James Shreeve, "Argument Over a Woman," *Discover* (Aug. 1990), 56.

24.   "Ware ware no sosen wa nijūman nen mae no Afurikajin nanoka," [I Wonder If Our Ancestor Who Lived 200,000 Years Ago Is an African], *AERA* (Dec. 12, 1990), 9. Afterwards, it was decided to invite Cann and Wolpoff to the second international symposium in Nov. 1992.

25.   Gunter Brauer, "The Origins of Modern Asians: By Regional Evolution or By Replacement," *Abstracts*, 7.

26. *Ibid.*

27. Geofrey G. Pope, "The Facial Evidence for Regionalism in the Far East," *Abstracts*, 31.

28. *Ibid.*

29. Christy G. Turner II, "Teeth and Prehistory in Asia," *Scientific American*, Vol. 260, No. 2 (Feb. 1989), 88-91.

30. Christy G. Turner II, "Microevolution of East Asian and European Populations: A Dental Perspective," *Abstracts*, 44.

31. Regarding exchange during special seminar of Oct. 16, 1990, see "Mongoroido no tanjō to kakusan [Birth and Dispersal of Mongoloid], *Mongoroido* [Mongoloid], No. 9 (spring 1991), 7-9. For Mongoloid dispersal project and the search for a Mongoloid Eve, see M. Hirai, *Mongoroido Evu* [Mongoloid Eve], *Mongoroido* [Mongoloid], No. 2 (fall 1989), 10-12.

32. Xinzhi Wu, "The Origin and Dispersal of the Anatomically Modern Homo Sapiens of China," *Abstracts*, 48.

33. Johan Kamminga and R. V. S. Wright, "The Upper Cave at Zhoukoudian and the Origins of the Mongoloids," *Journal of Human Evolution*, XVII (1988), 745.

34. Katsushi Tokunaga and Takeo Juji, "The Migration and Dispersal of East Asian Populations as Viewed from HLA Genes and Haplotypes," *Abstracts*, 39.

35. "Ware ware no sosen," 8.

36. *Ibid.*, 9-10. Wolpoff and Cann were present at the second international conference and NHK-G news covered their presentations and the discussions. According to Wolpoff, he took the culture of Japan into consideration in putting together his paper. His intention was to behave politely and emphasize the problems with both hypotheses. He indicated that he and Cann had agreed not to engage in a heated debate. After being interviewed by TV news, he had the feeling that the reporter was trying to pit him against Cann and stir up an exchange, but he related that he had refused to be drawn into a confrontation. The report containing interviews with Cann as well as Wolpoff was broadcast on the 9 PM news on Nov. 18, 1992. In view of the subdued atmosphere of the conference and the lack of loud voices, the NHK coverage was quite bland and consisted of explaining both theories in a highly educational way. It is noteworthy that Asahi Shimbun publications could find nothing new at the conference to attract their readers. However, Asahi did run a story during the conference concerning an announcement by the National Science Museum that an examination of teeth

184

from the Jomon and medieval periods revealed modern Japanese to belong to a Yayoi-type grouping. *Asahi Shimbun*, Nov. 18, 1992.

37.   "Ware ware no sosen," 9.

38.   *Asahi Shimbun*, Nov. 18, 1990.   Yukio Dodo, et. al, "Population History of Japan: A Cranial Nonmetric Approach," *Abstracts*, 11.

39.   *Asahi Shimbun*, Nov. 20, 1990, evening edition.   Bernard Vandermeersch, "The Near Eastern Hominids and the Origin of Modern Humans in Eurasia," *Abstracts*, 45.

40.   *Nihonjin no kigenten* [Japanese Origins' Exhibition], July 16-Aug. 31, 1988 (Tokyo: National Science Museum, 1988), 8-9, 40-51.   Faceless, nonidentifiable men have been found in Okinawa as well, e.g., Yamashita-cho man.

41.   *Ibid.*, 10-15.

42.   *Ibid.*, 14.

43.   *Ibid.*, 17.

44.   *Ibid.*, 17-25.

45.   Weaver, *op. cit.*, 608-609.

46.   *Nihonjin no kigenten*, 17.

47.   *Ibid.*, 28.

48.   Kamminga, *op. cit.*, 739, 744.

49.   *Ibid.*, 744.

50.   Xinzhi Wu, "Origins and Affinities of the Inhabitants of Japan in Different Periods," in *Preprint Papers: International Symposium on Japanese as a Member of the Asian and Pacific Populations, September 25-29, 1990* (Kyoto: International Center for Japanese Studies, 1990), 1. *Nihonjin no kigenten*, 31.

51.   *Nihonjin no kigenten*, 32.   See Wu, "The Origin and Dispersal of the Anatomically Modern Homo Sapiens of China," 48.

52.   *Nihonjin no kigenten*, 34.   For an overview of Paleolithic culture in Siberia, see Denis Sinor, ed., *The Cambridge History of Early Inner Asia* (Cambridge: Cambridge University Press, 1990), 53-62, 92-94.   A. P.

Derev'anko, *Paleolithic of North Asia and the Problem of Ancient Migrations* (Novosibirsk, 1990), 54-63.

53. *Nihonjin no kigenten*, 37.

54. *Ibid.*, 38-39.

55. *Ibid.*, 51.

56. *Ibid.*

57. *Ibid.*, 92-93.

58. *Ibid.*

59. *Ibid.*, 94-95.

60. Hisashi Suzuki, *Hone kara mita nihonjin no rūtsu* [Japanese Roots from the Point of View of Bones], (Iwanami Shinsho; Tokyo, 1983), 218-219. For Yasumoto's critical appraisal of the theory of continuous change, see Biten Yasumoto, *Shinsetsu: nihonjin no kigen* [New Theory: Japanese Origins], (Tokyo: JICC, 1990), 22-24.

61. Kazuro Hanihara, "Nihonjin no kigen," [Japanese Origins] in *Nihonjin doko kara kita ka* [Where Did the Japanese Come from?], ed. by Kazuro Hanihara (Tokyo: Shōgakukan, 1984), 28-41. Takeshi Umehara and Kazuro Hanihara, *Ainu wa gennihonjin ka* [Are Ainu the Original Japanese?], (Tokyo: Shōgakukan, 1982), 131-132.

62. Hanihara, "Nihonjin no kigen," 28-29.

63. *Yomiuri Shimbun*, July 11-15, 1988.

64. Hanihara bases his hypothesis on Jomon and Kofun population estimates made by Shuzo Koyama, of the National Museum of Ethnology, and studies of estimated population sizes and annual growth rates for European neolithic populations. According to Hanihara, a 0.2% natural population growth rate is not too high for agricultural populations and concludes that the ratio of Jomon to migrant lineages in the Kofun/early historic period would have been 1:9 or 2:8. In his opinion, it was very probable that a large-scale migration was responsible for the high population growth during the 1,000 years from Yayoi to the early historic age. Kazuro Hanihara, "Estimation of the Number of Early Migrants to Japan: A Simulative Study," *Journal of the Anthropological Society of Nippon*, Vol. 95, No. 3 (1987), 392-394, 400-401. For Koymana's study of demographics, see Shuzo Koyama, "Jinko kara mita nihon minzoku," [Japanese Race from the Point of View of Population] in *Nihonjin shin kigenron* [New Theory of

Japanese Origins], ed. by Kazuro Hanihara (Tokyo: Kadokawa Shoten, 1990), 172-182.

65.   *Nihonjin no kigenten*, 96.

66.   "Nihonjin no kigen," [Japanese Origins], *Newton*, Vol. 10, No. 5 (Apr. 1990), 58-59.

67.   *Ibid.*, 62. This 40,000-year date for the existence of stone tools is controversial. Oda and Keally write: "Rarely does anyone deny the existence of Paleolithic artifacts dating   12,000 to 30,000 years ago.   However, archaeological opinion is sharply divided on the question of artifacts of human origin predating 30,000 B.P. ...." Shuzuo Oda and Charles T. Keally, "A Critical Look at the Paleolithic and 'Lower Paleolithic' Research in Miyagi Prefecture, Japan," *Journal of the Anthropological Society of Nippon*, Vol. 94, No. 3 (1986), 325.

68.   "Nihonjin no kigen," 63-67.

69.   *Ibid.*, 58-59.

70.   *Ibid.*, 72-73, 85.

71.   *Ibid.*, 74-75.

72.   *Ibid.*, 74, 80-83. Also, on cold climate adaptation, see Hanihara, "The Origin of the Japanese in Relation to Other Ethnic Groups in East Asia," 78-79.

73.   "Nihonjin no kigen," 76-77.

CHAPTER III ENDNOTES

1.　*Asahi Shimbun*, Feb. 23, 1989.　According to Yoshinogari's chief researcher, Tadaki Ichida, when this Feb. 23 article appeared, Yoshinogari became known for the first time all over Japan.　He explained that from that day, huge numbers of visitors began to flock to the site and on Feb. 27, the construction of the industrial park was postponed.　See "Gendai no shōzō," [Modern Portrait], *AERA* (Nov. 7, 1989), 56.

2.　"Gishiwajinden ga toku kuni no hitotsuka Yayoi jidai no saidaikyū shūraku arawareru," [Is It One of the Countries Gishiwajinden Mentioned? Biggest-class Yayoi period shūraku appeared.], *AERA* (Mar. 21, 1989), 62-63.

3.　*Asahi Shimbun*, Feb. 23, 1989.

4.　Makoto Sahara, "Yoshinogari to Wajinden," [Yoshinogari and Wajinden], No. 7, *Yomiuri Shimbun*, July 4, 1989, 11.

5.　Matsumoto, *op. cit.*, 26-27.　"Nara Makimuku iseki no hakkutsu de Kyūshū to Yamato no yakusha sorou," [Because of the Excavation of Makimuku Ruins in Nara, Players of Kyushu and Yamato Gather], *AERA* (June 20, 1989), 68.

6.　See *Yoshinogari isekiten* [Yoshinogari Ruins' Exhibition], Sept. 9-29, 1989, (Tokyo: Ancient Orient Museum, 1989), 30-47.

7.　Tsuboi's comment on Yoshinogari and the *Wei Chronicle* was broadcast in Part 3 of NHK's "Resurrection of Yamatai Country."

8.　*Yamataikoku ga mieta! Yoshinogari Ōkoku*. [Yamatai Country Can Be Seen! Yamatai Kingdom.], (Saga Shimbun: Saga Prefecture, 1989), 1-2, 22-29, 36-37.

9.　"Gishiwajinden ga toku kuni no hitotsuka," 62-63.

10.　On Jofuku's travels, see Derk Bodde, China's First Unifier (Hong Kong University Press: Hong Kong, 1967), 116.　Also, Denis Twitchett and Michael Loewe, eds., *Cambridge History of China*, I (Cambridge: Cambridge University Press, 1986), 78.　For an interpretation of the Jofuku legend for Japanese history, i.e., the coming of the toraijin and rice cultivation, see Takeshi Umehara, "Jofuku densetsu ga imi suru mono," [What the Jofuku Legend Means], *Yayoi no shisha: Jofuku* [Yayoi Missionary: Jofuku], (Saga TV Publication, 1989), 26-29.

11.   "Yoshinogari wa toraijin no karutago? Roma?" [Was Yoshinogari Carthage or Rome for Toraijin?], *AERA* (Oct. 24, 1989), 34-37.

12.   Gari Ledyard, "Galloping Along with the Horseriders: Looking for the Founders of Japan," *Journal of Japanese Studies*, Vol. 1, No. 2 (spring 1975), 224-225, 228.

13.   Namio Egami and Makoto Sahara, *Kiba minzoku wa kita? Konai?* [Did Horseriding People Come or Not?], (Tokyo: Shōgakukan, 1990), 22-36, 120-124.

14.   *Asahi Shimbun*, Nov. 8, 1989, Dec. 31, 1989. "Ushinawareyuku Yayoi jidai," [Losing the Yayoi Period], *AERA* (Dec. 5, 1989), 72-74.

15.   Sonoko Sugimoto, "Kodai no kodō ga kikoeru," [We Can Hear the Beat of Ancient Times], *Asahi Shimbun*, Jan. 1, 1990, "Yomigaeru kodai," [Resurrection of Ancient Times] section, 1.

16.   *Asahi Shimbun*, Mar. 26, 1990.

17.   *Asahi Shimbun*, Mar. 30, 1990. Yoshinogari was designated a national history park on Oct. 27, 1992.

18.   *Asahi Shimbun*, Dec. 25, 1990.

19.   *Asahi Shimbun*, Dec. 1, 1990.

20.   For the two-paragraph report, see *Asahi Shimbun*, Nov. 6, 1990.

21.   *Asahi Shimbun*, Dec. 1, 1990.

22.   "Gendai no shōzō," 53-56. "Ushinawareyuku Yayoi jidai," 72-74.

23.   Ellul, *op. cit.*, 47.

24.   Ippei Iwata, "Haiteku de saguru Nihonjin no rūtsu 2: Jomon Nihon wa Yayoijin no furontia datta," [Japanese Roots Through Hi-Tech, 2: Jomon Japan Was Frontier of Yayoi People], *Shūkan Asahi* [Weekly Asahi], (Jan. 18, 1991), 154-156. The article included details and diagrams regarding Koyama's population studies upon which Hanihara based his calculations (see fn. 64, Chap. II). The article also related that Koyama's figures were derived from the correlation of population registers which were begun in the 7th century A.D. and data on ancient ruins. For Koyama's conceptualization of the effects of climate on food systems and population growth, see Koyama, *op. cit.*, 172-173.

25.   Iwata, *op. cit.*, 156-157.

26. *Ibid.*, 157.

27. Ippei Iwata, "Haiteku de saguru Nihonjin no rūtsu 3: Daisensō wo osameta Himiko no sekushī na miryoku," [Japanese Roots Through High-Tech 3: Himiko's Sexy Charms Put an End to a Big War], *Shūkan Asahi* [Weekly Asahi], (Feb. 1, 1991), 132-133.

28. *Ibid.*

29. *Ibid.*, 133-134.

30. *Ibid.*, 134-135.

31. The archaeologist Hiroshi Tsude, of Osaka University, is doubtful whether late Yayoi mounds evolved into key-shaped tombs. He notes that although there are some common features, scale and quality differ. He relates that one of the earliest key-shaped tombs, Nara's Hashihaka Tomb, is 100 times as large as Tatetsuki Tomb in terms of volume. In his explanation, the difference in quality is evident in the following: (1) the jut-out section of Hashihaka which is as high as 13 meters, (2) the long stone chamber, and (3) the wooden coffin which is about three times the length of the body. Hiroshi Tsude, ed., *Kofun jidai no ō to minshū* [King and People in Kofun Period], Vol. 6 of *Kodaishi fukugen* [Restoration of Ancient History], (Tokyo: Kodansha, 1989), 30.

32. Dower, *op. cit.*, 313.

CHAPTER IV ENDNOTES

1.   Wills, *op. cit.*, 139, 143, 150.

2.   Hideo Matsumoto, "Characteristics of Mongoloid and Neighboring Populations Based on the Genetic Markers of Human Immunoglobulins," *Human Genetics* LXXX (spring 1988), 208.

3.   Hideo Matsumoto, *Nihon minzoku no genryū* [Origin of the Japanese Race], (Tokyo: Tairiku Shobō, 1985), 5, 12, 38.

4.   Matsumoto, "Characteristics of Mongoloid," 208.

5.   *Ibid.* Matsumoto, *Nihon minzoku no genryū*, 38, 105-106.

6.   Arthur G. Steinberg and Charles E. Cook, *The Distribution of the Human Immunoglobulin Allotypes* (Oxford: Oxford University Press, 1981), 1.

7.   Matsumoto, *Characteristics of Mongoloid*, 208. Genetic drift refers to chance events that alter gene frequencies in small breeding populations. Genetic flow concerns the exchange of genetic material between populations due to dispersion of gametes through interbreeding. Definitions from Molnar, *op. cit.*, 243.

8.   Matsumoto, "Characteristics of Mongoloid," 208.

9.   Matsumoto, *Nihon minzoku no genryū*, 5. Matsumoto, "Characteristics of Mongoloid," 208.

10.   Matsumoto, "Characteristics of Mongoloid," 207.

11.   For quotation, *Ibid.* Also, see Matsumoto, *Nihon minzoku no genryū*, 265.

12.   Matsumoto, "Characteristics of Mongoloid," 211.

13.   V. N. Basilov, "Introduction" in *Nomads of Eurasia*, ed. by V. N. Basilov (Seattle: University of Washington Press, 1989), 5.

14.   Matsumoto, *Nihon minzoku no genryū*, 164, 236.

15.   *Ibid.*, 187.

16.   *Ibid.*, 206.

17.   *Ibid.*, 209-211.

18.   *Ibid.*, 211. Azekura refers to a structure with an elevated floor and triangular logs joined together without nails. In Nara, there are two of these structures in the vicinity of the front gate of Tamukeyama Shrine.

19.   *Dentsu Japan Market/Advertising Yearbook 1987* (Tokyo: Dentsu, 1986), 71.

20.   *Dentsu Japan Market/Advertising Yearbook 1985/86* (Tokyo: Dentsu, 1985), 1-36.

21.   J. Edward Kidder Jr., "The Fujinoki Sarcophagus," *Monumenta Nipponica*, Vol. 44, No. 4 (winter 1989), 415-421. *Asahi Evening News*, Oct. 17, 1988.

22.   On spread of micro-blade culture, see Komei Sasaki, *Nihon Tanjō* [Birth of Japanese History], Vol. 1 of Nihon no rekishi [History of Japan], (Tokyo: Shueisha, 1991), 63-65.

23.   Matsumoto, *Nihon minzoku no genryū*, 79-80.

24.   Matsumoto, "Characteristics of Mongoloid," 211. As late as 1993, Matsumoto still maintained that the Japanese people migrated to Japan 12,000 to 13,000 years ago. See interview with Matsumoto, *Nikkei Weekly*, Jan 18, 1993.

25.   Nihon Hoso Kyokai, ed., *NHK nenkan '90* [NHK Yearbook '90], (Tokyo: NHK, 1991), inside cover, 49.   Peter J. S. Dunnet, *The World Television Industry* (London: Routledge, 1990), 169.

26.   Goto, Hirahara, Oyama and Sata, *op. cit.*, 7.

27.   For further information on ATL, see: Y. Hinuma, et. al., "Antibodies to Adult T-cell Leukemia Virus Associated Antigens (ATLA) in Sera from Patients with ATL and Controls in Japan," *International Journal of Cancer*, XXIX (1982), 631-634. Kazuo Tajima, et. al., "Epidemiological Features of HTLV-1 Carriers and Incidence of ATL in an ATL-Endemic Island," *International Journal of Cancer*, XXXX (1987), 741, 744-745. Martine Y. K. Armstrong, et. al., "Prevalence of Antibodies Interactive with HTLV-1 Antigens in Select Solomon Islands Populations," *American Journal of Physical Anthropology*, LXXXI (1990), 469-470.

28.   For Matsumoto's observations that Ainu and Okinawans from Miyako have Gm patterns of northern Mongoloid type, see Matsumoto, "Characteristics of Mongoloid," 210-211.

29.   *Asahi Evening News*, Nov. 14, 1991.

30.   For the change in weather conditions leading to the disappearance of the mammoth, see S. A. Arutiunov and William W. Fitzhugh, "Prehistory of Siberia and the Bering Sea," in *Crossroads of Continents*, ed. by W. W. Fitzhugh and A. Croswell (Washington D.C.: Smithsonian Institution Press, 1988), 119.

31.   See Sasaki, *op. cit.*, 63-65.

32.   For an overview of the various hypotheses on the spread of rice cultivation in Asia, see T. Higuchi, "Yayoi bunka ni eikyō o ataeta Goetsu bunka," [Wu-Yueh Culture and Its Influence on Yayoi Culture] in *Nihon bunka kigenron* [Theory of the Origin of Japanese Culture], (Tokyo: Gakken, 1990), 22-27. Tadayo Watabe, "Origin and Dispersal of Rice in Asia," *East Asian Cultural Studies*, XXIV (Mar. 1985), 33-38. Komei Sasaki, "The Wa People and Their Culture in Ancient Japan: The Cultures of Swidden Cultivation and Padi-Rice Cultivation," *Acta Asiatica*, LXI (1991), 28-41.

33.   Matsumoto, "Characteristics of Mongoloid," 211.

34.   *Ibid.* Even Yasumoto comments on the wide gulf between Matsumoto's and Hanihara's perspectives on Japanese origins. See Yasumoto, *Shinsetsu*, 24-25.

35.   *Asahi Shimbun*, Oct. 8, 1990. Also, see Satoshi Horai, "Mitokondria DNA kara mita Mongoroido no tayōsei to kakusan," [Diversity and Dispersal of Mongoloid from Mitochondrial DNA], *Mongoroido* [Mongoloid], No. 11 (fall 1991), 23. Satoshi Horai, "Phylogenetic Affiliation of the Japanese Inferred from Mitochondrial DNA," *Preprint Papers*, 35-36.

36.   "Jinrui wa Afurika de umareta," [The Human Race Was Born in Africa], *Newton*, Vol. 1, No. 12 (Nov. 1991), 76-77.

37.   *International Herald Tribune*, Oct. 3, 1991. "Who We Were," *U.S. News & World Report*, Vol. 3, No. 12 (Sept. 16, 1991), 58. On genetic mixture, see Brown, *op. cit.*, 99.

38.   "Jinrui wa Afurika de umareta," 78-79.

39.   "Who We Were," 55.

40.   Shahin Rouhani, "Molecular Genetics and the Pattern of Human Evolution," in *The Human Evolution*, 57.

41.   M. Nei and A. K. Roychoudhury, "Genetic Relationship and Evolution of Human Races," in *Evolutionary Biology*, ed. by M. Hecht, B. Wallace and G. Prance (New York: Plenum Press, 1982), 43.

42.   "Jinrui wa Afurika de umareta," 80-83.

43.   *Ibid.*, 84-85.

44.   See special archaeology issue, "Ushinawareta kodai bunmei," [Lost Ancient Cultures], *Newton* (Dec. 1991), 132-191.

45.   Satoshi Horai, "Mongoroido no michi: DNA de tsuiseki suru," [Mongol Road: In Pursuit with DNA], *Kagaku Asahi, Monthly Journal of Science* (Jan. 1992), 111-112.

46.   Horai, "Phylogenetic Affiliation of the Japanese," *Preprint Papers*, 36.

47.   Horai, "Mongoroido no michi," 111-112.

48.   In the written summary for the lecture, the "guess" is provided with a little bit more substance, the indication being that it is in agreement with paleoanthropology.   See Satoshi Horai's summary for the 6th university science open symposium held in Tokyo from Jan. 24-25, 1992 in the program *Mongoroido chikyū o ugoku* [Mongoloid Movements], 38.

49.   Horai, "Mitokondria DNA," 23.

CHAPTER V ENDNOTES

1. *Asahi Shimbun*, July 10, 1990.

2. Masao Okuno, "Tēsondon kofungun to kiba minzoku seifuku ōchō setsu," [Taesung Tomb Group and Horserider Conquest Kingdom Theory], *Higashi Ajia no kodai bunka* [Ancient Culture of East Asia], LXVIII (summer 1991), 85.

3. Kyungcheol Shin, "Nikkan kodaishi kaimei," [Clarifying Japan-Korean Ancient History], *Gekkan Asahi* [Monthly Asahi], Vol. 3, No. 6 (June 1991), 61-63.

4. Okuno, "Tēsondon kofungun," 84-85, 93.

5. Namio Egami, "Kiba minzoku setsu wa jisshō sareta," [Horserider Theory Proven], *Gekkan Asahi* [Monthly Asahi], Vol. 3, No. 6 (June 1991), 52-53.

6. See the conversation between Egami and Mori in "Fune ni notta kiba minzoku miete kita," [Coming to See that Horseriding People Came by Boat], *Gekkan Asahi* [Monthly Asahi], Vol. 4, No. 3 (Mar. 1992), 130.

7. *Ibid.*, 128.

8. Toshiyaki Tanaka, "Tēsondon kofungun to Mimanaron," [Taesung Tomb Group and Mimana Theory], *Higashi Ajia no kodai bunka* [Ancient Culture of East Asia], LXVIII (summer 1991), 55-56.

9. Wontack Hong, *Relationship between Korea and Japan in Early Period* (Seoul: ILSIMSA, 1988), 243-244.

10. "Archaeology Pioneer: Kim W. Y.," *Korea Newsreview*, Vol. 21, No. 2 (Jan. 11, 1992), 26.

11. Y. Y. Kim, "Rewriting of Korea-Japan History," *Korea Newsreview*, Vol. 20, No. 29 (July 20, 1991), 31.

12. Tanaka, "Tēsondon kofungun to Mimanaron," 56-57.

13. *Ibid.*, 56.

14. Carter J. Eckert, Ki-baik Lee, et. al., *Korea Old and New History* (Seoul: ILCHOKAK, 1990), 14-18, 24-30. Ki-baik Lee, *A New History of Korea* (Cambridge: Harvard University Press, 1984), 41.

15. Eckert, Lee, et. al., *op. cit.*, 29, 42.

16. "Archaeology Pioneer," 27.

17. Egami, *op. cit.*, 53-54.

18. Tsunoda and Goodrich, *op. cit.*, 22.

19. Hong, *op. cit.*, 231-232.

20. *Asahi Shimbun*, Dec. 8, 1991.

21. *Ibid*. Also, see discovery of bronze mirrors, "Newly Excavated Kaya Relics Prove Foreign Contact," *Korea Newsreview*, Vol. 20, No. 51 (Dec. 21, 1991), 31. For the leader of this excavation's (Hyotaek Lim's) comments on the mirrors, see *Asahi Shimbun*, Mar. 16, 1992, evening edition.

22. *Asahi Shimbun*, Jan. 5, 1992.

23. "Kankoku no maboroshi no ōkoku Kaya iseki," [Phantom Kingdom in Korea, Kaya Ruins] *Asahi Gurafu* [Asahi Graph], (Mar. 27, 1992), 3-7. "Kiba minzoku to wajin kaikō: Bēru wo nuida kodai ōkoku Kaya," [Meeting of Horseriders and Wa: Ancient Kaya Kingdom Unveiled], Shūkan Asahi [Weekly Asahi], (Mar. 27, 1992), "Ancient Express" section. The meeting of horseriders and Wa referred to in this article concerns the cultural transmission through Kaya of north Asian cultural elements.

24. *Asahi Shimbun*, Mar. 19, 1992, evening edition.

25. *Asahi Shimbun*, Mar. 16, 1992, evening edition.

26. *Asahi Shimbun*, Mar. 31, 1992. The proceedings of the conference were later published at the end of the year by Kadokawa Shoten under the title of *Kyodai kofun to kaya bunka* [Gigantic Tombs and Kaya Culture]. By 1993, Shin had become resolute in the opinion that Kaya mokkakubo culture arose as a consequence of an invasion from north Asia. He explained that the building of late 3rd century graves over earlier graves indicated that the old population had been crushed by a new group of people. See Kyungcheol Shin, "Kankoku no Kaya bunka to Wa" [Kaya Culture of Korea and Wa], Gakushuin University lecture program of Wazoku to kodai Nihon [Wa Race and Ancient Japan], Jan. 8-9, 1993, inserted pages.

27. See Korean-language catalog, *Kaya Special Exhibition* (Seoul: National Central Museum, 1991), *passim*.

28. *Asahi Evening News*, Apr. 12, 1991.

196

29. Roger Cribb, *Nomads in Archeology* (Cambridge: Cambridge University Press, 1991), 1.

30. Sinor, ed., *op. cit.*, 19, 34, 39-40.

31. *Ibid.*, 7.

32. *Ibid.*

33. *Ibid.*, 9-10. Basilov, *op. cit.*, 8.

34. V. P. Kurylev, L. P. Pavlinskaya and G. N. Simakov, "Harness and Weaponry," *Nomads of Eurasia*, 137-138.

35. Sinor, ed., *op. cit.*, 97-99.

36. *Ibid.*, 98.

37. *Ibid.*, 102.

38. *Ibid.*, 117.

39. *Ibid.*, 38.

40. Ledyard, *op. cit.*, 224.

41. *Ibid.* "Fune ni notta kiba minzoku miete kita," 130.

BIBLIOGRAPHY

Primary Media Sources

Television

Fuji. "Minami no shima ni Nihon no kokyō o mita" [Japan Roots as Seen in the Southern Islands]. May 19, 1989.

_____. "Yayoi wo horu otokotachi" [Excavators of Yayoi]. June 22, 1992.

NHK-E. "ETV 8." Program on the roots of the Japanese race. Feb. 11, 1987.

_____. "ETV 8." Program on the ancient history of Japan and Korea. Feb. 12, 1987.

_____. "ETV 8." Program on Fujinoki tomb. Nov. 7, 1988.

_____. "ETV 8." Series on the period of Fujinoki tomb. Oct. 25-26, 1988.

_____. "ETV 8." Program on Mongoloid dispersals' project. July 3, 1989.

_____. "ETV 8." Program on tracing Japanese origins through blood analysis. Sept. 4, 1989.

_____. "Gendai jānaru" [Modern Journal]. Program on ancient Japan after Himiko. Feb. 5, 1991.

_____. "Doyō forum" [Saturday Forum]. Symposium on ancient Japanese history. Feb. 9, 1991.

_____. "Rekishi no naka no Nihonjin" [Japanese in History]. Open lectures by Makoto Sahara. Aug. 5-6, 1991.

_____. "Hello Science." High school correspondence course, human evolution program. Sept. 19, 1991.

_____. "Gendai jānaru" [Modern Journal]. Program on the analysis of the bones found in Fujinoki tomb. Oct. 9, 1991.

_____. "Gendai jānaru" [Modern Journal]. Program on Mongoloid dispersals' project. Mar. 9, 1992.

_____. "Rekishi de miru Nihon" [Japan as Seen Through History]. High school educational lectures of Makoto Sahara and Hiroshi Tsude. April 21, 28 (Sahara); May 5, 1992 (Tsude).

198

_____. "Gendai jānaru" [Modern Journal]. Program on Kaya excavations, with Kyungcheol Shin present, Sept. 2, 1992.

_____. "Gendai jānaru" [Modern Journal]. Program commemorating the award of the national culture medal to Namio Egami. Nov. 3, 1992.

NHK-G. "Kokuri no bi to chikara" [Beauty and Power of Koguryo]. May 9, 1986.

_____. "Yomigaeru Yamataikoku" [Resurrection of Yamatai Country]. May 17-19, 1989.

_____. "Tsuiseki Yoshinogari jidai" [In Search of the Age of Yoshinogari]. Nov. 3, 1989.

_____. "Koriataun no niseitachi" [Second Generation of Koreatown]. Jan. 15, 1990.

_____. "Rekishi tanjō" [Birth of History]. Program on Yamato rule and internal disorder. Aug. 29, 1990.

_____. "Rekishi tanjō" [Birth of History]. Program on the riddle of Mimana Japanese Government. Mar. 4, 1991.

_____. "Ajia to taiheiyō sensō" [Asia-Pacific War]. Program on Korean residents of Japan who served in Japanese Imperial Army. Aug. 14, 1991.

_____. "Kurabete mireba" [Compare]. Program on Japanese-style rice vs. Indian-style rice. Sept. 30, 1991.

_____. "Nazo no kiba minzoku" [Riddle of Horseriding People]. Nov. 3, 1991.

_____. "Hikyo Baikaru" [Unexplored Baikal]. Nov. 4, 1991.

_____. "Kurabete mireba" [Compare]. Program on Jomon vs. Yayoi. Nov. 4, 1991.

_____. "Rekishi hakken" [Discovery of History]. Program on the secret of Himiko's authority to rule. May 8, 1992.

_____. "Dai Mongoru" [Greater Mongolia]. Monthly series on the rise of the Mongol empire. Apr.-Aug. 1992.

_____. "Prime 10." Program on the golden race, the Scythians. July 2, 1992.

_____. "Asia's Pops' Queens in Yoshinogari." Oct. 24, 1992.

_____. NHK 9 PM News. Featured report on roots of human race. Nov. 18, 1992.

NTV. "Kodaishi Supesharu" [Ancient History Special]. Programs on Japanese roots from 1985-1988: Nov. 4, 1985, Nov. 24, 1986, Nov. 23, 1987, July 4, 1988.

_____. "Haruka naru Japan rōdo" [Trip to Japanese Roots]. Oct. 20, 1988.

_____. 11 PM News. Featured report on Yoshinogari ruins. May 2, 1989.

_____. "The Chase: Yoshinogari madonna ōkoku o fukugen" [The Chase: Restoration of Yoshinogari Madonna Kingdom]. Nov. 15, 1989.

_____. "Documentary '90." Program on discimination and third-generation Koreans resident in Japan. May 6, 1990.

_____. "Documentary '90." Program on Japanese labor relations in Korea. June 24, 1990.

_____. "Documentary '91." Program on the anger and grief of relatives of soldiers conscripted into the Japanese Imperial Army. Aug. 11, 1991.

_____. "Documentary '91." Program on the present lives of Koreans who fought in World War II. Aug. 18, 1991.

_____. "Chingisu Han no ryōbo wo sagase" [Search for Chinggis Khan's Grave]. Nov. 28, 1991.

_____. "Nippon tanjō" [Birth of Japan]. Program on the latest horserider theory. Feb. 15, 1992.

_____. NTV 11 PM News. Featured reports on a Yoshinogari-related excavation in Fukuoka. Dec. 14-15, 1992.

TBS. "Nikkan kōryū no kako" [Past Japan-Korea Relations]. Jan. 13, 1990.

_____. "Yamataikoku satsujin jiken" [Murder Incident in Yamatai Country]. TV drama. Oct. 12, 1990.

_____. "Shin Bīgurugō tankenki" [New Beagle Notebook]. First program of a series retracing the voyage of Darwin on the Beagle. Oct. 9, 1991.

_____. "Himiko wa korosareta?!" [Himiko Was Killed?!]. Dec. 22, 1991.

_____. "Sekai fushigi hakken" [Quiz: World Mysteries]. Two-part program on the origins of the Japanese. Apr. 11, 1992, Apr. 18, 1992.

TV Tokyo. "Kiwameru II" [Come to the Core II]. Program on Yoshinogari. Oct. 26, 1990.

_____. "Yomigaeru densetsu" [Resurrection of a Legend]. Program on the riddle of Kibi Kingdom. Mar. 20, 1991.

_____. "TV Columbus." Focus on changes in the facial characteristics of Japanese people. June 1, 1991.

TVK-42. "Compass U." Program on Yoshinogari and other ancient ruins. Nov. 17, 1990.

Newspapers

Asahi Evening News. 1985-1992.

Asahi Shimbun. 1985-1992.

Yomiuri Shimbun. 1988-1992.

Popular Magazines

"Bīgurugō kōkaiki" [Voyage Diary of the Beagle]. *Newton*, Vol. 11, No. 12 (Nov. 1991), 18-37.

Egami, Namio. "Kiba minzoku setsu wa jissho sareta" [Horserider Theory Proven]. *Gekkan Asahi* [Monthly Asahi], Vol. 3, No. 6 (June 1991), 52-60.

_____, and Mori, Koichi. "Fune ni notta kiba minzoku miete kita" [Coming to See that Horseriding People Came by Boat]. *Gekkan Asahi* [Monthly Asahi], Vol. 4, No. 3 (Mar. 1992), 128-135.

"Fujinoki hisōsha rēsu haran bukumi" [The Competition Among the Candidates for Person Buried in Fujinoki Storms On]. *AERA* (Oct. 25, 1988), 18-19.

"Fujinoki ni Kankoku no atsui shisen" [Korea Keeping a Hopeful Eye on Fujinoki]. *AERA* (Oct. 18, 1988), 43-45.

"Gendai no shōzō [Modern Portrait]. *AERA* (Nov. 7, 1989), 53-57.

"Gishiwajinden ga toku kuni no hitotsuka Yayoi jidai no saidaikyū shūraku arawareru" [Is It One of the Countries Gishiwajinden Mentioned? Biggest-class Yayoi Period Shūraku Appeared]. *AERA* (Mar. 21, 1989), 62-63.

Horai, Satoshi. "Mongoroido no michi: DNA de tsuiseki suru." *Kagaku Asahi, Monthly Journal of Science* (Jan. 1992), 108-112.

Iwata, Ippei (chief writer). "Haiteku de saguru Nihonjin no rūtsu" [Japanese Roots Through Hi-tech]. Parts 1-14. *Shūkan Asahi* [Weekly Asahi] (Jan. 4-11, 1991), 34-38; (Jan. 18, 1991), 154-157; (Feb. 1, 1991), 132-135; (Feb. 8, 1991), 138-141; (Mar. 1, 1991), 142-145; (Mar. 8, 1991), 148-151; (July 5, 1991), 172-175; (July 12, 1991), 144-147; (July 19, 1991), 156-159; (July 26, 1991), 114-117; (Aug. 2, 1991), 46-49; (Dec. 13, 1991), 84-87; (Dec. 20, 1991), 80-84; (Dec. 27, 1991), 72-75.

"Jinrui wa Afurika de umareta" [The Human Race Was Born in Africa]. *Newton*, Vol. 11, No. 12 (Nov. 1991), 62-85.

"Jomon Torippu" [Jomon Trip]. *AERA* (Aug. 27, 1991), 31-56.

Kadowaki, Kenji, Matsumoto, Seicho, and Sahara, Makoto. "Kodaishi no nazo wo toku" [Solving the Riddle of ancient History]. *Gendai* (Jan. 1992), 102-123.

"Kamimei Yoshinogari iseki no seiki" [Clarifying the Century of Yoshinogari Ruins]. *Rekishi dokuhon* [History Reader] (Sept. 1989), 66-181.

"Kankoku no maboroshi no ōkoku Kaya iseki" [Phantom Kingdom in Korea, Kaya Ruins]. *Asahi Gurafu* [Asahi Graph] (Mar. 27, 1992), 3-7.

"Kiba minzoku to wajin kaikō" [Meeting of Horseriders and Wa]. *Shūkan Asahi* [Weekly Asahi] (Mar. 27, 1992), "Ancient Express" section.

"Kodaishi hakkutsu sōmakuri, 1989 zenki" [All Ancient History Excavations, First Half of 1989]. *Asahi Gurafu* [Asahi Graph] (July 14, 1989), 4-47.

"Kodaishi hakkutsu sōmakuri, 1989 koki" [All Ancient History Excavations, Second Half of 1989]. *Asahi Gurafu* [Asahi Graph] (Dec. 29, 1989), 4-33.

"Kodaishi hakkutsu sōmakuri, 1990 zenki" [All Ancient History Excavations, First Half of 1990]. *Asahi Gurafu* [Asahi Graph] (July 6, 1990), 4-27.

"Kodaishi hakkutsu sōmakuri, 1990 koki" [All Ancient History Excavations, Second Half of 1990]. *Asahi Gurafu* [Asahi Graph] (Dec. 28, 1990), 4-33.

"Kodaishi hakkutsu sōmakuri, 1992 koki" [All Ancient History Excavations, Second Half of 1992]. *Asahi Gurafu* [Asahi Graph] (Dec. 25, 1992), 3-43.

Kuroiwa, Jugo, and Wada, Atsumu. "Kojiki wa gishō setsu no shinsō ni semaru" [Approaching the Truth Regarding the Theory that the *Kojiki* Is a Falsified Document]. *Gekkan Asahi* [Monthly Asahi], Vol. 3, No. 3 (Mar. 1991), 120-126.

202

Matsumoto, Seicho. "Reiryoku wo ushinatta Himiko wa jinmin ni korosareta ka?" [Himiko Who Lost the Shaman Power Was Killed by the People]. *AERA* (June 13, 1989), 26-27.

"Nara Makimuku iseki no hakkutsu de Kyushu to Yamato no yakusha sorou" [Because of the Excavation of Makimuku Ruins in Nara, Players of Kyushu and Yamato Gather]. *AERA* (June 20, 1989), 68.

"Nihon to dōyō gakusetsu wakareru" [Theory Differs Among Scholars Just Like in Japan]. *AERA* (Oct. 18, 1988), 46.

"Nihonjin no kigen" [Japanese Origins]. *Newton*, Vol. 10, No. 5 (Apr. 1990), 58-87.

"Rōkaku hakkutsu de Yamataikoku ronsō mata hazumu" [Because of Excavation of Castle-style Watchtower, Yamataikoku Debate Becomes Lively Once Again]. *AERA* (June 2, 1992), 62-63.

"Saga-ken ni futte waita nisen nen ni ichido no shōki" [Trading Opportunity Arises in Saga Prefecture for the First Time in 2,000 Years]. *AERA* (May 2, 1989), 75.

Sahara, Makoto, et. al., "Koko made wakatta 'Nihon no rūtsu'" [Japanese Roots Are Understood Up to This Point]. *Bungei Shunju* (Jan. 1992), 292-346.

Shin, Kyungcheol. "Nikkan kodaishi kaimei" [Clarifying Japan-Korea Ancient History]. *Gekkan Asahi* [Monthly Asahi], Vol. 3, No. 6 (June 1991), 61-63.

"Ushinawareta kodai bunmei" [Lost Ancient Civilizations]. *Newton* (Dec. 1991), 130-191.

"Ushinawareyuku Yayoi jidai" [Losing the Yayoi Period]. *AERA* (Dec. 5, 1989), 72-74.

"Ware ware no sosen wa nijūman nen mae no Afurikajin nanoka" [I Wonder If Our Ancestor Who Lived 200,000 Years Ago Is an African]. *AERA* (Dec. 12, 1990), 8-11.

Yamataikoku ga mieta! Yoshinogari ōkoku. [Yamatai Country Can Be Seen! Yoshinogari Kingdom]. Saga Shimbun: Saga Prefecture, 1989. Single issue publication.

"Yamataikoku wa Chūgokufū datta" [Yamatai Country Was Chinese in Style]. *Shūkan Asahi* [Weekly Asahi]. (June 5, 1992), 34-36.

"Yamataikoku yori furui Chūgokufū rōkaku" [Chinese-style Watchtower Older Than Yamatai Country]. *Asahi Gurafu* [Asahi Graph] (June 5, 1992), 3-5.

Yomiuri Special 31: Yoshinogari, Fujinoki, Yamataikoku. Tokyo: Yomiuri Shimbunsha, 1989. Special issue.

"Yoshinogari wa toraijin no Karutago? Roma?" [Was Yoshinogari Carthage or Rome for Toraijin?]. *AERA* (Oct. 24, 1989), 34-37.

204

Secondary Sources

*Abstracts: The First World Conference on Prehistoric Mongoloid Dispersals,
November 16-21, 1992.* Tokyo: Tokyo University Museum, 1992.

Aikens, C. Melvin. "From Asia to America: The First Peopling of the New
World." *Prehistoric Mongoloid Dispersals*, No. 7 (special issue 1990), 1-
34.

Akazawa, Takeru. "Introduction." *Prehistoric Mongoloid Dispersals*, No. 7
(special issue, 1990), v-vi.

_____. Symposium invitation letter. Feb. 21, 1990.

_____, and Aikens, C. Melvin, eds., *Prehistoric Hunter-Gatherers in Japan.*
Tokyo: University of Tokyo Press, 1986.

_____, Aoki, Kenichi, and Kimura, Tasuku. *The Evolution and Dispersal of
Modern Humans in Asia.* Tokyo: Hokusen-sha, 1992.

_____, et. al. "Introduction." *Abstracts: The Evolution and Dispersal of
Modern Humans in Asia, November 14-17, 1990.* Tokyo: Tokyo
University Museum, 1990.

"Archaeology Pioneer: Kim W. Y." *Korea Newsreview*, Vol. 21, No. 2 (Jan.
11, 1992), 26-27.

Armstrong, Martine Y. K., et. al. "Prevalence of Antibodies Interactive with
HTLV-1 Antigens in Select Solomon Islands Populations." *American
Journal of Physical Anthropology*, LXXXI (1990), 465-470.

Ashton, W. G., trans. *Nihongi.* Tokyo: Charles E. Tuttle, 1972.

Barnes, Gina L. *Protohistoric Yamato.* Ann Arbor: University of Michigan,
Center for Japanese Studies, 1988.

Basilov, V. N. "Introduction." *Nomads of Eurasia.* Edited by V. N. Basilov.
Seattle: University of Washington Press, 1989.

Beane, Wendell C., and Dotty, William G., eds. *Myths, Rites, Symbols: A
Mircea Eliade Reader.* Vol. 1. New York: Harper and Row, 1976.

Best, Jonathan W. "Horserider Reruns: Two Recent Studies of Early
Korean-Japanese Relations." *Journal of Japanese Studies*, Vol. 16, No.
2 (summer 1990), 437-442.

Bodde, Derke. China's First Unifier. Hong Kong: Hong Kong University Press, 1967.

Bodmer, W. F., and Cavalli-Sforza, L. L. *Genetics, Evolution and Man*. San Francisco: W. H. Freeman and Co., 1976.

Brauer, Gunter. "The Evolution of Modern Humans: A Comparison of the African and non-African Evidence." *The Human Evolution*. Edited by Paul Mellars and Chris Stringer. Princeton: Princeton University Press, 1989.

_____. "The Origins of Modern Asians: By Regional Evolution or By Replacement." *Abstracts: The Evolution and Dispersal of Modern Humans in Asia, November 14-17, 1990*. Tokyo: Tokyo University Museum, 1990.

Brown, Michael H. *The Search for Eve*. New York: Harper and Row, 1990.

Campbell, Bernard G., ed. *Humankind Emerging*. 5th ed. Boston: Little Brown and Company, 1985.

Cann, Rebecca L. "In Search of Eve." *The Sciences*, XXVII (Sept.-Oct. 1987), 30-37.

_____. "DNA and Human Origins." *Annual Review of Anthropology*, XVII (1988), 127-143.

_____, Stoneking, Mark, and Wilson, Allan C. "Mitochondrial DNA and Human Evolution." *Nature*, CCCXXV (Jan. 1987), 31-36.

Cribb, Roger. *Nomads in Archeology*. Cambridge: Cambridge University Press, 1991.

Cummings, Michael R. *Human Heredity*. St. Paul, Minn.: West Publishing Co., 1988.

Dentsu Japan Market/Advertising Yearbook 1985/86. Tokyo: Dentsu, 1985.

Dentsu Japan Market/Advertising Yearbook 1987. Tokyo: Dentsu, 1986.

Derev'anko, A. P. *Paleolithic of North Asia and the Problem of Ancient Migrations*. Novosibirsk, 1990.

Diamond, Jared. "Blood, Genes and Malaria." *Natural History* (Feb. 1989), 8-18.

Dobzhansky, Theodosius, and Boesiger, Ernest. *Human Culture*. New York: Columbia University Press, 1983.

Dower, John. *War Without Mercy*. Pantheon: New York, 1986.

Dunnet, Peter J. S. *The World Television Industry*. London: Routledge, 1990.

Eckert, Carter J., Lee, Ki-baik, et. al. *Korea Old and New History*. Seoul: ILCHOKAK, 1990

Edwards, Walter. "Event and Process in the Founding of Japan: The Horserider Theory in Archeological Perspective." *Journal of Japanese Studies*, Vol. 9, No. 2 (summer 1983), 265-295.

_____. "Buried Discourse: The Toro Archeological Site and Japanese National Identity in the Early Postwar Period." *Journal of Japanese Studies*, Vol. 17, No. 1 (winter 1991), 10-23.

Egami, Namio. *Kiba minzoku kokka: Nihon kodaishi e no apurōchi* [Horserider Theory: An Approach to Ancient Japanese History]. Tokyo: Chūō Kōron, 1967.

_____, and Sahara, Makoto. *Kiba minzoku wa kita? Konai?* [Did Horseriding People Come or Not?]. Tokyo: Shōgakukan, 1990.

Eldredge, Niles, and Tattersall, Ian. *The Myth of Human Evolution*. New York: Columbia University Press, 1982.

Eliade, Mircea. *Myths, Dreams and Mysteries*. New York: Harper and Row, 1960.

_____. *Shamanism: Techniques of Ecstasy*. Translated by Willard R. Trask. Princeton: Princeton University Press, 1964.

Ellul, Jacques. *Propaganda*. New York: Alfred A Knopf, 1968.

Fiske, John. *Television Culture*. London: Methuen, 1987.

_____. *Introduction to Communication Studies*. London: Routledge, 1988.

Fitzhugh, William W. "Prehistory of Siberia and the Bering Sea." *Crossroads of Continents*. Edited by W. W. Fitzhugh and A. Croswell. Washington D.C.: Smithsonian Institution Press, 1988.

Garrett, Wilbur E. "The Peopling of the Earth." *National Geographic*, Vol. 177, No. 4 (Oct. 1988), 434-437.

"Gishi Wajin-den." *The East*, Vol. 25, No. 5 (Jan.-Feb. 1990), 7-10.

Goto, K.; Hirahara, H.; Oyama K.; and Sata M. *A History of Japanese Television Drama*. Tokyo: Japan Association of Television Broadcasting Art, 1991.

Gould, Stephen Jay. *The Mismeasure of Man*. New York: W. W. Norton, 1981.

_____. "Grimm's Greatest Tale." *Natural History* (Feb. 1989), 20-28.

_____. "Through a Lens Darkly." *Natural History* (Sept. 1989), 16-24.

_____. *Wonderful Life*. London: Penguin, 1991.

Gowlett, John A. J. *Ascent to Civilization*. New York: Alfred A. Knopf, 1984.

Hanihara, Kazuro. "Nihonjin no kigen" [Japanese Origins]. *Nihonjin doko kara kita ka* [Where did the Japanese Come from?]. Edited by Kazuro Hanihara. Tokyo: Shōgakukan, 1984.

_____. "The Origin of the Japanese in Relation to Other Ethnic Groups in East Asia," *Windows on the Japanese Past: Studies in Archeology and Prehistory*. Edited by Richard Pearson. Ann Arbor: Center for Japanese Studies, University of Michigan, 1986.

_____. "Estimation of the Number of Early Migrants to Japan: A Simulative Study." *Journal of the Anthropological Society of Nippon*, Vol. 95, No. 3 (1987), 391-403.

Herman, Edward F., and Chomsky, Noam. *Manufacturing Consent: The Political Economy of the Mass Culture*. New York: Pantheon, 1988.

Higuchi, T. "Yayoi bunka ni eikyō o ataeta Goetsu bunka" [Wu-Yueh Culture and its Influence on Yayoi Culture]. *Nihon bunka kigenron* [Theory of the Origin of Japanese Culture]. Tokyo: Gakken, 1990.

Hinuma, Y., et. al. "Antibodies to Adult T-cell Leukemia Virus Associated Antigens (ATLA) in Sera from Patients with ATL and Controls in Japan." *International Journal of Cancer*, XXIX (1982), 631-635.

Hirai, M. "Mongoroido Evu" [Mongoloid Eve]. *Mongoroido* [Mongoloid], No. 2 (fall 1989), 10-12.

Hong, Wontack. *Relationship between Korea and Japan in Early Period*. Seoul: ILSIMSA, 1988.

Horai, Satoshio. "Phylogenetic Affiliation of the Japanese Inferred from Mitochondrial DNA." *Preprint Papers: International Symposium on*

Japanese as a Member of the Asian and Pacific Populations, September 25-29, 1990. Kyoto: International Center for Japanese Studies, 1990.

_____. "Mitokondria DNA kara mita Mongoroido no tayōsei to kakusan" [Diversity and Dispersal of Mongoloid from Mitochondrial DNA], *Mongoroido* [Mongoloid], No. 11 (fall 1991), 19-23.

Hudson, Mark, and Barnes, Gina L. "Yoshinogari." *Monumenta Nipponica*, Vol. 46, No. 2 (summer 1991), 211-235.

International Herald Tribune, Oct. 3, 1991.

Ishinomori, Shotaro. *Manga Nihon no rekishi* [Cartoon: History of Japan]. Vol. 2. Tokyo: Chūō Kōron, 1990.

Ito, Youichi and Hattori, Takaaki. "Mass Media Ethics in Japan." *Communication Ethics and Global Change.* Edited by Thomas Cooper. New York: Longman, 1989.

Japan, 1991 Marketing and Advertising Yearbook. Tokyo: Dentsu, 1990.

"Jinshu to minzoku wo kangaeru" [Thinking about Race and Nation]. *Mongoroido* [Mongoloid], No. 5 (summer 1990), 2-9.

Johanson, Donald, and Shreeve, James. *Lucy's Child.* New York: William Morrow, 1989.

Jorde, L. B. "Human Genetic Distance Studies." *Annual Review of Anthropology*, XIV (1985), 343-373.

Kamminga, Johan, and Wright, R. V. S. "The Upper Cave at Zhoukoudian and the Origins of the Mongoloids." *Journal of Human Evolution*, XVII (1988), 739-767.

Kaya – Ancient Kingdoms of Korea. Japanese-language exhibition catalogue with English-language listing of exhibits. Tokyo: Asahi Shimbun, 1992.

Kaya Special Exhibition. Korean-language catalogue. Seoul: National Central Museum, 1991.

Kidder Jr., J. Edward. "The Newly Discovered Takamatsuzuka Tomb." *Monumenta Nipponica.* Vol. 27, No. 3 (autumn 1972), 245-251.

_____. "The Archeology of the Early Horse-Riders in Japan." *Transactions of the Asiatic Society of Japan*, Third Series, Vol. 20 (1985), 89-123.

_____. "The Fujinoki Sarcophagus." *Monumenta Nipponica*, Vol. 44, No. 4 (winter, 1989), 415-460.

Kim, Y. Y. "Rewriting of Korea-Japan History." *Korea Newsletter*, Vol. 20, No. 29 (July 20, 1991), 30-31.

Kimura, Motoo. "The Neutral Theory of Molecular Evolution." *Scientific American*, Vol. 241, No. 5. (Nov. 1979), 98-126.

Klein, Richard G. *The Human Career.* Chicago: University of Chicago Press, 1989.

Kobayashi, Yasuko. *Shotoku Taishi no shōtai* [True Character of Shotoku Taishi]. Tokyo: Bungei Shunjū, 1990.

"Kofun jidai no Nihon to Chugoku/Chosen" [The Tomb Period of Japan and China/Korea]. *Kikan Kokogaku* [Archeology Quarterly], XXXIII (Nov. 1, 1990), 1-88.

Kokuritsu Hakubutsukan Nyusu [National Museum News]. July 1, 1992.

Kolakowski, Leszek. *The Presence of Myth.* Chicago: University of Chicago Press, 1989.

Koyama, Shuzo. "Jinkō kara mita nihon minzoku" [Japanese Race from the Point of View of Population]. *Nihonjin shin kigenron* [New Theory of Japanese Origins]. Edited by Kazuro Hanihara. Tokyo: Kadokawa Shoten, 1990.

Kuhn, Thomas. *The Structure of Scientific Revolutions.* Chicago: University of Chicago Press, 1962.

Kurylev, V. P., Pavlinskaya, L. P., and Simakov, G. N. "Harness and Weaponry." *Nomads of Eurasia.* Edited by V. N. Basilov. Seattle: University of Washington Press, 1989.

Ledyard, Gari. "Galloping Along with the Horseriders: Looking for the Founders of Japan." *Journal of Japanese Studies*, Vol. 1, No. 2 (spring 1975), 217-254.

_____. "Horse-rider Theory." *Kodansha Encyclopedia of Japan*, Vol. 3 (1983), 229-231.

Lee, Ki-baik. *A New History of Korea.* Cambridge: Harvard University Press, 1984.

Lee, Martin A., and Solomon, Norman. *Unreliable Sources.* New York: Lyle Stewart, 1990.

Levi-Strauss, Claude. "The Structural Study of Myth." *Myth: A Symposium.* Bloomington: Indiana University Press, 1958.

Lewin, Roger. *Bones of Contention.* New York: Simon and Schuster, 1987.

_____. *In the Age of Mankind.* Washington D.C.: Smithsonian Books, 1988.

_____. *Evolution.* Boston: Blackwell Scientific Publications, 1989.

Lubo-Lesnichenko E. "The Huns, Third Century B.C. to Sixth Century A.D.." *Nomads of Eurasia.* Edited by V. N. Basilov. Seattle: University of Washington Press, 1989.

Matsumoto, Hideo. *Nihon minzoku no genryū* [Origin of the Japanese Race]. Tokyo: Tairiku Shobō, 1985.

_____. "Characteristics of Mongoloid and Neighboring Populations Based on the Genetic Markers of Human Immunoglobulins." *Human Genetics*, LXXX (spring 1988), 207-218.

Molnar, Stephen. *Human Variation: Races, Types and Ethnic Groups.* Englewood Cliffs, N.J.: Prentice Hall, 1983.

Mongoroido chikyū o ugoku [Mongoloid Movements]. Program of 6th University Science Open Symposium, Tokyo, Jan. 24-25 1992.

"Mongoroido no tanjō to kakusan [Birth and Dispersal of Mongoloid]." *Mongoroido* [Mongoloid], No. 9 (spring 1991), 2-9.

Mori, Koichi, ed. *Wajin no tōjō* [Appearance of Wajin], Vol. 1 of *Nihon no kodai* [Ancient Japan]. Tokyo: Chūō Kōron, 1985.

Mouer, Ross, and Sugimoto, Yoshio. *Images of Japanese Society.* London: Kegan Paul International, 1986.

_____. eds. *Constructs for Understanding Japan.* London: Kegan Paul International, 1989.

Murayama, Shichiro, and Miller, Roy Andrew. "The Inariyama Tumulus Sword Inscription." *Journal of Japanese Studies*, Vol. 5, No. 2 (summer 1979), 405-438.

"My Granddad, Neanderthal?" *Newsweek* (Oct. 16, 1989), 50-51.

"Mysterious Ancient Mirrors: Triangular-Edged Mirrors with Designs of Deities and Animals." *The East*, Vol. 25, No. 2 (July-Aug. 1989), 36-41.

Naoki, Kojiro, et. al. *Yamataikoku no nazo ni idomu* [Trying to Solve the Riddle of Yamatai Country]. Tokyo: Gakuseisha, 1988.

Nei, M., and Roychoudhury, A. K. "Genetic Relationship and Evolution of Human Races." *Evolutionary Biology*. Edited by M. Hecht, B. Wallace and G. Prance. New York: Plenum Press, 1982.

New York Times. Dec. 23, 1990.

"Newly Excavated Kaya Relics Prove Foreign Contact." *Korea Newsreview*, Vol. 20, No. 51 (Dec. 21, 1991), 31.

Nihon Hoso Kyokai, ed. *Yamataikoku ga mieru* [Yamatai Country Can Be Seen]. Tokyo: NHK, 1989.

_____. *NHK nenkan '90* [NHK Yearbook '90]. Tokyo: NHK, 1991.

Nihonjin no kigenten [Japanese Origins' Exhibition], July 16-Aug. 31, 1988. Tokyo: National Science Museum, 1988.

Nikkan kodaishi no nazo [Puzzle of Japanese-Korean Ancient History], Program of an Asahi Shimbun symposium, May 16, 1990.

Nikkei Weekly. Jan. 18, 1993.

Obayashi, Taryo. "The Ethnological Study of Japan's Ethnic Culture." *Acta Asiatica*, No. 61 (1991), 1-23.

Oda, Shuzuo, and Keally, Charles T. "A Critical Look at the Paleolithic and 'Lower Paleolithic' Research in Miyagi Prefecture, Japan." *Journal of the Anthropological Society of Nippon*, Vol. 94, No. 3 (1986), 325-361.

Okuno, Masao. *Yamataikoku wa kodai Yamato o seifuku shita* [Yamatai Country Conquered Ancient Yamato]. Tokyo: JICC, 1990.

_____. *Yamataikoku wa koko da* [Yamatai Country Was Here]. Tokyo: Tokuma Bunko, 1990.

_____. *Himiko: Yamataikoku eiyūden* [Himiko: The Heroic Story of Yamatai Country]. Tokyo: President, 1991.

_____. "Tēsondon kofungun to kiba minzoku seifuku ōchō setsu" [Taesung Tomb Group and Horserider Conquest Kingdom Theory]. *Higashi Ajia no kodai bunka* [Ancient Culture of East Asia], LXVIII (summer 1991), 84-93.

Olson, Alan M., ed., *Myth, Symbol and Reality*. Notre Dame: University of Notre Dame Press, 1980.

Onuki-Tierney, Emiko. *The Monkey as Mirror*. Princeton: Princeton University Press, 1987.

Otomasu, Shigetaka. "Yoshinogari iseki to Yamataikoku" [Yoshinogari Ruins and Yamatai Country]. *Yoshinogari iseki wa kataru* [What Yoshinogari Tells Us]. Tokyo: Gakuseisha, 1992.

Pope, Geogrey G. "The Facial Evidence for Regionalism in the Far East." *Abstracts: The Evolution and Dispersal of Modern Humans in Asia, November 14-17, 1990*. Tokyo: Tokyo University Museum, 1990.

Powers, W. R. "The Peoples of Eastern Beringia." *Prehistoric Mongoloid Dispersals*, No. 7 (special issue 1990), 53-74.

Public Opinion Poll on Leisure and Travel, Prime Minister's Office, 1986. Foreign Press Club.

Putnam, John J. "The Search for Modern Humans." *National Geographic*, Vol. 174, No. 4 (Oct. 1988), 438-477.

Robinson, G. W. "Early Japanese Chronicles: The Six National Histories." *Historians of China and Japan*. Edited by W. G. Beasley and E. G. Pulleyblank. London: Oxford University Press, 1961.

"Roots of the Japanese in Southeast Asia?" *The East*, Vol. 25, No. 5 (Jan.-Feb. 1990), 18.

Rouhani, Shahin. "Molecular Genetics and the Pattern of Human Evolution." *The Human Evolution*. Edited by Paul Mellars and Chris Stringer. Princeton: Princeton University Press, 1989.

Rubin, Bernard, ed. *When Information Counts*. Lexington, Mass.: Lexington Books, 1985.

Sahara, Makoto, et. al. *Yoshinogari tairan to wakoku* [Yoshinogari: Turmoil and Wa Country]. Tokyo: Yamakawa Shuppansha, 1990.

Saishin Yamataikokuron [Latest Yamatai Country Theory]. Tokyo: Gakken, 1990.

Sakamoto, Taro. *The Six National Histories of Japan*. Translated by John S. Brownlee. Tokyo: University of Tokyo Press, 1991.

Saga Prefecture Education Committee, ed. *Yoshinogari iseki* [Yoshinogari Ruins]. Tokyo: Yoshikawa Kobunkan, 1990.

San-kuo chih [Account of the Three Kingdoms].

Sasaki, Komei. *Nihon tanjō* [Birth of Japanese History], Vol. 1 of *Nihon no rekishi* [History of Japan]. Tokyo: Shueisha, 1991.

_____. "The Wa People and Their Culture in Ancient Japan: The Cultures of Swidden Cultivation and Padi-Rice Cultivation." *Acta Asiatica*, LXI (1991), 24-46.

Sha, Meijin. *Yamataikoku Chugokujin wa kō yomu* [Chinese interpret Yamatai Country this way]. Tokyo: Tokuma Shobo, 1990.

Shin, Kyungcheol. "Kankoku no Kaya bunka to Wa" [Kaya Culture of Korea and Wa]. Gakushuin University lecture program of Wazoku to kodai Nihon [Wa Race and Ancient Japan], Jan. 8-9, 1993. Inserted pages.

_____, et. al. *Kyodai kofun to Kaya bunka* [Gigantic Tombs and Kaya Culture]. Tokyo: Kadokawa Shoten, 1992.

Shreeve, James. "Argument Over a Woman." *Discover* (Aug. 1990), 52-59.

Sinor, Denis, ed. *The Cambridge History of Early Inner Asia*. Cambridge: Cambridge University Press, 1990.

Spencer, Frank, ed., *A History of American Physical Anthropology, 1930-1980*. New York: Academic Press, 1982.

Spiess, Eliot B. *Genes in Population*. New York: John Wiley & Sons, 1977.

Steinberg, Arthur G., and Cook, Charles E., *The Distribution of the Human Immunoglobulin Allotypes*. Oxford: Oxford University Press, 1981.

_____, and Larrick, James W. "Immunoglobulin Allotypes in Peoples from Five Villages in Nepal." *Journal of Human Evolution*, Vol. 10, No. 4 (May 1981), 329-334.

_____, and Matsumoto, Hideo. "Studies on the Gm, Inv, Hp and Tf Serum Factors of Japanese Populations and Families." *Human Biology*, XXXVI (1964), 77-84.

Stoneking, Mark, and Cann, Rebecca L. "African Origin of Human Mitochondrial DNA." *The Human Evolution*. Edited by Paul Mellars and Chris Stringer. Princeton: Princeton University Press, 1989.

Strensky, Ivan. *Four Theories of Myth in Twentieth-Century History*. London: MacMillan Press, 1987.

Sugawara, Makoto. "The Yayoi Japanese." *The East*, Vol. 25, No. 3 (Sept.-Oct. 1989), 34-38.

214

Suzuki, Hisashi. *Hone kara mita nihonjin no rūtsu* [Japanese Roots from the Point of View of Bones]. Iwanami Shinsho: Toyko, 1983.

_____, and Hanihara, Kazuro. *The Minatogawa Man*. Tokyo: University of Tokyo Press, 1982.

Takahashi, Toru, and Amano. Yukihiro. *Hakkutsu sareta kodaishi* [Excavation of Ancient History]. Tokyo: Nihon Bungeisha, 1989.

Takashima, Juhei, et. al. *Yoshinogari iseki* [Yoshinogari Ruins]. Tokyo: Gakken, 1989.

_____, and Harashima, Reiji, eds. *Yoshinogari to kodai iseki tanbō* [Inquiring into Yoshinogari and Ancient Ruins]. Tokyo: Kodansha, 1991.

Tajima, Kazuo, et. al. "Epidemiological Features of HTLV-1 Carriers and Incidence of ATL in an ATL-Endemic Island." *International Journal of Cancer*, XXXX (1987), 741-746.

_____. "HTLV-1 no bumpu kara mita nanbei mongoroido no kakusan to ijū" [Dispersal and Migration of South American Mongoloid from Distribution of HTLV-1]. *Mongoroido* [Mongoloid], No. 12 (winter 1991), 28-36.

Takeuchi, Hitoshi. *Mūtairiku kara kita Nihonjin (futatabi)* [Japanese who came from Mu continent (again)]. Tokyo: Takuma Shoten, 1990.

Tanaka, Migaku. *Wajin Sōran* [Wa Disturbances], Vol. 2 of *Nihon no rekishi* [History of Japan]. Tokyo: Shūeisha, 1991.

Tanaka, Toshiyaki. "Tēsondon kofungun to Mimanaron" [Taesung Tomb Group and Mimana Theory]. *Higashi Ajia no kodai bunka* [Ancient Culture of East Asia], LXVIII (summer, 1991), 55-69.

"The First Humans." *U.S. News & World Report* (Feb. 27, 1989), 52-59.

"The Search for Adam and Eve." *Newsweek* (Jan. 11, 1988), 46-52.

Tokunaga, Katsushi, and Juji, Takeo. "The Migration and Dispersal of East Asian Populations as Viewed from HLA Genes and Haplotypes." *Abstracts: The Evolution and Dispersal of Modern Humans in Asia, November 14-17, 1990*. Tokyo: Tokyo University Museum, 1990.

_____. "HLA kara miru Higashi Ajia jinruishūdan no kakusan to idō" [Dispersal and Movement of East Asian Peoples from HLA Viewpoint]. *Mongoloido*, No. 4 (spring 1990), 15-18.

215

Tsuboi, Kyotari, ed. *Recent Archeological Discoveries in Japan.* Translated by Gina Barnes. Paris: UNESCO, 1987.

Tsude, Hiroshi, ed. *Kofunjidai no ō to minshū* [King and People in Kofun Period], Vol. 6 of *Kodaishi fukugen* [Restoration of Ancient History]. Tokyo: Kodansha, 1989.

Tsunoda, Ryusaku, and Goodrich, L. Carrington. *Japan in the Chinese Dynastic Histories.* S. Pasadena: P.D. and Ione Perkins, 1951.

Tsutsumi, Senjo. Review of *Jomon jidai* [Jomon Period] by Shuzo Koyama. *Yamataikoku Jinkōron* [Yamatai Country Population theory]. Edited by Biten Yasumoto. Tokyo: Kashiwa Shobō, 1991.

Turner II, Christy G. "Ancient Peoples of the North Pacific Rim." *Crossroads of Continents.* Edited by W. W. Fitzhugh and Aron Crowell. Washington D.C.: Smithsonian Institution Press, 1988.

_____. "Teeth and Prehistory in Asia." *Scientific American,* Vol. 260, No. 2 (Feb. 1989), 88-96.

_____. "Microevolution of East Asian and European Populations: A Dental Perspective." *Abstracts: The Evolution and Dispersal of Modern Humans in Asia, November 14-17, 1990.* Tokyo: Tokyo University Museum, 1990.

Twitchett, Denis, and Loewe, Michael, eds. *Cambridge History of China,* I. Cambridge: Cambridge University Press, 1986.

Umehara, Takeshi. "Jofuku densetsu ga imi suru mono" [What the Jofuku Legend Means]. *Yayoi no shisha: Jofuku* [Yayoi Missionary: Jofuku]. Saga TV Publication, 1989.

_____, and Hanihara, Kazuro. *Ainu wa gennihonjin ka* [Are the Ainu the Original Japanese?] Tokyo: Shōgakukan, 1982.

Watabe, Tadayo. "Origin and Dispersal of Rice in Asia." *East Asian Cultural Studies,* XXIV (Mar. 1985), 33-39.

Watanabe, Masao. *The Japanese and Western Science.* Philadelphia: University of Pennsylvania Press, 1988.

Weaver, Kenneth F. "The Search for Our Ancestors." *National Geographic,* Vol. 168, No. 5 (Nov. 1985), 560-623.

"Who We Were." *U.S. News & World Report,* Vol. 3, No. 12 (Sept. 16, 1991), 53-60.

216

Wills, Christopher. *The Wisdom of the Genes*. New York: Basic Books, 1989.

Wolpoff, Milford H. "Multiregional Evolution: The Fossil Alternative to Eden." *The Human Evolution*. Edited by Paul Mellars and Chris Stringer. Princeton: Princeton University Press, 1989.

Wu, Xinzhi. "Origins and Affinities of the Inhabitants of Japan in Different Periods." *Preprint Papers: International Symposium on Japanese as a Member of the Asian and Pacific Populations, September 25-29, 1990*. Kyoto: International Center for Japanese Studies, 1990.

_____. "The Origin and Dispersal of the Anatomically Modern Homo Sapiens of China." *Abstracts: The Evolution and Dispersal of Modern Humans in Asia, November 14-17, 1990*. Tokyo: Tokyo University Museum, 1990.

Yamamoto, S. *Kūki no kenkyu* [A Study of "Kuuki"]. Tokyo: Bungei Shunjūsha, 1977.

Yasumoto, Biten. *Shinsetsu: nihonjin no kigen* [New Theory: Japanese Origins]. Tokyo: JICC, 1990.

_____. *Nakoku no metsubo* [The Downfall of Na Country]. Tokyo: Mainichi Shimbun, 1990.

_____. *Yamataikoku e no michi* [The Road to Yamatai Country]. Tokyo: Tokuma Bunko, 1990.

_____. *Kyodai kofun no nushi ga wakatta!* [The Identify of the Person Buried in the Gigantic Burial Bound Found Out!]. Tokyo: JICC, 1991.

_____. *Yamataikoku ronsō ni kecchaku ga tsuita!* [Yamataikoku Debate Has Been Concluded!]. Tokyo, JICC, 1992.

_____. ed. *Yoshinogari wa Yamataikoku nanoka* [Wondering if Yoshinogari Is Yamatai Country]. Tokyo: Tokuma Bunko, 1990.

_____. et. al. *Edo no Yamataikoku* [Yamatai Country in Edo Period]. Tokyo: Kashiwa Shobo, 1991.

Yoshinogari isekiten [Yoshinogari Ruins' Exhibition], Sept. 9-29, 1989, Tokyo: Ancient Orient Museum, 1989.

Young, Steven. "Beringia: An Ice Age View." *Crossroads of Continents*. Edited by W. W. Fitzhugh and Aron Crowell. Washington D.C.: Smithsonian Institution Press, 1988.

INDEX

218

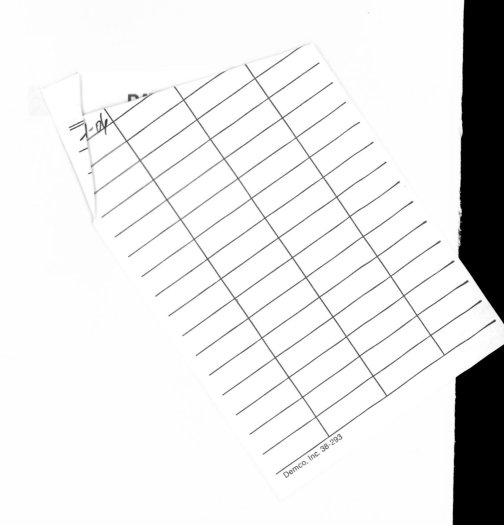

Demco, Inc. 38-293